Emotion in the Tudor Court

Rethinking the Early Modern

Emotion in the Tudor Court

Literature, History, and Early Modern Feeling

Bradley J. Irish

Northwestern University Press
Evanston, Illinois

Northwestern University Press
www.nupress.northwestern.edu

Printed in the United States of America

10 9 8 7 6 5 4 3 2 1

ISBN 978-0-8101-3640-3 (cloth)
ISBN 978-0-8101-3639-7 (paper)
ISBN 978-0-8101-3641-0 (ebook)

Library of Congress Cataloging-in-Publication data are available from the Library of Congress.

To Frank

CONTENTS

Acknowledgments ix

List of Abbreviations xi

Introduction 3

Chapter 1
The Disgusting Cardinal Thomas Wolsey 19

Chapter 2
The Envious Earl of Surrey 55

Chapter 3
The Rejected Earl of Leicester, the Rejected Sir Philip Sidney 93

Chapter 4
The Dreading, Dreadful Earl of Essex 137

Notes 179

Index 231

ACKNOWLEDGMENTS

Emotion in the Tudor Court originated during my doctoral studies at the University of Texas at Austin, where I had the great fortune of being supervised by Frank Whigham. An unequaled scholar, mentor, and friend, it is to him that I dedicate this final product.

I am grateful to the countless instructors who have provided me with the tools to undertake such a project. As an undergraduate at Boston University, my thought was shaped by Laurence Breiner, William Carroll, Geoffrey Hill, Christopher Martin, Erin Murphy, and James Siemon. My graduate career was tirelessly supported both by the rest of my dissertation committee—James Loehlin, Jason Powell, Wayne Rebhorn, and Marjorie Curry Woods—and by the vibrant community of University of Texas scholars, including Samuel Baker, Douglas Bruster, Jean Cannon, Ann Cvetkovich, Linda Ferreira-Buckley, Gregory Foran, Elizabeth Hedrick, Hala Herbly, Jessica Kilgore, Jonathan Lamb, Eric Mallin, Noël Clare Radley, and Hannah Wojciehowski.

At Arizona State University, I have the privilege of working alongside a generous and talented group of colleagues. I am especially indebted to my friend and regular collaborator Cora Fox, whose critical eye has never failed to sharpen both my thinking and its presentation. I owe thanks also to Heather Ackerman, John Henry Adams, Karen Adams, Aaron Baker, Sally Ball, Lee Bebout, Dan Bivona, Robert Bjork, Ron Broglio, Joe Buenker, Gregory Castle, Deborah Clarke, Jessica Early, Melissa Free, Maureen Daly Goggin, David Hawkes, Kalissa Hendrickson, Julia Himberg, Cynthia Hogue, Tara Ison, George Justice, Devori Kimbro, Kristen Larue-Sandler, Devoney Looser, Mark Lussier, Ruby Macksoud, Edward Mallot, Heather Maring, Bruce Matsunaga, T. M. McNally, Keith Miller, Ian Moulton, Richard Newhauser, Krista Ratcliffe, Alberto Ríos, Kristin Rondeau-Guardiola, Bradley Ryner, Sarah Saucedo, Karen Silva, Robert Sturges, Linda Sullivan, Ayanna Thompson, Victoria Thompson, Elly van Gelderen, and Doris Warriner.

I am equally grateful for the wisdom and guidance of scholars elsewhere—many of whom I only know electronically. I thank Simon Adams, Amanda Bailey, Katie Barclay, Lisa Feldman Barrett, Todd Borlik, Susan Broomhall, Sukanta Chaudhuri, Mario DiGangi, Thomas Dixon, Natalie Eschenbaum, Charles Ess, Tiffany Florvil, Lisa Ford, Erika

Gaffney, Terry Gifford, Stephen Guy-Bray, Andrew Hadfield, Paul Hammer, Peter Herman, Allison Hobgood, Lalita Hogan, Patrick Hogan, Peter Holland, Paulina Kewes, Arthur Kinney, Roger Kuin, Russell Leo, Katherine Little, Andrew Lynch, Steven May, Richard Meek, Gail Kern Paster, Curtis Perry, Mark Rankin, Will Rossiter, Gary Sherman, Cathy Shrank, Raymond Siemens, Freya Sierhuis, Malcolm Smuts, Alan Stewart, Richard Strier, Erin Sullivan, Stephanie Trigg, Michael Ullyot, Owen Williams, Heather Wolfe, Michael Woods, and Daniel Woolf.

I thank Cassie Miura and Marjorie Curry Woods for their assistance with the translation of foreign quotations.

Part of my work was funded by a grant from Arizona State University's Institute for Humanities Research Fellows Program. I thank Sally Kitch, Jennifer Quincey, Rena Saltzman, and the IHR staff for their support.

A portion of chapter 1 was published as "Coriolanus and the Poetics of Disgust," *Shakespeare Survey* 69 (2016): 198–215. A portion of chapter 2 was published as "The Rivalrous Emotions in Surrey's 'So Crewell Prison,'" *SEL Studies in English Literature 1500–1900* 54, no. 1 (2014): 1–24. I am thankful for the right to reprint this content here.

I am grateful to Lambeth Palace Library for permission to quote from their holdings.

I am especially indebted to Gianna Mosser and the staff of Northwestern University Press for their tireless support of this project. I owe great thanks to Anne Gendler, Maggie Grossman, Liz Hamilton, Marianne Jankowski, Paul Mendelson, Steven Moore, JD Wilson, and the anonymous readers of my manuscript. I also thank Marcus Keller, Ellen McClure, and Feisal Mohamed for including me in the Rethinking the Early Modern series.

Finally, this work, and all my work, would be impossible without the endless love of my family. To my parents, my grandmothers, Olivia and Penelope, and Jenny—thank you.

ABBREVIATIONS

BL British Library, London.

CP Cecil Papers, Hatfield House, Hertfordshire.

CSPS *Calendar of Letters, Despatches, and State Papers, Relating to the Negotiations between England and Spain*. Ed. G. A. Bergenroth et al. 17 vols. London, 1862–1954.

Folger Folger Shakespeare Library, Washington, D.C.

L&P *Letters and Papers, Foreign and Domestic, of the Reign of Henry VIII*. Ed. J. S. Brewer et al. 23 vols. London, 1862–1932.

ODNB *Oxford Dictionary of National Biography*. Oxford: Oxford University Press, 2004. http://www.oxforddnb.com.

OED *Oxford English Dictionary Online*. Oxford: Oxford University Press, 2015. http://www.oed.com.

TNA The National Archives, Kew.

When quoting from manuscripts, I have aimed for semi-diplomatic transcription. When necessary for the sake of clarity, minor punctuation has been silently added. All unattributed translations are mine. When quoting from calendars of state papers, I cite by document number.

Emotion in the Tudor Court

INTRODUCTION

Nowadayes, as the early moderns were fond of saying, there's no doubt that scholarship has gotten emotional—and this mood shows little sign of passing, if recent work is any indication. In both the sciences and humanities, countless scholars are now participating in the "affective turn," an interdisciplinary movement that traces the social, psychological, and material contours of emotional experience, a subject long taken for granted in many corners of the modern academy.[1]

In literary and cultural scholarship of early modern England, the fruits of this research cluster are already apparent.[2] Though there has long been interest in certain discrete areas of Renaissance emotional thought—such as attitudes toward grief, or the discourse of melancholy[3]—about a decade ago there began to emerge a body of work, marshaled by Gail Kern Paster's *Humoring the Body: Emotions and the Shakespearean Stage* (2004) and her mutually edited (with Mary Floyd-Wilson and Katherine Rowe) collection *Reading the Early Modern Passions: Essays in the Cultural History of Emotion* (2004), that sounded a new charge for emotion as an object of explicit historical study in the period.[4] Grounded in a rigorously historicist treatment of Galenic humoral physiology—which envisioned a materially porous boundary between the environment and self—this scholarship seeks to "discover the phenomenological character" of Renaissance affect, by imagining "the early modern embodiment of emotion in terms that challenge the post-Cartesian divisions between thought, soma, and world."[5] A boom of important scholarship followed in this mode, variously attending to the Galenic context of early modern emotion.[6] Complementing the interest in humoralism, other historicist work on early modern emotion has taken a variety of forms: Robert Cockcroft, Wendy Olmsted, Lynn Enterline, and R. S. White consider Renaissance affect through the lens of the contemporary rhetorical tradition; Susan C. Karant-Nunn, Joseph Campana, and Steven Mullaney explore the emotional consequences of the Reformation; and Daniel Juan Gil, Jennifer C. Vaught, and Cora Fox emphasize the relationship between literary works and the period's changing emotional modes.[7] Emotion, indeed, is pervasive in recent scholarship on the period: in 2015 alone, there emerged no fewer than nine new essay collections on emotion in the Renaissance.[8]

Following suit, *Emotion in the Tudor Court* is an attempt to imagine the emotional world of the sixteenth-century English court.[9] It is also an attempt to imagine how the workings of emotion more generally might prove valuable to the study of literature, history, and culture. Textual forms, in their capacity to record the textures of emotion, provide the spark for my imaginings. But *Emotion in the Tudor Court* doesn't seek to historicize early modern discourses of emotion (like so much of the valuable work described above), nor to explore Renaissance emotionality via the models of affect currently dominant in contemporary cultural studies.[10] Instead, I mount in what follows three nested, escalating claims about the literary and historical study of emotion. A specific *historical* argument, about the role of emotion in the Tudor court, is developed in service of a broader, *methodological* argument about the manner of deploying emotion as a generalized analytical mode, itself serving a broader still *disciplinary* argument, about what aggregate model of emotion can best undergird this affective analysis for literary studies and cultural history. Taken together, these three arguments offer new direction for the study of emotion in the early modern period—with implications, I hope, for the study of emotion more broadly in the literary disciplines.

For the last several decades, historians of the early modern period have become increasingly devoted to a "socially derived understanding of Tudor politics."[11] This agenda, epitomized by Patrick Collinson's now-famous cry for "an account of political processes which is also social," has guided the efforts of many of the most prominent and influential scholars of sixteenth-century British history.[12] Thanks to the efforts of David Starkey and many others, the great beneficiary of this trend has been the early modern court—which, as the amorphous, dynamic social core of interpersonal engagement between monarchs and their power-players, has been thought to unseat more public, formalized institutions like Parliament and the Privy Council as the "centre of political politics" in Tudor England.[13] Though like-minded historians still fiercely debate just *how* such interaction should be assessed, there is nonetheless a growing consensus in current scholarship: in Tudor England, sociality was paramount to political power, and in Tudor England, the sociality of political power was most evident in the royal court.

In its historical mode, *Emotion in the Tudor Court* thus argues most basically that the operation of the Tudor courtly sphere, including its production of literary and cultural texts, is made fully comprehensible only by acknowledging the centrality of emotion to social and political action. In the sixteenth-century court, I suggest more specifically, particular moments of political crisis generated sociotextual nodes that are best processed by tending to the dynamics of a particular governing emotion. In the chapters that follow, I examine the textual field surrounding such incidents—for example, the rise and fall of Cardinal Thomas Wolsey, or the Earl of Essex's ill-fated rebellion—via the discourse of an operative emotion like *disgust* or *dread*. Accordingly, I treat the Tudor court as what Ann Cvetkovich valuably terms an "archive of feeling," viewing its "cultural texts as repositories of feelings and emotions, which are encoded not only in the content of the texts themselves but in the practices that surround their production and reception."[14]

My historical claim finds contemporary support in the increasing sense among modern thinkers that many post-Enlightenment models of the rational political subject don't give just due to the emotional components of politics.[15] Perhaps most notably, Chantal Mouffe's influential critique of the Habermasian tradition argues that a crucial "mistake of liberal rationalism is to ignore the affective dimension" of the political realm: the "prime task of democratic politics," she advocates instead, "is not to eliminate passions nor to relegate them to the private sphere in order to render rational consensus possible, but to mobilise those passions towards the promotion of democratic designs."[16] Such work in political theory is complemented by research in contemporary neuroscience: the oft-cited Antonio Damasio has spent decades arguing for the intimate anatomical coupling of reasoning and emotional processes, while Jonathan Haidt has similarly refined a thesis that moral and political judgments owe as much to intuitive, emotional responses as to reasoned deliberation.[17] Several mass-market books, such as Damasio's *Descartes' Error: Emotion, Reason, and the Human Brain* (1994), *The Feeling of What Happens: Body and Emotion in the Making of Consciousness* (1999), and *Looking for Spinoza: Joy, Sorrow, and the Feeling Brain* (2003), as well as Haidt's *The Righteous Mind: Why Good People Are Divided by Politics and Religion* (2012), have brought these theories to a nonspecialist audience, and there appears to be a growing interest in the emotional underpinnings of the "Political Brain," which calls into question "intellectualist and deliberationist models" of political analysis.[18] This suspicion of the Habermasian "rational cognitive subject" dovetails with a common inclination of many post-structuralists, and theorists working on affect have similarly foregrounded the connection between emotions and politics; for example, John Protevi's recent analysis of "affective cognition in social contexts" gives rise to a perspective he provocatively calls "political physiology."[19] In fact, the affective turn has birthed a research cluster known as "public feelings," an interdisciplinary collective that attempts to correct "how the division between public and private spheres has problematically confined feelings and emotional life to the domain of the personal and private," thus obscuring the important political stakes of emotionality.[20]

And though, as we will see, *Emotion in the Tudor Court* attempts to model a mode of affective analysis that is applicable to any domain of literary and cultural study, the political operation of the early modern court is an especially rich arena for emotional investigation. The "promise of affect theory," in Donovan Schaefer's formulation, is "the possibility of sliding together analytical tools used to pick apart *both* highly individuated and highly social contact zones"—and, as a context in which the stakes of emotional life were unforgivingly interpersonal, the court is one such contact zone in which it is paramount to consider individuated and social experience jointly.[21] Produced by men and women who are, by definition, some degree proximate to the center of political power, courtly literature particularly encodes the affective negotiation between the private and public spheres, in a way that reflects how many modern theorists understand the operation of emotion more generally. Indeed, current research in the affective sciences insists that the subjective experience of emotion is socially situated: the "social functions of emotions" are apparent across "the individual, dyadic, group, and cultural levels of analysis," and it has recently been argued that, as a primary component of "relationship reconfiguration" strategy, emotions are fundamentally "designed to function in a social context."[22] As early as Petrarch and Salutati, in fact, early modern thinkers acknowledged the proximity of the social and emotional domains: for many in the Renaissance, Richard Strier has shown, "sociality and affectivity are seen as defining the human, and as inextricably linked."[23] The court is the social heart of Renaissance politics, and emotion is its lifeblood. Tending to emotion, I suggest, can freshly situate the social operation of the courtier within the social operation of the court, and can freshly illuminate the literary, cultural, and historical texts that are generated by this interplay.

My suggestion that understanding emotion is paramount to understanding the Tudor court raises an immediate question: what critical method best facilitates this analysis? As we've seen above, recent work on Renaissance emotion has largely focused on how literature reflects and refracts early modern discourses of the emotional body, revealing how notions of the humors and passions dynamically shaped the relationship between early modern subjects and their natural world. But despite the certain value of this approach, there remains a sense in which its dominance has obscured the larger possibilities of emotionality as a framework for literary, cultural, and historical analysis.

My methodological argument, then, entails reconceptualizing how we might study Renaissance emotionality, by looking beyond the historical phenomenology that has dominated the field. I posit emotion not only as a source of inquiry—that is, not only as a set of historical discourses to be analyzed and inhabited—but rather as the mode of inquiry itself, by leveraging the inherent affectivity of textual, social, and biographical data to uncover new sites of meaning and new channels of inspection. My primary aim is not to historicize the features of emotionality in early modern experience, but rather to use features of emotionality to historicize early modern experience more broadly: I am concerned not so much with how early modern subjects understood a sentiment like disgust, but rather with how a wide engagement with models and discourses of disgust can inform our understanding of how they, and the texts they construct, participate in the Renaissance social world. A historicist reconstruction of the Tudor court, grounded largely in archival data, provides the raw material of my analysis; sensitivity to the varied contours of emotion, as understood by a variety of discourses, is how that analysis proceeds.

For reasons explained above, this project is a treatment of emotion in the literature and politics of the sixteenth-century English court. But its methodological approach is portable, and it is my hope that this form of affective analysis, and the more specific discourses of emotion I explore throughout, will be of value to other studies in both the Renaissance and beyond. "Affect," Brian Massumi argues, "like thought or reflection, could be extended to any or every level" of analysis—and indeed, much like ideology, emotion is implicated in every feature of human engagement.[24] As collective theoretical effort proceeds, it is my hope that we will continue to speak more regularly of performing an "affective" reading of text and culture. Rather than historicizing emotion as an end in itself, *Emotion in the Tudor Court* is committed to performing such broader analysis of the Tudor court and its productions.

I have claimed that emotion is crucial to understanding literary and political interaction in the Tudor court, and I have claimed that scholars of both the Renaissance and other fields might benefit from treating emotion not as an object, but as a method of analysis. But a final question remains: how should we develop our understanding of emotion?

In response, my disciplinary argument is that those of us working in the humanities can benefit from pursuing a model of emotion that is deeply informed by the current, ongoing research programs of the social and natural sciences.[25] On some level, this should be uncontroversial. Few, I think, would bristle at the notion that there's something to be gained by cross-field interaction, which is already integrated into the conceptual architecture of much contemporary scholarship—and more specifically, as we'll see below, cognitive studies of the early modern period (a lineage in which *Emotion in the Tudor Court* is generally enrolled) routinely anchor their analysis in scientific approaches. But the precise treatment of literary emotion has been thornier. In theory, inquiry into humoral subjectivity indeed "uses cognitive theory in a historicist context," and it is true that treatments of emotion and affect in literary studies are sometimes peppered with references to the prominent work of scientists like Damasio, Joseph LeDoux, Paul Ekman, and Richard Dawkins.[26] But in practice, it seems to me that the routinely effusive claims of interdisciplinarity often mask an engagement with other fields that remains underdeveloped. (The work of Lalita Pandit Hogan and Patrick Colm Hogan is a crucial exception.)[27] As Constantina Papoulias and Felicity Callard sharply note, the limited scope of affect studies' scientific borrowings necessarily risks reductive and distorted conclusions, while such interdisciplinary maneuvers may ultimately be little more than rhetorical gestures.[28] In fact, Ruth Leys reveals, some literary and cultural studies of affect have stumbled into their own version of the vulgar New Historicist anecdote—in which a particular empirical study or concept, often decontextualized and misrepresented, is made to bear the burden of a theoretical argument surpassing its capacity to be responsibly supported.[29]

A more thoroughly interdisciplinary approach, in the manner that I'm advocating, requires a more thorough effort to engage other fields in their own terms—acknowledging, of course, that our status as disciplinary tourists will inevitably shape our encounters there, and will help select the souvenirs we take home. As such, this book converses widely with a variety of other disciplines, since the promise of interdisciplinarity cannot be realized by casual glances at other fields. But more specifically, the project's interdisciplinary approach is premised on the fact that contemporary scientific discourses of emotion—rooted, as they are, in our very specific historical, cultural, and epistemological moment—can reach back some 400 years into the past, to tell us something nontrivial about the early modern world. This conviction does not, it must be said, oblige us to lazily essentialize or universalize emotion, or to slip into naive anachronism: a compelling body of evidence, as we will see below, suggests that it is still possible to find currents of transhistorical and transcultural continuity in the culturally inflected experience of human emotion, and it is possible to use these currents to seek new ground in the study of historically situated phenomena.

In some instances, scientific models of emotion lead me to conclusions that might otherwise be derived independently from humanistic methods, a feature that suggests the proximity between fields that are often seen as professionally and intellectually disparate. I would never claim that scientific approaches are the *only* way to generate every textual reading in this book—and indeed, part of my aim is to demonstrate how the sciences can offer corroborating evidence for the kind of work we're already doing in the humanities. In this sense, *Emotion in the Tudor Court* partly resembles what has been termed "correlational criticism"—that which is "often the initial phase of a new theoretical approach to literary analysis."[30] But more often, I think we'll find, such scientific models offer complementary knowledge that helps enrich and extend the discoveries of our own and related fields. To wield the sharpest possible critical tool, it seems sensible to integrate this perspective into our interrogation of early modern emotionality—and indeed, the editors of *Reading the Early Modern Passions* acknowledge that "empirical science and cultural studies ought to create more space for each other in their conceptual nesting grounds."[31] I very much agree, and in this sense my project aligns with the vital comparativist work of Patrick Colm Hogan—a program thoroughly grounded in contemporary scientific research—whose transparently titled *What Literature Teaches Us about Emotion* (2011) has recently argued that "literature provides a vast and largely unexplored body of data for emotion research" in the sciences.[32] I concur that the science of emotion and literary/historical analysis should be better friends, and in its disciplinary argument, this book attempts to nurture such a relationship.

In advocating this method, my project broadly attempts to advance a new position in the larger, longer critical conversation about how literary scholars engage with the past. When a previous generation of thinkers—the so-called old historicists—glanced backward, they found a human subjectivity that looked suspiciously like their own; "what those scholars lacked," Gail Kern Paster reflects, "was our theorized notion of the interior historicity of the subject."[33] New Historicism, of course, changed all of that. Seeking instead a history that is radically alien, New Historicist and cultural materialist scholars actively sought in their work "a stubborn, unassimilable otherness, a sense of distance and difference"; finding little in early modern subjects that recalled our contemporary sense of autonomous interiority, they convincingly urged us to "resist speciously imputing modern assumptions about 'the self' to a historically distant culture."[34] Reflecting "the post-1980 fashion for theorising the body and affect, and the post-1990 fashion for inventing fresh paradigms for historicising subjectivity," the recent turn to Galenic humoralism in early modern studies is, most fundamentally, an inheritor of this legacy.[35] To be sure, humoralism is not merely a manifestation of New Historicism; the previous generation of historicists, it has been argued, "shared a suspicion of emotions as calculated constructions of power," and recent scholars of emotion and affect are more rightly thought to focus on "physiocultural rather than sociocultural formations."[36] But the fact remains that, rooted as it is in New Historicism, the historical phenomenology of the scholarship described above has been fundamentally committed to honoring temporal distance: it emphasizes "historical differences in modes of emotional self-experience" by reconstructing "how emotions might have been experienced differently by early modern subjects."[37]

My project, however, takes a very different approach. In applying the insights of the modern sciences to historical phenomena, my aim is not to affirm the subjective continuity of past and present: I acknowledge absolutely that emotions have a history, that understandings of emotion change over time, and that cultural forces crucially shape how emotions are experienced. But I am equally uninterested in defamiliarizing the past beyond recognition. Instead, I attempt to employ intellectual frameworks anchored in modern understandings to account for the historically situated conditions of early modern culture, always with the knowledge that such understandings might help us make sense of, but distinctly do not *determine*, the experience of past subjects. In such, I am aligned with the more recent position of Paster herself—who, having "come to believe [that] basic human emotions are fundamentally trans-historical and trans-cultural," now suggests employing "a heuristics of similarity, even perhaps of sameness" in the study of early modern emotional life.[38] Modern theories of emotion offer a guide to thinking about historical affect, but it is not one contingent on absolute congruence between temporal moments. In the moment of New Historicism's rising ascendancy, Jean E. Howard wisely observed that "a phenomenon in one period, which *seems* analogous to a phenomenon in another, may arise amid such different social conditions and play such a different role in a culture's power relations and discursive systems that the two phenomena cannot be seen as continuous with one another."[39] A historicist practice like the one I'm advocating makes space to acknowledge the messy interplay of phenomenal analogy, a unique opportunity to examine both points of contact and points of divergence between our world and those worlds of the past—honoring, as Paster again puts it, "the productive spaces between sameness and difference."[40]

Finally, it is important to note that engaging the sciences in the manner I'm suggesting need not entail any epistemological commitments—there is intellectual benefit whether or not one assents to the objectivity of their methods and findings. Whatever one's disposition, the sciences (to borrow a famous phrase) can be good to think with: such research on emotion, I find, helps me see new things about early modern literature and culture, and is for that reason worthy of attention.[41] Hedging on the truth value also alleviates the consequences attached to the mistakes and misunderstandings that inevitably creep into interdisciplinary translation. I am not a trained scientist, or a trained historian, and I will undoubtedly err in my attempts at disciplinary crossing. But by making a good faith effort to engage other fields in their own terms, and by seeking in them not answers, but new ways of questioning, even such missteps can be ultimately productive.

These three arguments guide my study of emotion in the Tudor court. They do, however, require some further justification, especially insofar as the project embraces the insights of the modern sciences: with good reason, literary and cultural studies tend to be skeptical about the transhistorical and transcultural investments of much scientific discourse. It is now long ago that critical theory dismissed ideas of human essentialism as "vacuous and untenable"—and in Renaissance studies more specifically, the emerging practitioners of the New Historicism were quickly associated with a shared conviction that "there is no transhistorical or universal human essence and that human subjectivity is constructed by cultural codes which position and limit all of us."[42] It is thus an important question to ask: given what we know about the social construction of reality, how are the empirical findings of the sciences compatible with the analysis of historically and culturally contingent phenomena?

Vulgar determinism and essentialism are rightly rejected by modern scholars. But "in their laudable attempt to ward off one type of reductionism," William E. Connolly suggests, "too many cultural theorists fall into another"—an alternate reductionism "that ignores how biology is mixed into thinking and culture and how other aspects of nature are folded into both."[43] An adequate theory of lived experience can't neglect the interaction of biological and cultural phenomena; what's needed, as Catherine Belsey has recently argued, is to account for how "the biology that constitutes human beings always interacts with the relatively autonomous culture their evolved brains make possible."[44] In this spirit, John Dupré advocates for a pluralism that "draws both on the empirical knowledge derivable from the (various) sciences, and on the wisdom and insight into human nature that can be derived from more humanistic studies."[45] F. Elizabeth Hart, more specifically, imagines such a framework integrating both biological and cultural elements, a "*third* epistemological position nestled between the polar extremes of realism and relativism":

> a third position that effectively reshapes their relations from a binary structure to an epistemological continuum on which realist and relativist positions occupy opposite—but not all-encompassing—ends. This third position is actually a *set* of positions that together define the continuum connecting its two ends, positions that manifest varying degrees of combinatory possibilities of both realism and relativism but that do not have to fully commit to either.[46]

Despite skewing, quite naturally, toward one end or the other of Hart's continuum, scholars working on the nature/culture divide have been increasingly vocal in advocating for such a flexible third position—whether it is called "soft essentialism,"[47] weak constructionism (including "weak biological constructionism" *and* "weak social constructionism"),[48] "constrained constructivism,"[49] or "componential compatibilism."[50]

"Far from being inconsistent with post-structuralist thought," Ellen Spolsky importantly argues, the "assumptions that emerge from the study of evolved human brains in their successive contexts" can actually work to "extend and enrich it"—and indeed, the work of her colleagues in cognitive and evolutionary literary studies have led the way in this regard.[51] For though scholars in the humanities (and social sciences) once seemed "so afraid of being labeled essentialist, reductionist, or biological," the game is starting to change: as Paul Cefalu and Bryan Reynolds recently observed, a growing number of "literary critics are now participating in the cognitive revolution, partly because some of the seeming bogeys like universalism, essentialism, and eliminative materialism have been shorn of their odious sociobiological implications."[52] Though this trend is evident throughout the discipline—and here Patrick Colm Hogan was also a vanguard—it has a particular concentration in early modern studies, where scholars like Amy Cook, Mary Thomas Crane, Arthur Kinney, and Evelyn Tribble have made groundbreaking contributions to our understanding of literary cognition.[53]

And most crucially of all, this third epistemological position is gaining particular ground in the study of emotionality, as scholars from across disciplinary lines increasingly argue that emotions are neither "strictly biological or chemical occurrences" nor "wholly created by language and society": though having a clear "neurological basis," they are still crucially "shaped, repressed, expressed differently from place to place and era to era."[54] In 2012 William A. Mason and John P. Capitanio observed that, although "opinions continue to differ among emotion theorists about the relative contributions of biology and experience to the expression of emotions, a consensus seems to be building that both factors must be included in an integrated theory of emotional expression."[55] This is a sound way to account for the wealth of emerging data, which suggest both "undeniable variability and irrefutable evidence of consistencies in emotional responses across situations, individuals, and cultures."[56] The philosopher John Protevi, for example, offers one intriguing model for thinking through this "interface of somatic and social":

> We can accommodate universal patterns of basic emotions, which although not genetically determined, do reliably develop from our shared genetic makeup, given minimally shared developmental contexts, such as some form of providing nutrition and care. I think we can satisfy the social constructivists, however, by noting that the thresholds and triggers of these basic emotional patterns develop during the singular contacts of unique somatic endowments and complex socialization practices, as do the patterns, thresholds, and triggers of higher emotions. These socialization practices instill "emotion scripts" that indicate culturally specific forms of acceptable performance of emotions.[57]

In a different discipline, the spirit of this formulation is echoed by Jonathan H. Turner and Jan E. Stets, both sociologists of emotion:

> People occupy positions in social structures and play roles guided by cultural scripts. They are able to do so because of their cognitive capacities to perceive and appraise the situation (its structure and culture), themselves (as objects), others, and their own physiological responses. Emotions are ultimately aroused by the activation of body systems. This arousal generally comes from cognitive appraisals of self in relation to others, social structure, and culture. Once activated, emotions will be constrained by cognitive processes and culture.[58]

These formulations, of course, are just two of many advanced by scholars of emotion, but are representative of the growing transdisciplinary commitment to collapse the traditional nature/culture binary. It is to this end that Simon Clarke promotes "an interdisciplinary perspective in the study of emotions which has elements of sociology, social constructionism, interactionism, and psychoanalysis and addresses issues such as social action, agency, gender, and the embodiment of the emotions"—but, most crucially, doesn't "wholly [discount] elements of biology or the social."[59]

There is little doubt in my mind that emotions are the dual products of biological and social construction. This categorical hybridity, I argue, is what fundamentally underwrites the emotional power of literature itself, which transcends time and place to affect us. Literary emotion, it seems to me, so often evokes the sense of meeting a familiar stranger: the rage of Achilles, the envy of Iago, and the indifference of Bartleby resist full assimilation into our contemporary modes of emotional knowing, yet still demand to be acknowledged as kin to something in ourselves. As such, models from the sciences guide, but do not command, my search for literary and historical feeling. In developing this approach over the years, I have encountered (exceptionally smart) scholars of historical emotion that soundly reject the premise on which my work is founded. And indeed, a reader committed absolutely to the position that modern understandings have nothing to tell us about the emotions of the past is not likely to be satisfied by the book that follows. But scholarly disagreement is the sign of a healthy field. I can only say that I am convinced that the particular form of interdisciplinarity outlined above does generate valuable insights into this most interdisciplinary of phenomena. The method that I'm advocating is certainly not the only way to approach the study of early modern emotions—but it is one, I hope will become apparent as the chapters unfold, that does offer many virtues.

In four chapters, *Emotion in the Tudor Court* tries to account for the operation of some prominent courtly emotions in sixteenth-century England. Beginning with the early reign of King Henry VIII, chapter 1 considers the literary portrayal of Cardinal Thomas Wolsey, the much-hated *alter rex* who gripped English politics for nearly two decades. I argue that contemporary slanders and satires of Wolsey, insistent in their images of illness, appetite, and intrusion, are animated by a core notion of *disgust*, a primal response through which the cardinal is cast as a physical and social blight contaminating both King Henry and the commonweal. Despite Wolsey's profound role in shaping his early reign, King Henry ultimately fulfills the trajectory of disgust anticipated by the poets, diagnosing the now-abject cardinal as a foreign pathogen and purging him from the symbolic body of the court. Chapter 2 explores the life and art of Henry Howard, Earl of Surrey, a young man who, from atop the pinnacle of the Henrician court hierarchy, produced some of the period's greatest literary achievements—but whose short, volatile life never fulfilled the promise of its aristocratic upbringing. I argue that Surrey's courtly experience is best understood through the dynamics of *envy*, an emotion that not only colored his celebrated friendship with King Henry's illegitimate son (Henry Fitzroy, Duke of Richmond), but also ultimately underwrote the terms of his destruction, just weeks before King Henry's own demise.

The book's second half is devoted to the court of Henry's most famous daughter. Turning to the earlier reign of Queen Elizabeth I, chapter 3 considers the techniques through which Robert Dudley, Earl of Leicester (famed Elizabethan courtier par excellence) and his nephew Sir Philip Sidney (the equally famed shepherd knight), managed courtly *rejection*, by converting the sting of political failure into a source of affective solidarity. In the 1570s, I argue, the discontented Leicester party utilized a series of pageants and entertainments, ostensibly designed for royal flattery, to tacitly imagine a liberating community of outlaw courtiers. By finding emotional strength in mutual opposition, their strategy reveals the social and psychic advantages of performing one's incompatibility with official crown policy, even under the guise of endorsing it. The project concludes by considering what is perhaps the most memorable event of the Tudor dynasty's final years: the infamous, stillborn rising of Robert Devereux, Earl of Essex, and his followers in February 1601. Chapter 4 argues that the political experience of Elizabeth's final decade, in which anxiety over the aging queen, the unsettled succession, and unrest at home and abroad transformed the court into a factional battleground, was marked by an atmosphere of *dread*—a flexible term, in early modern usage, that could attach to both a terrified subject and the object that terrifies it, and that reflects the affective ambivalence between Elizabeth's courtiers and their own dread sovereign. In literary and cultural texts associated with Essex, members of his circle attempt to find political mastery in the affective mode of dread, a mode the crown desperately wished to keep as its own prerogative. The struggle for the Elizabethan court in the 1590s was a struggle to control the definition of dread, and was one in which Essex and many of his followers would finally pay a dreadful price.

The emotions I consider—*disgust, envy, rejection*, and *dread*—proved elemental to the affective atmosphere of the early modern court, and interrogating them in turn will help to situate moments of literary and historical interest within it. It is important to note, however, that while this book's early modern content is considered via the emotion I found to be most illuminating, the pairings are not indivisible; considering Wolsey, for example, through the lens of dread, or Essex through the lens of envy, would undoubtedly yield different and useful results. Indeed, though the models of emotion here are necessarily bound to individual chapters, they are all ultimately scalable: I can imagine each forming the basis of its own full-length study of the Tudor court, as there undoubtedly would be value in exploring their operation more broadly in the period. My aim, however, is to consider a variety of approaches to emotion in the period, as a foundation for more focused studies in the future.

My presentation, most obviously and importantly, is chronological, as I proceed through major moments of courtly interest in the sixteenth century. Other organizing factors also contribute to the overall design. The book's movement from *disgust* (according to scholars, the most bodily of emotions) to *dread* (one considerably more metaphysical) is, in general, a progression of increasing abstraction. And there is something of a birds-eye thematic narrative, as the era's political rise of middle-class bureaucrats and newly made men provoked disgust and envy among many onlookers at Henry VIII's court—the same types of men who would find themselves rejected by the too-shrewd-to-be-tractable Elizabeth, whose management of the realm in her final years ultimately left many courtiers in a perilous state of dread. But I wouldn't want to push on this too hard: such a broad accounting is necessarily a casual one, and its explanatory value is accordingly so. Given the complexity of affective experience, macro-narratives of emotional change (transformation, development, rupture, etc.) are particularly vulnerable to oversimplification and exaggeration, and it is crucial not to extrapolate too widely from one's analytical frame. My aim is not to offer a rigid taxonomy of the court's emotional modes, or to expose, in the manner famously envisioned by Raymond Williams, a sweeping structure of feeling that undergirds sixteenth-century England—tasks, I think, that risk obscuring the complexities of affective experience.

Two more notes on the project's limitations. The first concerns the valence of the emotions I investigate: there is no doubt that this book overwhelmingly dwells on the negative, a feature that aligns it with the preexisting bias of current scholarship on early modern emotion. As noted above, a focus on grief and melancholy dominated the field prior to the "affective turn," and Richard Strier rightly observes that even more recent work on emotion usually "presents the period in dark and dour terms."[60] This book offers no remedy—partly because the court, as a social arena dominated by the mechanics of competition and rivalry, was structurally primed to generate and amplify negative interpersonal feelings. But this does not mean, of course, that courtly life was uniformly dour: it was also filled with love, with camaraderie, with enthusiasm, with pride, and such positive sentiments certainly deserve more attention than they've garnered to date.[61] Space prevents me from including a transitory chapter that considers the reigns of Edward VI and Mary I as a period of *hope*—in which soldiers on both sides of the post-Reformation battlefield were marshaled by optimism for England's religious future—though I hope to publish it shortly as a separate study. I am also coediting (with Cora Fox and Cassie Miura) an essay collection on positive affect in the early modern world, designed to help give a more complete accounting of emotional life in the Renaissance.

There is also a gender imbalance in the project's subject matter. Though Queen Elizabeth figures prominently in the book's second half, its focus ultimately settles on several of the prominent men whose courtly experience provides a nexus of literary and political interest. This is partly because of the inescapable realities of Tudor social organization—in which men, of course, had vastly unequal access to the center of political power—and partly because of the realities of the extant historical and literary record. But, again, this does not at all mean that the emotional life of courtly women was any less complicated than that of their male counterparts. While I have elsewhere explored some of the emotional dynamics of women's manuscript circulation in the Henrician period, it is clear that this is an area that demands further study.[62]

These shortcomings, I hope, will be partly softened by what the book does offer. Most fundamentally, *Emotion in the Tudor Court* is interested in uniting archives of literary, historical, social, and biographical data to tell a few discrete stories about the affective world of the early modern courtly sphere. In what follows, I'll try to demonstrate the value in telling them this particular way.

CHAPTER 1

The Disgusting Cardinal Thomas Wolsey

In 1544 the Flemish painter Cornelis Metsys produced an engraving of King Henry VIII, a man with three more years to live.[1] (See the front cover of this book.) In the image, a modern commentator observes, the king's appearance is "ravaged by a combination of overindulgence, disease, and ever-increasing suspicion of those around him"; this Henry resembles an old toad, perched with "shoulders hunched, his face bloated, his mouth pinched, and his wary eyes reduced to mere slits."[2] The king of Metsys's portrait—and the king immortalized in history—bears little physical resemblance to the youthful Henry, whose beauty was sung in the courts of foreign princes:

> And first of all, his Majesty is twenty-nine years old, and extremely handsome; nature could not have done more for him; he is much handsomer than any other sovereign in Christendom, a great deal handsomer than the King of France; very fair, and his whole frame admirably proportioned.[3]

Henry remained the stud of Christendom for the first half of his reign—a role more widely acknowledged of late, thanks not only to the work of historians like David Starkey, but also to Jonathan Rhys Meyers's portrayal of the king in Showtime's popular television series *The Tudors* (2007–2010).[4]

But Henry's reign would have a second half, and age would not prove kind to him within it. At about the time of his infamous break with Rome, the king first complained of the "sore legge" that would increasingly plague his life; when this ulcerated wound clogged in 1538, Henry was found "without speaking, black in the face, and in great danger," and when the same occurred three years later, he was again "really thought to be in danger."[5] Though the king's mobility was severely limited, his appetite did not follow suit, and he soon swelled to infamous proportions. His condition in the final years is perhaps best indicated by an entry in the postmortem inventory of the royal household: "Twoo Cheyres called trauewes" had been commissioned for the ailing Henry, "for the kinges Majestie to sitt in to be carried to and fro in his galleries and Chambres."[6] The mighty King Henry VIII—who once, "placing his hand on his thigh," had boasted to an Italian diplomat of what "a good calf" he had—spent his last days being "moved by engines and art rather than by nature," the same leg unable to hoist his decaying body.[7] Time, we know, ravages all, but Henry went less gracefully than most, and did so far more publicly.

But even back in Henry's younger days, when the lusty king kept his vigor with a steady diet of hunting, harping, and hawking, his court was still home to—and indeed dominated by—an "unwieldy hulk of corrupted flesh bearing perilously [a] supple, powerful brain, a demoniac incandescence of ambition and pride driving and lighting from within the bloating, rotting body."[8] This is how Garrett Mattingly assessed the life and career of Cardinal Thomas Wolsey, the lord chancellor and papal legate whose meteoric rise starting in 1509 was capped by an equally spectacular fall in 1529. During the years of his ascendancy, Wolsey extended his reach into virtually every facet of English monarchal politics—a political mastery that was not unnoticed by contemporaries, for whom he eventually assumed the qualities of *alter rex* ("other king").[9] Having little of his father's taste for bureaucratic tasks, the young King Henry left much of his realm's daily operation to Wolsey, whose control of the Great Seal ensured that his own court at Hampton was in many ways an unmatched administrative and political center.

Nearly a century after his death, it is Wolsey who plays the villain role in Shakespeare's *King Henry VIII*, a domineering royal minister whose arrogance and treachery pervade the first half of the play. ("The devil speed him!" exclaims his chief adversary, Edward, Duke of Buckingham, "No man's pie is freed / From his ambitious finger.")[10] But Shakespeare's depiction of a churlish, self-interested cardinal emerges from a pool of anti-Wolsey sentiment that had festered in England for nearly a century—and that has, despite some recent revisionist efforts, largely shaped the subsequent historical tradition.[11] I begin my study of emotion in the Tudor court by considering one aspect of how this reputation was generated: the portrayal of Wolsey in Henrician literary culture. Ripe with images of gluttony and disease, contemporary satires of Wolsey—such as John Skelton's *Why Come Ye Nat to Courte?*, William Roy and Jerome Barlowe's *Rede Me and Be Nott Wrothe*, and a variety of anti-Wolsey ballads—are underwritten by the affective energy of disgust, a visceral response through which the cardinal is cast as a physical and spiritual contaminant, dangerously infecting both King Henry and his realm.

In this chapter, I suggest that the dynamics of disgust, as articulated by modern researchers in the humanities and sciences, can help us situate Wolsey's place in the Henrician imagination. As the governor of ingestion and rejection, disgust is a key force in the emotional arsenal that was fielded against Wolsey; as we will see, contemporary attacks insistently invoke the rhetoric of disgust in their attempts to discredit the cardinal and his political influence. Furthermore, this sentiment of disgust ultimately guides the terms of Wolsey's ruin: despite his profound role in shaping the first half of Henry's reign—in which he is so fully incorporated into the body politic that he is often indistinguishable from the king—the cardinal is finally imagined as a sickness of the *res publica*, a disease that is only cured by purging him from the symbolic body of the court.

"From the Donge Carte": The Rise of Cardinal Thomas Wolsey

"Cardynall wolsey," so writes George Cavendish, the cardinal's former gentleman usher and contemporary biographer, "was an honest poore mans Sonne borne in Ipsewiche with in the Countie of Suffolk."[12] Though few imagined that a butcher's son would grow to become the most formidable subject in England, Wolsey apparently showed a remarkable early promise: in 1486 he took his B.A. from Oxford at just fifteen years old, earning him the famous moniker "boy bachelor." As he continued his studies, he advanced to fellow and eventually dean of his alma mater, Magdalen College; he then turned his attention to an ecclesiastical career, taking his first benefice in 1500 at Limington and gradually acquiring more over the next decade. After securing a position as royal chaplain to Henry VII (and aligning himself with Richard Fox, Bishop of Winchester), Wolsey made his ventures into the political realm, embarking on notable ambassadorial journeys to the Low Countries and Scotland in 1508.[13]

At the death of Henry VII, Wolsey was named almoner to the new king; by 1511, he was a fixture in Henry VIII's council, starting the rise to power that would see, by the end of 1515, the butcher's son named archbishop of York, cardinal, and lord chancellor. As Cavendish records, King Henry, who lacked his father's passion for bureaucracy, soon granted his cardinal the daily operation of the realm:

> [Wolsey was happy] to disborden the kyng of so waytie a charge & troblesome busynes, puttyng the kyng in Comfort that he shall not

> nede to spare any tyme of his pleasure for any busynes that shold necessary happen in the Councell as long as he beyng there hauyng the kynges auctorytie & commaundenment, doughted not to se all thynges sufficiently furnysshed & perfected.[14]

Wolsey gradually installed himself as head minister and proxy to the king, displacing the de facto series of conciliar checks that had developed in the first years of the new reign.[15]

The cardinal's career enjoyed another crescendo in 1518: after a series of maneuverings, he was named papal legate *a latere*, making him England's foremost ecclesiastical authority.[16] That year Wolsey also secured his greatest diplomatic coup to date: the Treaty of London, a pact in which Europe's leading political players agreed to cease (at least temporarily) the nationalist conflicts that had for the last decade fractured the Christian world. Though Henry received nominal credit for the proceedings, Wolsey was widely acknowledged as the true architect; in the flattering words of Erasmus, it was the cardinal who "cemented with such close-knit treaties that peace which all the greatest monarchs had long desired."[17]

Over the next decade, Wolsey would continue to guide English policy—especially as it concerned the ever-warring powers in Europe, whose enthusiasm for peace quickly waned. England forged ties first with Holy Roman Emperor Charles V (1521) before defecting to his rival Francis I of France (1525); with such flexible commitments, the cardinal hoped to keep Henry a player on the international scene, while blocking either of the superpowers from achieving real supremacy. At the same time, Wolsey was occupied with tending fires at home (such as widespread resentment of the levies that funded his foreign endeavors), and soon enough, matters foreign and domestic became perilously entwined, in a thread that would unravel the very fabric of Henrician court and culture.

That's because sometime in the middle of the 1520s, King Henry had become enamored with a woman named Anne Boleyn.[18] It is difficult to assess Wolsey's initial role in the infamous scheme that soon unfolded; some contemporaries saw "the Cardinal as the cause . . . of the intended divorce," while Cavendish claims that Wolsey made "perswasion to the contrarie. . . . vppon his knees" after learning of Henry's plan to separate from Catherine of Aragon.[19] Reluctant or not, however, the cardinal was to orchestrate this mission, and it was an inability to secure his master's wish that ultimately secured his own downfall. It does seem that he tried in earnest: Wolsey and his agents spent months canvassing possible grounds for the separation, and in May 1527 he convened a secret, exploratory trial at Westminster to adjudge the validity of the king's current marriage to Queen Catherine. (The famous point of contention concerned the young Catherine's prior marriage to Prince Arthur Tudor, King Henry's deceased older brother.) After initial arguments, on both the spiritual legality of the match and the validity of the papal bull that dispensed it, it became clear that Wolsey and Henry would have to look to Rome for satisfaction.

But conflict between Francis and Charles continued to ravage Europe, making it rather untimely for Pope Clement VII, caught in the crossfire, to pass judgment on so realm-shaking a matter. (To make matters worse, Queen Catherine was aunt to Charles V, whose imperial troops had seized Rome in the spring of 1527 and taken the pope into custody.) In 1528 the pope would eventually order Cardinal Lorenzo Campeggio to London, ostensibly armed with a commission to try the case within England—but Clement had no intention of allowing a judgment there, preferring instead that proceedings unfold within his own jurisdiction in Rome.[20] After months of further legal maneuverings, the trial was finally convened at Blackfriars in May 1529; Campeggio successfully stalled the operation, leaving no choice but to nullify the current action and reconvene in Rome.[21] Wolsey's fate, it is often said, was sealed at this moment.

I will save the climax of the story for later in the chapter, as it belongs to a different, final phase of Wolsey's career. The cardinal's time at the top of fortune's wheel was much longer than that at the bottom, and it was during his long ascendancy that he provoked the ire of so many of Henry's subjects, both noble and common—including those with sharp tongues and sharp pens.[22] In the decade preceding his downfall and death, the cardinal was a subject of considerable literary interest, figuring in a robust corpus of surviving satires and slanders. Collectively, these texts have been largely ignored by modern scholars, despite their tempting position at an intersection of literary and cultural concerns.

Writing Wolsey

The best known of the anti-Wolsey poems flow from the pen of John Skelton, tutor to Henry VIII and self-styled poet laureate of the English realm.[23] Though he may have first assailed the cardinal in the allegorical interlude *Magnyfycence* (c. 1516–19)[24]—in which a king is corrupted by his courtly minions—Skelton is most remembered for a trilogy of explicit poetic attacks against the cardinal in the early 1520s, setting much of the satirical agenda that would subsequently define sixteenth-century anti-Wolsey slander.[25] The first salvo was the infamously opaque *Speke,*

Parott, a virtuoso performance that embeds a critique of Wolsey within a tapestry of linguistic fragments; often regarded as a masterpiece of Skelton's canon, the poem lampoons the cardinal on a variety of grounds, including his usurpation of royal authority and his lavish expenditures. [26] Wolsey equally figures in Skelton's *Collyn Clout*, a descendant of medieval ecclesiastical satire; here, the cardinal epitomizes clerical negligence, an unchecked tyrant whose oppressive policies have left the commonwealth both spiritually and financially bankrupt.[27] Finally, *Why Come Ye Nat to Courte?* is perhaps the most direct of Skelton's attacks; framed as a warning to the English nobility, the poem records the degradation of court culture under the base-born cardinal's malevolent influence. Taken together, these three poems entail a major assault on Wolsey's personal and political character—and as we will see, they do so in a surprisingly consistent affective mode.[28]

In addition to Skelton's well-known corpus, attacks on Wolsey appear elsewhere in the records of Henrician literature. George Cavendish, Wolsey's biographer, also penned a lesser-known poetic treatment of the cardinal; as part of his *de casibus* cycle of Henrician worthies, he conjures Wolsey's doleful ghost, who laments the ruthless ambition that brought about his ruin.[29] Equally interesting is what may be called the populist tradition of anti-Wolsey poems. At least two anonymous ballads denounce the cardinal's ruinous authority; "Of the Cardnall Wolse" (c. 1521) is cast as a direct complaint to King Henry himself, while "An Impeachment of Wolsey" (c. 1528) develops the cardinal's unfavorable comparison with Thomas Becket into a prophecy of Wolsey's inevitable fall.[30] At the other end of the social spectrum is the anonymous courtly interlude *Godly Queene Hester*—a hybrid-morality drama that, in the spirit of Skelton's *Magnyfycence*, attacks Wolsey directly in the guise of the treacherous advisor Aman.[31]

But perhaps the most elaborate anti-Wolsey invective is *Rede Me and Be Nott Wrothe*, a nearly 4,000-line salvo composed by the Lutheran exiles William Roy and Jerome Barlowe. Writing from Strassburg in 1527, the authors leave little unscathed in their treatment of England's spiritual shortcomings; as the realm's premier churchman, Wolsey is accordingly blasted throughout as the quintessential example of ecclesiastical corruption.[32] This satire is most notable for its intricate paratextual structure: the complete edition consists of (1) a mock-display of Wolsey's coat of arms, explicated in the accompanying stanzas; (2) a series of fictionalized letters between two would-be readers of the text, designed to obscure the poem's true origin; (3) a prefatory dialogue between the author and the book, in which the personified text fears reprisal for its contents; (4)

an ironic lamentation, in which a Catholic clergyman mourns the recent death of the Mass; and (5) finally, the main satire itself, a two-part dialogue on all matters religious by a pair of simple serving men.[33] This long, demanding text—smuggled secretly into England, to the ire of Wolsey and his agents—suggests again how easily the cardinal could serve as a flashpoint for extensive religious critique.

Such works comprise a dispersed, yet surprisingly consistent rejoinder to Wolsey's stranglehold on Henrician politics. United in their apparent disdain for the low-bred, ambitious cardinal, they inevitably return to Wolsey's unseemly place in the contemporary political scene: he is painted as a base usurper, slowly poisoning the commonwealth with his unchecked, unmatched power. As such, I argue that these poetic satires and slanders are ultimately animated by a core response of disgust, the affective mode that dominated literary reaction to what might be called the "Wolsey crisis." Disgust, to be sure, is often central to the generic operation of satire—which has, in the tradition of the ancients, long deployed scatological tropes in efforts to purge social ills.[34] (Indeed, in emphasizing the connection between bodily and moral revulsion, modern scientific treatments of disgust offer much to elucidate the general psychological underpinnings of satiric conventionality.) But literary disgust for Wolsey, I suggest, cannot be satisfactorily attributed to mere convention: given the cardinal's place in the Henrician social order, we will see how the emotion proves especially apt for denouncing Wolsey's precise role as a noxious, foreign body infecting the English court. First, however, we must pause to consider what it means to be repulsed.

A Brief History of Disgust

Nowhere do the Henrician satirists employ the term "disgust," a word that began its career in the English language at approximately the same time that Shakespeare was starting his as a playwright.[35] Yet there is little doubt that the sentiment of disgust, as we would now describe it, was richly featured in early modern life, and the basic condition that evokes it—"matter out of place," in anthropologist Mary Douglas's memorable phrase—was of obvious interest to a culture so invested in the management of social, political, and spiritual hierarchies.[36]

Since Darwin's pioneering work on emotional expression, disgust has been considered a core emotion of human experience; disgust elicitors in a cross-cultural context[37] reliably predict a stereotypical set of responses, including facial behavior,[38] physiological changes,[39] and neuro-anatomical activation.[40] Yet disgust has long been an undertheorized emotion, and has become subject to serious investigation only in the last several decades.[41] Since then, new contributions to the literature on disgust have been published every year, and the emotion has occasioned several recent full-length treatments indebted to theories from both the sciences and humanities.[42]

At its core, disgust is an emotion about food—or, to be more precise, spoiled food. It is an emotion about vomit, about nausea, about noxious, putrid smells; it is about how we know what we can eat, and how we know what we cannot. In evolutionary terms, natural selection obviously favored those organisms with higher avoidance tendencies toward spoiled or rotten food, and it's likely that this safeguard was internalized into the disgust response during the long process of human development. In fact, disgust's basic, biological response is so integrated into human adaptive behavior that some theorists question whether it is an emotion at all—it might be closer, they suggest, to a motivational state like thirst or hunger.[43]

Food and its rejection have long been recognized as central to the operation of the disgust response, since Darwin's initial investigation in *The Expression of the Emotions in Man and Animals*.[44] In the early twentieth century, A. Angyal confirmed that fear of "oral incorporation" was disgust's fundamental motivation, and in subsequent decades researchers have largely agreed that the primary domain of disgust was the mouth, the site of both ingestion and vomit.[45] In a foundational article of modern research, Paul Rozin and April E. Fallon offer a concise definition of "disgust as a food-related emotion": the feeling of disgust, they suggest, entails "revulsion at the prospect of (oral) incorporation of an offensive object. The offensive objects are contaminants; that is, if they even briefly contact an acceptable food, they tend to render that food unacceptable."[46] As subsequent research has confirmed, food-aversion behavior seems the fundamental component of disgust's physiological response, which includes, most centrally, the induction of nausea.[47] The emotion is, in other words, the "guardian of the mouth"—that which crucially prevents us from incorporating infectious or dangerous substances.[48]

Yet disgust is also an emotion about much more than food: it is an emotion about blood, about pus, about excrement, about wounds, about corpses. Despite the theoretical foundation outlined above, it is clear that issues of oral incorporation alone cannot account fully for the phenomenology of disgust, which occurs in many circumstances that have little to do with food or orality. Accordingly, investigators have located a variety of domains in which disgust triggers can be identified, radiating outward from the emotion's origins as an oral defense. Unsurprisingly, many of these domains continue to constellate around the issue of contamination, but the conceptualization of this contamination becomes increasingly abstract as we travel further out on the spectrum from disgust's original purview. In an influential essay, Jonathan Haidt, Clark McCauley, and Paul Rozin introduced the "Disgust Scale," an articulation of the emotion's forms across a series of discrete domains.[49] Their research suggests that disgust elicitors can be broadly categorized into two tiers. The first set, elicitors of *core disgust*, attends to the emotion's origins in orality: when we are disgusted by food, bodily products, or animals (particularly organisms associated with food or excrement, such as maggots, cockroaches, or rats), we are experiencing a visceral, somatic warning against oral incorporation. In evolutionary terms, these foundational elicitors originate as an oral prophylactic for a "species living with the constant threat of microbial contamination."[50]

Alternately, the second set of disgust elicitors has little to do with orality. In a process of cultural evolution, core disgust seems to have enlarged its purview, adapting to regulate matters of sex, hygiene, the body envelope (i.e., the physical integrity of the human body), and death. These domains, the researchers suggest, have in common their ability to remind human beings of their fundamentally animal origins—and as such, this category of *animal-reminder disgust* serves an important cultural function, as a "defensive emotion that guards us against the recognition of our animality." They continue:

> Humans cannot escape the evidence of their animal nature. In every society people must eat, excrete, and have sex. They bleed when cut, and ultimately they die and decompose. We propose that most cultures have found ways to "humanize" these activities, through rituals, customs, and taboos that serve to differentiate humans from animals. People who violate their local food and sex taboos risk being shunned and reviled by their peers, and in many cultures they are labeled as "animals."

Because of the human need to distinguish ourselves from mere animals—to insist that our lives have a higher meaning, and perhaps even extend beyond death—we have evolved an emotional mechanism that discourages us from engaging that in the world which suggests the opposite.[51]

To be sure, the disgust domains outlined here are not exhaustive; in their recent revision of the disgust scale, Bunmi O. Olatunji and colleagues have suggested adding *contamination* as a third category of disgust elicitors, while other researchers have advanced an entirely different taxonomy, around the categories of *pathogen avoidance*, *mate choice*, and *social interaction*.[52] But the consensus is that disgust is an emotion of avoidance, by which we attempt to limit our exposure to those objects that may endanger us, either with the physical threat of illness or with the existential threat of confronting our own material nature.[53] Taken wholly, this entails the basic notion of "pure disgust," the feeling of disgust "devoid of moral connotations."[54]

But more challenging, and more pertinent to our analysis of literature, history, and culture, are the instances in which disgust seems occasioned by violations of the *moral* order—or does, at least, according to ordinary language. Some researchers have claimed that the lay sense of "moral" disgust is, strictly speaking, a linguistic slippage: that is, when we claim to be disgusted by an act of racism, for example, we are really just mislabeling the experience of anger.[55] Yet there is compelling evidence that suggests the deep connection between the visceral, embodied experience of pure disgust and the so-called disgust that is elicited by sociomoral transgressions. While the elicitors of this sociomoral disgust are shaped by culturally specific variation,[56] the semantic congruence of disgust's visceral and sociomoral forms occurs across a wide linguistic range: we can point to examples from the Indo-European, Afroasiatic, and Sino-Tibetan language families in which a single word signifies both eruptions of the stomach and eruptions of the social order.[57] As the guardian of social contamination, sociomoral disgust is a culturally inflected elaboration of core disgust's biological purview.[58]

In her groundbreaking study of purity regulations, Douglas tentatively explored "the relations between pollution and morals"—but it is the modern research tradition that fully articulates the deep linkage between visceral and moral disgust, and it is this tradition that helps to account for their dual operation in anti-Wolsey satire.[59] That sociomoral infractions elicit a genuine disgust response—sometimes called the "moral dyspepsia" thesis—has received ample substantiation in the laboratory setting.[60] The recent work of Gary D. Sherman and his colleagues reveals that viewing morally offensive images predicts the same somato-visceral responses typically associated with food-based, core disgust. That morally objectionable content should elicit the tightening of the throat and queasiness in the chest and stomach—involuntary behaviors poised to block the ingestion of offensive food, and, if necessary, expel it—suggests the deep continuity between the biological origins of disgust and its culturally conditioned adaptations.[61] The hypothesis is further substantiated by Edward B. Royzman and his colleagues, who find that laboratory subjects asked to imagine an act of consensual sibling incest still experience a state of "oral inhibition," consisting of nausea, gagging, and diminishing of the appetite.[62] That the orality of the disgust response adheres in such moral examples suggests that these emotional elaborations are mapped across a spectrum. To this point, neurological research indicates that both pure and moralized disgust responses are underpinned by a similar anatomical architecture: functional MRI reveals that both domains "recruited remarkably overlapping neural substrates" in the medial and lateral orbitofrontal cortex.[63]

The evidence, it follows, suggests that humans have evolved a "primary" disgust system as a biological safeguard, which became elaborated in a set of culturally and historically determined "complex" forms.[64] In its complex form, moral disgust guards not the human body, but the human soul: it is that which involves "the protection of the self as a spiritual entity from degrading and polluting influences," as articulated within a particular cultural context.[65] Charged with "the protection of the soul or the world from degradation and spiritual defilement," moral disgust thus keeps vigil over "regulative concepts such as sacred order, natural order, tradition, sanctity, sin, and pollution," just as disgust in its core form stands watch over the literal violation of our material self.[66] The transition from disgust's role as guardian of the body to guardian of sociomoral conventions seems to be an example of what evolutionary theorists call "exaptation," the process by which an organism's fitness is enhanced by features serving a purpose other than that for which they were evolutionarily built.[67] In its primary form, the emotion of disgust helps us determine what sorts of (material) things we should allow within our physical body; in its extended, culturally elaborated form, it helps social groups collectively determine what sort of (behavioral) things should be allowed within their symbolic body. Or, as Jonathan Haidt and his colleagues aptly put it: disgust, having "evolved to help our omnivorous species figure out what to *eat* in the physical world, now helps our social species figure out what to *do* in the cultural world."[68]

Unsurprisingly, then, disgust is an emotion particularly implicated in the production of automatic, affective moral judgment. In fact, we can even go so far, as has been recently argued, to label the response of disgust as an "embodied moral judgment": there is a "causal relationship between feelings of physical disgust and moral condemnation," and the emotion's visceral activation makes it particularly suited to influence cognitive processes.[69] This connection has been confirmed in the laboratory, where individuals who have been primed with disgust elicitors have been shown to appraise moral situations more severely.[70] This is not at all, of course, to imply that disgust *ought* to be a criterion of moral assessment; the interaction of politics, morality, and disgust is incredibly fraught, as evidenced by any number of contemporary debates in the public sphere, and there is no doubt that the rhetoric of disgust has been routinely invoked to justify any number of discriminatory and dehumanizing practices, such as prohibitions against miscegenation or same-sex marriage.[71] And dehumanizing is indeed a key term, because "disgust in humans serves as an ethnic or outgroup marker" that establishes "a social bond or attraction that distinguishes the ingroup from outgroups"—a distinction, in its most extreme iteration, that leads to the denial of interiority, subjectivity, and sociality to the target subject or outgroup.[72] "When people fail to take the perspective of dehumanized targets," it has been suggested, "they feel disgust, a strictly negative emotion often linked to perceived moral violations and subsequent aggressive responses"—and indeed, these dehumanized targets elicit activity in neural structures associated with disgust (the insula and amygdala), but *not* in the medial prefrontal cortex, the "brain region reliably implicated in mentalizing and social cognition."[73] In other words, the dehumanized disgust target does not register as worthy (or perhaps even possible) of social intercourse. This is hardly pleasant stuff—but current thinking suggests that, whether we like it or not, the moral politics of disgust is an issue with which we must contend, as did those in the early modern period.

The term "disgust"—a cognate of the Italian *disgusto* and French *desgoust*, derived ultimately from the Latin *gustus* (taste)—came into the English language at the close of the sixteenth century; the earliest printed appearance that I've located occurs in John Florio's Italian dictionary *A Worlde of Words* (1598). Florio's translation reveals the semantic congruence of disgust's visceral and sociomoral forms: the Italian *disgusto/sgusto* is rendered with the English cluster "disgust, distast, vnkindnes, dislike."[74] This dual usage is confirmed in Randle Cotgrave's *A Dictionary of the French and English Tongues* (1611), which renders *Desappetit* as "a queasinesse, or disgust of stomacke" and *Desaimer* as "to fall into dislike, or disgust."[75] When the Catholic loyalist Anthony Copley denounces both Jesuit and Protestant prophecy, his expression equally suggests the proximity between moral disgust and distaste:

> So likewise of her Maiesties end how disasterously they haue prophecied, and do expect, I am sure you haue heard and do disgust as much as I. But what talke I of Protestants, seeing that also vpon very religious Catholikes they haue augured no lesse fatally, for being their known or but suspected distasters?[76]

That, in 1602, both "disgust" and "distaste" are deployed in this context suggests the immediate connection between the concept's gastric origins and its moral elaboration. In fact, in the years immediately after Florio's rendering, "disgust" is used quite regularly in its sociomoral form: in the first years of the seventeenth century, the word appears often in religious polemics, as a term of moral derision.[77] Though some researchers assert that the sociomoral usage of "disgust" is merely a figurative extension of the emotion's true visceral form (the form suggested by its etymological origins in "distaste"), it is telling, I think, that both the gustatory and sociomoral usage enter the English language simultaneously. And indeed, in the pre-Cartesian physiology of the sixteenth century, the deep association between an individual's corporal state and their higher-order existence has an organic connection to the disgust spectrum I have articulated throughout.[78] Though Skelton and the anti-Wolsey satirists would probably not have known the word "disgust," its imminent, multivalenced entry into the language suggests the general saliency of its varied forms in the early modern period.

I have reviewed this literature in such detail because the contemporary poetic reaction to Cardinal Wolsey was underpinned by these very dynamics of disgust. The domains of disgust—issues of contamination, infection, rottenness, corporality—dominate the satirical response to Wolsey's role in Henrician politics, and disgust is the primary affective state that is elicited by the cardinal. As an emotion flexible enough to account for both visceral and symbolic alienation, disgust provided the disenchanted observers with a poignant affective vocabulary with which to denounce Wolsey. Armed with the rhetoric of disgust, they cast him as a rotten blight on the English body politic, repulsive in both body and soul.

Stomaching Wolsey

Suitable for indicting both material and moral failings, revulsion is the affective touchstone of anti-Wolsey sentiment; as we will see, attacks on Wolsey are punctuated with references to appetite, indulgence, beastliness, and disease, reflecting the domains of disgust I have just examined. In this sense, portrayals of Wolsey take pains to bar the cardinal from any association with the Bakhtinian classical body, that "strictly completed, finished product . . . isolated, alone, fenced off from other bodies."[79] But at the same time, this emphasis on the grotesque is hardly carnivalesque; there is little festive about the cardinal's open body, which elicits revulsion and terror, not celebration and empowerment.[80] For the Henrician satirists, the disgust that Wolsey evokes is the index to his moral status—and it is this disgust that guides their smear campaign, which denounces both the cardinal and his polluting influence on England's social body.

We can begin with food, the core domain of disgust. Among his many traits, Thomas Wolsey seems to have been a larger man—at least according to (some) early modern portraiture, and at least according to John Skelton.[81] In the poetic context, Wolsey's weight was an easy metonym for his greater tendencies toward gluttony and avarice; the satires routinely invoke eating habits as indicative of Wolsey's general character, condemning his "myche bely-joye, and so wastefull banketyng" as viscerally taxing and morally sickening.[82]

There is little doubt that Wolsey liked to eat, and he seems to have made a show of it: during his many feasts and banquets, Cavendish records, Wolsey's tables were stocked with "ijcc [200] disshes or above of wonderouse costly meates & devysys, subtilly devysed."[83] In 1527 he produced a particularly lavish spread for the visiting French ambassadors:

> Anon came vppe the second Course with so many disshes, subtilties, & curious devyses whiche ware above an Cth in nomber of so goodly proporcion and Costly that I suppose the Frenchemen neuer sawe the lyke. The wonder was no lesse than it was worthy indeade. There ware castelles with Images in the same, powlles Churche & steple in proporcion for the quantitie as well counterfeited as the paynter shold haue paynted it vppon a clothe or wall. There ware beastes, byrdes, fowles of dyuers kyndes and personages most lyvely made & counterfet in dysshes. Some fightyng (as it ware) with swordes, some with gonnes and Crosebowes, Some vaughtyng & leapyng, Some dauncyng with ladyes, Some in complett harnes Iustyng with speres. And with many more devysis than I ame able with my wytt to discribbe.[84]

For good reason, Wolsey's dining habits became the stuff of diplomatic legend, though not always to his credit: the Venetian ambassador Sebastian Giustinian, for example, records that during public functions "no one is served with the viands of the sort presented to the Cardinal, until after their removal from before him."[85] Yet even with this notable appetite, food didn't sit well with Wolsey's stomach; he long suffered from digestive issues, which he tried to relieve in 1520 by securing papal approval to continue eating meat during the Lenten season.[86] Skeptics like Skelton railed against his motives:

For he hath suche a bull,
He may take whom he wull,
And as many as him lykys,
May ete pigges in lent for pikys,
After the sectes of heretykis!
For in lent he wyll ete
All maner of flesshe mete.[87]

In light of such criticism, Wolsey eventually thought it wise to extend permissions to the populace; according to Polydore Vergil, in 1522 he overturned the Lenten restrictions on dairy products, in order to "lessen the stigma attaching to his name."[88]

The tension between the pleasure and pain of the gourmand's life has a formal correlation in the literary rendition of Wolsey's diet. For Skelton, so apt at producing rhetorical excess, the elaborate description of Wolsey's "banketynge braynlesse" becomes stomach-turning, and the excessiveness of the catalog stands as an obvious indictment of the cardinal's moral appetite.[89] *Why Come Ye Nat to Courte?* offers a pointed example:

To drynke and for to eate
Swete ypocras and swete meate.
To kepe his flesshe chast
In lent, for a repast,
He eateth capons stewed,
Fesaunt and partriche mewed,
Hennes, checkynges, and pygges.
He foynes and he frygges;
Spareth neither mayde ne wyfe.
This is a postels lyfe.[90]

The rapid-fire enumeration of Skelton's signature style renders this menu nauseating, a cumulative effect inducing sensory exhaustion. And exhaustion is a concern, given the apparent scope of Wolsey's consumptive habits: the transitional rhyme *pygges/frygges* indicates a temporary shift in registers, and the corresponding turn from conquests digestive to conquest sexual suggests the flexibility of *appetite* as a category of moral critique, which readily expands (like the spectrum of disgust) from the gustatory to the genital. Indeed, the legend of the cardinal's appetite endured long after his death—so much so, in fact, that in Thomas Churchyard's Elizabethan portrayal of Wolsey (in *The Mirror for Magistrates*), it serves as the generalized vehicle for the cardinal's *de casibus* trajectory:

So, tasting some, of Fortunes sweete consayts,
I clapt the hoode, on shoulder, braue as Son,
And hopt at length, to bite at better bayts,
And fill my mouth, ere banket halfe were don.
Thus holding on, the course I thought to ron:
By many a feast, my belly grue so big.[91]

Churchyard's Wolsey learns to enjoy dining above his station—a trope originated by Skelton, whose condemnation of Wolsey's more physical stomach is perhaps most salient in the depiction of what the upstart cardinal is *not* eating:

Howe ye were wonte to drynke
Of a lether bottell
With a knavysshe stoppell,
Whan mamockes was your meate,
With moulde brede to eate—
Ye cowde none other gete
To chewe and to gnawe,
To fyll therwith your mawe—
Lodged in the strawe,
Couchynge your drousy heddes
Somtyme in lousy beddes.[92]

In these lines, we find the most naked connection between food and disgust; a man of Wolsey's social standing and moral character (so the associative logic goes) should be eating rotten table scraps. As above, this gastric association soon extends to other disgust elicitors: if the world was just, the cardinal would be spending his nights not in the elaborate chambers of Hampton Palace, but in the muck and filth of its stables.

This image of the "lousy" Wolsey introduces another key disgust trope in the contemporary satires: the cardinal as a site of disease and infection. As noted above, Wolsey's health was routinely ailing; he may have suffered from adult-onset diabetes, bouts of gallstones and jaundice, and regular infections.[93] The poetic tradition, however, emphasized the illness that contained the most obvious moral dimension: Wolsey's alleged struggle with the effects of syphilis. Roy and Barlowe broach the issue with little subtlety:

Ief: O naye, for he hath no wyfe,
  But whoares that be his lovers.

Wat: Yf he vse whoares to occupy,
It is grett marvell certanyly,
That he escapeth the frenche pockes.

Ief: He had the pockes with out fayle,
Wherfore people on hym did rayle,
With many obprobrious mockes.[94]

Though it is impossible to ascertain the validity of this rumor, Wolsey apparently did have a perennial ailment of the eye, which Skelton took as sign of a venereal infection:

So fell and so irous,
So full of malencoly,
With a flap afore his eye,
Men wene that he is pocky.[95]

A Spanish dispatch of 1522 confirms that Wolsey had an issue with his sight, but it acquires here a very different moral valence:

> Henry leads his usual life, leaving all the cares of state to Wolsey, who is so very ill that he is in danger of losing an eye, and the rest of his body seems almost equally affected. There seems little hope of his immediate recovery, especially as he will not abandon the affairs of the kingdom to others and must see many people daily.[96]

Wolsey's "flap," Gwyn suggests, was likely "some kind of disfigurement," which "gave Skelton the opportunity to make an easy gibe."[97] Nonetheless, the gap between truth and tradition is instructive: Wolsey's physical form still provokes a disgust response, which is, in turn, still correlated with the moral loathsomeness his behavior displays.

And Skelton would gibe, ruthlessly: *Why Come Ye Nat to Courte?* concludes by comparing this "morbilloso Thoma" to a host of ancient lepers, monsters, and incurables.[98] Most humorously, he imagines a scene in which Wolsey seeks aid from Balthasar de Guercis, the queen's physician:

He is nowe so overthwart,
And so payned with pangis,
That all his trust hangis
In Balthasor [who] . . .
Hath promised to hele our cardinals eye.

Yet sum surgions put a dout
Lest he wyll put it clene out,
And make him lame of his neder limmes.
God sende him sorowe for his sinnes![99]

It is telling that Skelton concludes his poem, an invective of over a thousand lines, with a meditation on Wolsey's health: after enumerating the cardinal's social and moral maladies, the poet leaves the reader with an unmistakable sense that Wolsey is rotten to the core, body and soul. In fact, after the poem proper concludes, Skelton again lampoons Wolsey's health in a Latin epilogue, which continues to correlate his physical and moral decay:

> Oppressed with the Neapolitan disease, laid low under plaster poultices, pierced by the surgeon's iron instrument, relieved by nothing, nor made better by any medicine . . . If only, therefore, that profligate, that bad Cretan lord, more aptly called disgusting, a mad fanatic, would keep away from the brothel.[100]

A convergence of disease, decay, and sexual depravity, the syphilis trope is a particularly damning example of disgust-based rhetoric.

We have seen how the anti-Wolsey satirists coordinate their attacks along various points of the theoretical disgust spectrum, clothing their barbs in images of food and orality, physical illness and degeneration, and sexual indiscretions. They also routinely dehumanize Wolsey through animal associations, another of the central categories in the taxonomy of disgust. These images are not, to be clear, the conventional figures of the beast fable, which had long deployed animal allegory in a satiric mode; instead, Skelton and company employ animalization specifically to debase the hated cardinal, to strip him of his pomp and dignity, to reduce him to the barest matter. Much like the example of syphilis, animal metaphors have little trouble invoking a network of overlapping disgust elicitors: when, for example, Skelton observes that "So fatte a magott, bred of a flesshe-flye / Was nevyr suche a fylty gorgon, nor suche an epycure," a single couplet activates images of animality, appetite, orality, rottenness, and excrement.[101] Though merely a pest in this instance, Wolsey most often takes on a more sinister form; he is famously cast in the satiric tradition as the "Bochers Curre," a ferocious mastiff who treats the realm as his chew-toy.[102] Again, the concurrent association with orality is inevitable: the cardinal, "An Impeachment of Wolsey" laments, "gnawen hys pepyll as A dogge dothe a Catte."[103] Skelton confirms that the cardinal is on the heels of England's nobility, who

Rynne away and crepe;
Lyke a mayny of shepe,
Dare nat loke out at dur
For drede of the mastyve cur,
For drede of the bochers dogge . . .
He pluckes them by the hode,
And shakes them by the eare.[104]

Happily for the satirists, the cardinal's surname seemed to indicate his canine form, as when Roy and Barlowe denounce him as a "Ragynge courre, wrapped in a wolues skynne."[105] Because of the typographical and paleographical properties of the early modern "long" form of the minuscule *s*, detractors relished the visual similarity between *wolfe* and *wolse*.

In concert with their general strategy of debasement and desublimation, the satirists also harped more generally on Wolsey's humble beginnings, quite apart from any animal association. (Though, to be sure, his father's trade ensured that any discussion of Wolsey's origin implicitly activates both food and animal concerns.) The poems abound with broad harangues against Wolsey's undue elevation; "Of the Cardnall Wolse," for example, begs King Henry to free himself "from that Churle borne by kynde / and from that vyle bochers Blode."[106] But the cardinal's origin is also cast more basically as a source of inherent revulsion. In the Renaissance, Frank Whigham has shown, anxieties about a changing cultural order were encoded within an elaborate literary discourse of the alimentary tract, and it is thus unsurprising that early modern social warfare also borrowed more inclusively from the rhetoric of disgust.[107] The satires insistently expose from "whatt vilnes [Wolsey's] pompe did aryse," an indictment with both moral and material force.[108] Again, Skelton is tellingly caustic:

He ruleth all at wyll
Without reason or skyll.
How be it the primordyall
Of his wretched originall,
And his base progeny,
And his gresy genealogy,
He came of the sank royall
That was cast out of a bochers stall![109]

It seems to me that the phrase "greasy genealogy" is a mark of Skelton's unique genius—one would be hard-pressed to express the sentiment in a more revolting manner. In *Collyn Clout*, Skelton is even more precise in locating Wolsey's origin:

> With pryde inordynate,
> Sodaynly upstarte
> From the donge carte,
> The mattocke and the shovll,
> To reygne and to rule.[110]

Cast away with the butcher's viscera, and cast up from the dung-cart; as Skelton tells it, Wolsey is a phoenix rising from a pile of filth. What's more, his physical defilement accrues a moral analogue, when we recall that in early modern England carts were used to convey all manner of social and legal offenders to sites of public punishment and execution: by revealing the "carte" as the site of Wolsey's generation—from which he sprang, it seems, like Athena from the head of Zeus—Skelton suggests that the corrupt cardinal is destined for that "vile deathe that is ordained for wretchede theves."[111] That Wolsey has traded the cart and the shovel (the tools of his station) for the scepter and a cardinal's hat suggests the extent to which the natural order has been perverted by his undue elevation.

There are myriad ways in which contemporary satires attempt to construct Wolsey's physical body as a site of revulsion: he is associated materially with images of overindulgence, illness, sexual decadence, rottenness, excrement, filth, and animality. Yet as we have seen, disgust is an emotion elicited by stimuli both physical and symbolic, a reflection of its dual role as guardian of the body and the soul. And while descriptions of the cardinal's corporeal repulsiveness carry an obvious symbolic freight, another strand of anti-Wolsey discourse tends to exhibit the ways that Wolsey enacts the more figurative dynamics of disgust.

For example, the satires condemn Wolsey as a general intruder in the courtly sphere: his very authority, quite apart from his physical loathsomeness, entails an encroachment and violation of the king's prerogative. In this sense, Wolsey doubly relates to the notion of defilement: he both is defiled (by his low birth, polluted body, and physical repulsiveness) and threatens to defile those in his proximity, such as the king.[112] After spending four years in the court of the young King Henry, the Venetian ambassador Giustinian concluded that the "Cardinal is the person who rules both the King and the entire kingdom"; this sentiment was apparently shared by many English observers, and a general anxiety about

Wolsey's prominence pervades the contemporary poems.[113] For Skelton, Wolsey exemplifies the worst type of statesman, he

> That wolde conquinate,
> That wolde contemminate,
> And that wolde vyolate,
> And that wolde derogate,
> And that wolde abrogate[114]

the sanctity of the English realm. Wolsey's rule has descended upon the country like a plague, to the despoilment of King Henry and his subjects. This usurpation is attacked prominently in the ballad tradition: "Of the Cardnall Wolse," for example, warns the king that "As long as one / Dothe Reyne & Rule, as ye do see, / So long in poverte this Realme shalbe."[115] Alternately, "An Impeachment of Wolsey" directs its address at the cardinal himself:

> of yngland the Rule, & Souerente
> of yngland thow haste had . . .
> Vsurpyd awtoryte is thy defence;
> no man darre the Resyste.[116]

As Skelton records in his trilogy, the most damaging aspect of Wolsey's influence is its unending scope; whether in Star Chamber, Chancery, or the Common Law courts, the cardinal's unilateral authority demonstrates how dangerous it is "For one man to rule a kynge . . . To governe over all / And rule a realme royall."[117]

But as a social pathogen, Wolsey was most dangerous in his capacity to infect Henry himself. The cardinal's influence on the king was a regular concern of contemporary observers, many of whom could not believe that King Henry would willingly subject himself to such a monster. According to legal records, an Englishman named Anthony Irby proffered (quite unwisely) one such suggestion:

> It is a wonder to see the kyng, how he is ordered now a days: For the Cardynall & the duke of Suffolk, which the kyng haith brought vpp of noughte, do rewle hym in all thynges as they lyst; whedr it be by Negramancy, wytchecrafte, or pollycy no mann knoweth, but as it is thought the oon of them by his Negramancy and the other by his wytchecrafte.[118]

More broadly, this charge was echoed by William Tyndale in *The Practice of Prelates*, in the midst of an anti-Wolsey diatribe:

> And, as I heard it spoken of divers, he made by craft of necromancy graven imagery to bear upon him; wherewith he bewitched the king's mind, and made the king to dote upon him more than ever he did any lady or gentlewoman; so that now the king's grace followed him, as he before followed the king.[119]

Finally, Skelton invokes the witchcraft trope in *Why Come Ye Nat to Courte?*:

> The kynges grace
> Is toward hym so mynded,
> And so farre blynded,
> That he can nat parceyue
> How he doth hym disceyve.
> I dought, lest by sorsery,
> Or suche other loselry
> As wychecraft or charmyng;
> For he is the kynges derlyng.[120]

Whether or not such claims were literally believed by contemporaries, this textual record suggests that Wolsey's social infection could have the imaginative quality of a demonic possession. In the nineteenth century, anthropologists argued that cultural laws of contagion were a brand of "sympathetic magic"; in these early modern accounts, Wolsey is imagined as a magician who casts his contagion into being.[121]

The stakes of this symbolic inhabitation were not small. The latent anxiety in much of the anti-Wolsey literature is that the cardinal will eventually come to supplant King Henry entirely—a virus that has overrun its host, so to speak. A report of Giustinian's experience in England suggests one possible form that this effacement might take:

> On the ambassador's first arrival in England, [Wolsey] used to say to him,—"*His Majesty will do so and so*:" subsequently, by degrees, he went forgetting himself, and commenced saying, "*We shall do so and so*:" at this present he has reached such a pitch that he says, "*I shall do so and so.*"[122]

Ten years later, in the midst of Wolsey's undoing, a "boke of articles whiche the Lordes had put to the kynge agaynste the Cardinall" would similarly complain that "in all writynges which he wrot to Rome or any other forayn Prince, he wrot *Ego et Rex meus*, I and my kyng, as who woulde say that the kyng were his seruant."[123] In this linguistic slippage, Wolsey's assumption of Henry's voice nonetheless entails a symbolic occupation of the royal person—and it exemplifies, I think, a more pressing concern about monarchal integrity. This dilemma is anchored at the heart of *Why Come Ye Nat to Courte?*, as elaborated in its most famous passage:

> Why come ye nat to court?
> To whyche court?
> To the kynges courte?
> Or to Hampton Court?
> Nay, to the kynges court!
> The kynges courte
> Shulde haue the excellence;
> But Hampton Court
> Hath the preemynence![124]

There is little frivolous about Skelton here, who identifies a troubling ambiguity at the center of Henrician politics. To entertain the notion that Henry's authority may not be absolute—that it might be flexible, or porous, or even contingent—inherently entails a major destabilization of the social order of Skelton's England. In order to account for Wolsey's power, Skelton must essentially deconstruct the governing discourse of his political world: he must come to terms with the fact that, quite unhappily, "court" is no longer an unambiguous signifier. What happens to England, and to the English people, when one can no longer distinguish between the king's court and Wolsey's court? What does it mean that we must even ask "whyche court"? These questions belong to a much different conceptual register than those regarding Wolsey's weight, or those concerning his poxy eye. Yet they share an equal concern with the mechanics of disgust—the guardian of the moral order, and the emotion to which Skelton and his allies turn to guide their response to Wolsey's social intrusion.

As we have seen, contemporary satirists employed a regular thematic vocabulary in the denunciation of Wolsey. Poets routinely railed upon his infamous low birth, his insatiable appetite, his unseemly entry into English politics—all domains that correlate with the associative matrix of disgust. To conclude, there is a particular instance that exemplifies these trends, but that also warrants specific consideration of its own: the mock-display of Wolsey's crest, perhaps the most immediately compelling feature of *Rede Me and Be Nott Wrothe*.[125] Proudly emblazoned on the title page, the crest

Fig. 1. "The Descripcion of the Armes," from Folger STC 1462.7. Used by permission of the Folger Shakespeare Library under a Creative Commons Attribution-ShareAlike 4.0 International License.

offers a seductive visual guide to the contents within the volume. On the verso, the image is complimented by a verse "descripcion of the armes," three stanzas of rhyme royal that both explicate the visual parody and introduce many of the central terms of the satire that follows.[126] (See figure 1.) The shield, supported by "two angels off Sathan," exemplifies in its ornaments Wolsey's status as a lightning rod of social conflict and dissention:

> The sixe blouddy axes in a bare felde
> Sheweth the cruelte of the red man,
> Whiche hath devoured the beautifull swan.
> Mortall enmy vnto the whyte Lion,
> Carter of Yorcke, the vyle butchers sonne.[127]

In these opening lines, Roy and Barlowe deploy the groundwork for the associative network that accrues as their project progresses; Wolsey's affinity with red, for example, suggests his numerous identities as cardinal, antichrist, bloodthirsty tyrant, and butcher's son.

Wolsey's social presumptions are implicitly underscored by the beast allegory, in which the cardinal is framed in opposition to his noble adversaries the dukes of Buckingham and Norfolk, invoked by their heraldic icons ("beautiful swan" and "whyte Lion"). The animal motif is balanced by a description of Wolsey's own mascot:

> The bandog in the middes doth expresse
> The mastif Curre bred in Ypswitch towne
> Gnawynge with his teth a kynges crowne.[128]

It is no coincidence that Wolsey's canine form chews upon the symbol of royalty; he incorporates Henry's power into his own form, just as he has incorporated himself into the political center of the court. Furthermore, his predation is specifically construed as an act of leisure, suggesting the luxury that his usurped position affords; the "gnawynge" dog is one that savors the bone he chews, and there is a sense of oral sadism that attaches to Wolsey's mastery over the crown. The poem concludes by reflecting upon the more general consequence of this usurpation ("The cloubbe signifieth playne hys tiranny / Covered over with a Cardinals hatt"), before delivering a final warning to the upstart Wolsey: "Wherfor prest take hede and beware they croune."[129] Though they had no way to know it in 1527, Roy and Barlowe would not have to wait long to see this prophecy fulfilled; in two years Wolsey would be cast from the court, and in three he would be dead.

Half a century later, when lamenting that very fall, Churchyard's rendition of Cardinal Wolsey reflects upon his own cardinal sin in a telling register:

> Pryde is a thing, that God and man abores,
> A swelling tode, that poysons euery place,
> A stinking wounde, that breedeth many sores,
> A priuy plague, found out in stately face,
> A paynted byrd, that keeps a pecocks pace,
> A lothsome lowt, that lookes like tinkers dog,
> A hellish hownd, a swinish hatefull hog
> That grunts and groanes, at euery thing it sees,
> And holds vp snowt, like pig that comes from draffe.[130]

In Churchyard's act of poetic necromancy, Wolsey addresses his pride via the imagery of food, animals, and disease—the very elicitors of disgust that dominated the cardinal's satirical identity during his life.

The Abject *Alter Rex*: Thomas Wolsey's Fall

In the final movement of Skelton's *Magnyfycence*, the virtuous counselor Good Hope frames a telling consolation to the titular king, newly repentant for squandering his fortunes on courtly leeches and usurpers:

> Good Hope, your potecary, assygned am I,
> That Goddes grace hath vexed you sharply
> And payned you with a purgacyon of odyous poverte,
> Myxed with bytter alowes of herde adversyte.
> Nowe must I make you a lectuary softe—
> I to mynster it, you to receyve it ofte—
> With rubarbe of repentaunce in you for to rest;
> With drammes of devocyon your dyet must be drest.[131]

The conclusion of Skelton's interlude, framed in the disgust-based language of diet and purgation, anticipates the thematic terms that would dominate the conclusion of the cardinal's own story a decade later. Long cast as a source of social illness, Wolsey was a piece of spoiled meat in the belly of the body politic—and in his final years, he is ultimately purged from the Henrician social body, cast away in a remarkable, repentant act of political expulsion.

In the summer of 1529, things were not going particularly well for Cardinal Wolsey. Unable to muster enough leverage to force Pope Clement's hand, the cardinal and his agents watched hopelessly as King Henry's divorce proceedings were recalled to Rome—a devastating blow to the English party, who had hoped to convert its home field advantage into a favorable judgment before the case was ensnared in the papal courts. In the months preceding the unsuccessful legatine trial, Henry had already become suspicious of Wolsey's enthusiasm for the cause; despite the cardinal's long-standing protestations that he was "redy to expone [his] body, life, and blod for the accheving of the same," Henry received reports that both Campeggio and Wolsey could not be trusted.[132] The trial's relocation to Rome was a blow to Wolsey, and his weakness in its aftermath was apparently not lost upon contemporaries. According to a report in Hall, after the legatine adjournment—and after it had become apparent that "the kings fauor was from the Cardinal sore minished"—the royal council presented Henry with a book of "thirtie and foure" articles against Wolsey; by setting out "with what dissimulacion and clokyng, he had handeled the kynges causes," the cardinal's enemies successfully "moued the kyng against hym" further.[133] After the conclusion of the legatine proceedings in mid-July, Wolsey was quietly barred access from the king's presence, and his role in decision-making was severely restricted.

By early autumn, the writing was on the wall. In mid-September, letters make reference to "the reports which are circulated" against the cardinal, and in a dispatch of October 4, the French ambassador Jean du Bellay remarked that he could "see clearly [that] Wolsey is to lose his influence entirely" in the upcoming session of Parliament.[134] Having failed to make headway in the divorce, and having made an enemy of the would-be Queen Anne, Wolsey was left virtually unprotected. On October 9 he was formally indicted with the jurisdictional crime of *praemunire*: by exercising his legatine powers on English soil, Wolsey was said to have imported a foreign legal authority into the realm, to the prejudice of the king's royal prerogative. (That Henry had both enabled and exploited Wolsey's legatine standing for over a decade was ignored.)[135] Wolsey was soon commanded to "surrender and delyuer vppe the great Seale"; in late October, he admitted to the charge of *praemunire*, and threw himself on the king's mercy.[136]

The initial stage of Wolsey's downfall was complete. He would never regain his former place by Henry's side, and his vast fortunes were confiscated by the crown.[137] But his ruin was not final, at least not yet. In the fall of 1529, Henry seems to have had no desire to annihilate his long-trusted minister, and there is even evidence that the king assured Wolsey of his general good standing.[138] With Wolsey in this limbo—disgraced, but not destroyed—his enemies seized the offensive, attempting to muster a mass of evidence too damning to be ignored. In this campaign, the anti-Wolsey sentiment again seems to activate the mechanics of disgust that we have explored throughout this chapter. Wolsey's narrative culminates in this fundamental act of rejection and repulsion: like an ill humour, his malignant influence is drained away from the king and his council, so that new blood might circulate in its place. Even the sudden, surprising charges of *praemunire* mirror this trajectory: Wolsey's legatine authority was construed, appropriately enough, as an intruding foreign body, needing to be purged and expelled to restore the integrity of the English realm.[139]

One such example is deployed by the new lord chancellor, Thomas More, who addressed his predecessor's ground-shaking fall in his opening remarks to the Parliament of November 1529. In the midst of a general meditation on the state of the realm, in which King Henry is figured as the nation's shepherd, More reflects upon the recent woes that have plagued the English flock:

> As you se that emongest a great flocke of shepe some be rotten and fauty which the good sheperd sendeth from the good shepe, so the

> great wether which is of late fallen as you all knowe, so craftely, so scabedly, ye & so vntruly iuggled wyth the kyng.[140]

Given the timing of More's oration, there is little doubt that Wolsey is the anecdote's referent; the new lord chancellor takes care to smear his predecessor with the raw material of disgust. We've already seen how the poetic satires regularly dehumanize Wolsey by means of bestial identification, invoking an alleged animality as grounds for moral condemnation. In this elaboration, More imagines a dangerously infected Wolsey: he is portrayed as an ailing animal, a communicable threat that must be cast off for the greater good of the flock. "Rotten and fauty" accommodates both the material and moral registers of Wolsey's alleged disease, and More accordingly affirms the proximity of disgust's literal and figurative domains. Wolsey's designation as "wether" pushes the metaphor even further: signifying both a neutered ram (and by natural extension) a courtly eunuch, the term configures the cardinal as a deviant sexual subject, another damning witness to his moral disfigurement. (With this castration, More perhaps also enforces the clerical celibacy that Wolsey infamously flouted.) Little doubt remains when Wolsey is finally denounced as scabbed, an image triply suited to More's rhetorical aim: in Henrician usage, the word might entail a literal "disease of the skin," a "moral or spiritual disease," or, a specific "cutaneous disease in animals, esp. sheep."[141] Consistent with the general trend in anti-Wolsey satire, More's oration constructs a cardinal who is repulsively compromised; his rejection from the metaphoric flock was a necessity for the well-being of the whole, as was his purgation from the room of state.

More's rhetoric is echoed (and intensified) elsewhere. To supplement the *praemunire* charge, the House of Lords apparently drafted a more inclusive catalog of Wolsey's offenses. Many of the charges in the 44-item list concern his abuse of legatine authority, as a clear usurpation of King Henry's royal prerogative. But the sixth item is rather different:

> Whereas your grace is our soveraign lord and head, in whom standeth all the surety and wealth of this realm; the same lord cardinall knowing himselfe to have the foule and contagious disease of the great pocks broken out upon him in divers places of his body, came daily to your grace, rowning in your eare and blowing upon your most noble grace with his perilous and infective breath, to the marvellous danger of your highnesse, if God of his infinite goodnesse had not better provided for your highnesse. And when he was once

> healed of them, he made your grace to believe, that his disease was an imposthume in his head, and of none other thing.[142]

Hall succinctly confirms the charge that Wolsey, "hayvng the Frenche pockes presumed to come & breth on the kyng."[143] In this passage, we find Wolsey's association with disgust nakedly literalized: not only a symbolic sore on the commonweal, he also imperils the king quite concretely with his infectious breath. Given their general emphasis on Wolsey's coercive influence, the Lords' complaint thus reveals how the literal and metaphoric domains of disgust find respective targets in the king's body natural and his body politic: an assault converging here in the oral image of Wolsey's whisper ("rowning"), the unifying act in which the sly minister pollutes the kingdom with his policy and the king with his contagions.[144] This bifurcated sense of disgust is further suggested in the particular emphasis on Wolsey's syphilitic condition; his illness entails not just a corporeal infection, but a moral one as well. Finally, there may be some irony in how the cardinal is said to have obfuscated his specifically venereal illness: though "impostume" had a generalized meaning of "sore" or "abscess," in the sixteenth century it equally developed a figurative sense of "moral corruption in the individual, or insurrection in the state."[145]

But despite the efforts of his opponents, the cardinal endured into the New Year—and in fact, as Henry's position continued to soften, Wolsey was granted a pardon in mid-February 1530. In return for this partial restoration, the cardinal was commanded to take residency in York—the seat of his archbishopric, and a diocese in which the absentee cardinal had never set foot—in a domain far removed from court. In the spring and summer months, Wolsey made the slow trek northward, a spatial literalization of his expurgation from Henrician politics. Yet despite his disgrace, observers suggested that the cardinal still cut an impressive figure:

> It has been reported in the court that he rode in such sumptuous fashion that some men thought he was of as good courage as in times past, and that there was no impediment but lack of authority. Certain people came to him, some for debt, and some for restitution of things wrongfully taken by him; to which he answered that the King had all his goods, and he could neither pay nor restore.[146]

The journey north offered many such moments of image rehabilitation, in which Wolsey embraced (or at least embraced the performance of) a pastoral care that stands in sharp contrast to his conventional guise as the courtly wolf. In his *imitatio Christi*, the abject cardinal embraced in his parishioners that which might otherwise evoke revulsion: Cavendish records, for example, how Wolsey tended to "lix [59] poomen whos feet he than wasshed wyped & kyssed."[147] As the journey progressed, Wolsey remained a formidable politician, propped by (in Gwyn's words) a "surprising degree of confidence that all would be well."[148]

But the increasing goodwill of his flock could not save Wolsey from his king—and only months later, in the fall of 1530, further consideration found use at home for a disgraced cardinal. On November 4, amidst a backdrop of increasing papal resistance to Henry's matrimonial aims, Wolsey was suddenly taken into crown custody for the crime of high treason; the cardinal, it was alleged, had for several months been secretly plotting with the European powers to derail the divorce proceedings and expel Anne Boleyn from Henry's side. The precise motive for this maneuver remains obscure, but it is clear that the king had decided (or, depending on the account, had been convinced) to ruin his *alter rex* completely.[149] In a humiliating parody of his first exile, Wolsey now began the return journey back to the court—where he looked forward not to pomp and splendor, but to looming death.

Wolsey never had to face those charges; he died of illness on November 29, 1530, at Leicester Abbey. Accordingly, we'll never know what Henry had planned for his former minister—though it seems unlikely, perhaps he would have issued a second pardon, or found another way to secure Wolsey's obedience. What is clear, however, is that subsequent accounts of Wolsey's life shared a profound interest in these final days, chronicling the suffering cardinal's decay in rich detail; the relevant passages are insistently corporeal in description, demanding that we remain focused on Wolsey's malfunctioning body. They are concerned with the alimentary component of the cardinal's painful death, abounding with images of eating, excrement, and vomit. There is thus an implicit irony, a kind of poetic justice, in these portrayals of Wolsey's demise: long cast as a contaminant, a noxious figure whose very presence infected the realm, Wolsey finally finds the tables to be turned. The domains of disgust turn inward, and in a striking act of self-consumption, he becomes destroyed by the same feelings of repulsion and revulsion that he so often invoked in others.

Though doubtlessly embellished, Cavendish's eyewitness account is the most elaborate chronicle of Wolsey's demise—and it is one that seems strangely keen on foregrounding the gustatory textures of its subject's final days. The motif is established early in the narrative, when, on the evening of his arrest, Wolsey shares a symbolic meal with his servants:

> With that came vppe my lordes meate, and so we left our comynycacion. I gave hyme water & sett hyme down to dynner . . . notwithstandyng my lord did eate very littill meate but wold many tymes burst owte sodenly in teares with the most sorowfullest words that hathe byn hard of any wofull creature. And at the last he fetched a great sighe frome the bottome of his hart . . . [He was] more fed & moysted with sorowe & teares than with owther pleasaunt metes or dylicate drynkes.[150]

Tears do little to satisfy a man of such infamous appetite: the scene, despite its tenderness, cannot help but parody Wolsey's infamous gluttony, which now can do little but vomit sighs. But while food is sublimated in this example, Cavendish goes on to reveal the gruesome materiality of his master's digestion, anticipating the gastric illness that will eventually overtake him.

In a statement that recalls the category of *animal-reminder* disgust, Wolsey feared that he would "dye lyke a beast" on his journey back to London, a remark confirming the sociomoral linkage of human dignity and corporeal integrity.[151] Cavendish, however, does little to shield us from the animalistic details of Wolsey's physical deterioration, which is chronicled by moments of agonizing urination and defecation. On one evening, after observers "perceyved hys color often to chaynge and alter dyuers tymes," Wolsey announced that he had been "sodenly taken abought my stomake with a thyng that lyethe ouerthywart my brest as cold as a whetston."[152] With the help of an apothecary's purgative, he "avoydyd, excedyng myche wynd vppward," but the relief was only temporary.[153] As the evening continued, there "came vppon hyme suche a laske that it caused hyme to goo to his stoole," and later "he rose vppe and went in to his chamber, to his cloose stoole, the Fluxe trobled hyme so sore."[154] Plagued with "laske" ("looseness of the bowels, diarrhœa") and "flux" ("an abnormally copious flowing of blood, excrement, etc. from the bowels"), Wolsey's entrails turn inside-out, with a violence that recalls his own sudden expulsion from the court.[155] After his horrific local description, Cavendish next works to quantify his master's agony:

> Whan nyght came that we shold goo to bed, my lord waxed very syke thoroughe hys newe desease, the which caused hyme contynually frome tyme to tyme to goo to the stolle all that nyght. In so myche frome tyme that his desease toke hyme vnto the next day. He had above l [50] stooles, so that he was that day very weke.[156]

Wolsey's dozens of evacuations serve as a bathetic parallel to the dozens of dishes that once filled his banquet table. In this account, I find it hard to ignore the moral resonance of Wolsey's hyper-purgation; in his final days, the cardinal's long-accumulated sins are slowly (and excruciatingly) drained from his body, in a corporal prelude to the spiritual purification of death.[157]

In fact, as the end unfolded, the expulsions of Wolsey's body become an index to his degenerating condition. As Cavendish records, the cardinal himself first proffered the diagnosis:

> The matter that he avoyded was wonderous blake, the which phisicions call color adustum. And when he perceyved it he sayd vnto me "if I haue not" quod he "some helpe shortly yt will cost me my lyfe." With that I caused oon doctor . . . to loke vppon the grosse matter that he avoyded, vppon sight wherof he determyned howe he shold not lyfe past iiij or v dayes.[158]

By reading his own waste, the sorcerer Wolsey performs a de facto act of extispicy—though in this demonic divination, it is his own entrails that foretell the future. Even without the physician's confirmation, Wolsey could see that the end was near: his symptoms, he reflected, promised an imminent "excorriacion of the Intraylles, or Francye [frenzy], or elles present deathe, and the best ther of is deathe."[159] After a farewell to Cavendish and a (famed) speech of repentance, he expired around daybreak the following morning.

Though it is impossible to determine the precise cause of Wolsey's death, there is little doubt that Cavendish encodes his master's suffering in terms that are insistently alimentary. As suggested by the spectrum of disgust, the thematic matrix of illness, purgation, and excretion that pervades his account is an affective linkage to the revolting sociomoral violations that are levied in the anti-Wolsey satires.[160] The chronicle tradition largely echoes (and in some cases, elaborates) the gastric focus of Cavendish's narrative, ensuring that wretched purgation would mark the standard account of Wolsey's final days. Consistent with early modern physiological theory, the Italian historian (and friend of Machiavelli) Francesco Guicciardini links Wolsey's physical degeneration with a corresponding psychological/dispositional analogue: Wolsey, he notes, "was suddenly taken with a fluxe, engendred either of the humour of disdaine, or of the passion of feare."[161] In his chronicle of the age, Charles Wriothesley curtly observes (without further comment) that some "recken he killed himselfe with purgations"—a statement vague enough, at least as

I take it, to entail either an unintentional overdose or a doctor-assisted suicide.[162] The more scandalous suggestion is made explicit by an anonymous (and questionably reliable) Spanish chronicle of the age, which gossips that Wolsey "took some poison to die, to avoid a more shameful death."[163] This notion of a "more shameful death" reveals an intriguing contest between the domains of disgust: the indignity of corporeal decay is thought preferable to the moral revulsion of dying a traitor in a public spectacle. (Though, to be sure, the manner of Wolsey's agonizing death recalls the execution rites of a common traitor: both entail, echoing Wolsey's words above, excoriation of the entrails.)

The Protestant martryologist John Foxe similarly fixes on the physical indignity of Wolsey's death—the result of "purgations and vomites" that were "so blacke, that the stayning therof could not be gotten out of his blankets by any means."[164] But Foxe takes the most pleasure in his elaborate postmortem description:

> It is testified by one, yet being aliue, in whose armes the sayde Cardinall dyed, that hys body being dead, was blacke as pitch, also was so heauie, that sixe coulde scarse beare it. Furthermore, it did so stinke aboue the grounde, that they were constrayned to hasten the buriall thereof in the night season, before it was daye. At the which buriall, such a tempest, with such a stinch there arose, that all the torches went out, and so he was throwne into the tombe, and there was layde.

The trope of the putrid Catholic corpse was a favorite of Foxe, whose usage ranged historically from the "rotting stinch" of the dead Roman emperor Maximinus to the "stincking death" of his own contemporary Bishop Edmund Bonner—and when recording the demise of the Marian persecutor Stephen Gardiner, Bishop of Winchester, Foxe further wondered "whether he stonke before he dyed, as Cardinall wolsey did."[165]

It is Edward Hall's account, finally, that offers the most detailed connection between Wolsey's death and his alimentary distress:

> When the Cardinal saw the capitaini of the garde, he was sore astonnyed and shortly became sicke, for then he perceiued some great trouble toward him, and for that cause men sayd that he wilyngly toke so much quantitie of strong purgacion that his nature was not able to beare it . . . [He was then brought to the Abbey of Leicester], wher for very feblenes of nature cause by purgacions and vomites he dyed the second night folowyng.[166]

The scene is concluded with a telling summation: "This Cardinal as you may perceiue in this story was of a great stomacke, for he compted himselfe egall with princes, and by craftie suggestion gatte into his handes innumerable treasure." In early modern usage, the concept of *stomach* entailed not only "the pipe wherby meate goeth dowen," but also sentiments like "indignation, anger, vehement wrath, hatred, displeasure, abhorring of anie thing that liketh not"—a set of emotions with an obvious proximity to moralized disgust.[167] In fact, the earliest examples of the verb "to stomach" (as in 1523, when Thomas Cromwell could barely "stomak . . . the high Inuries done by the saide Francoys") entail only the moral application of indignation, resentment, and reluctant toleration: it is not until the nineteenth century that the verbal form reflects a more literal concern with digestive tolerance.[168] Wolsey was a man of great stomach, both literally and figuratively—and as such, he was a man who routinely activated the affective circuits of disgust, in both how he lived and how he died.

Given the nature of contemporary attacks on Wolsey, it is no surprise that motifs of contamination, illness, and purgation are literalized in the depictions of his death. In such accounts, the metaphors of political disgust are desublimated, inscribing themselves nakedly on Wolsey's increasingly hollow form. The cardinal, in fact, seemed aware of the implicit analogy between this evacuation of his body and the larger evacuation of his moral, even spiritual identity: according to Cavendish, in his final days he referred to himself as "a very wretche, replett with mysery, not worthy to be estemed but for a vile abiecte, vttirly cast a way."[169] This remark is telling—for it is in the discourse of abjection, as famously articulated by Julia Kristeva, that modern critical theory most squarely engages with the issue of disgust. As the "jettisoned object" of the symbolic order, the abject exists "on the edge of non-existence and hallucination"; it is those necessary preconditions of existence that must, in their loathsomeness, be forcefully cast from sight.[170] Kristeva explains the notion further in a catalog of abjection:

> Loathing an item of food, a piece of filth, waste, or dung. The spasms and vomiting that protect me. The repugnance, the retching that thrusts me to the side and turns me away from defilement, sewage, and muck. The shame of compromise, of being in the middle of treachery. The fascinated start that leads me toward and separates me from them.

Kristeva's understanding of the abject is a meditation on the dynamics of disgust—yet it also helps account for the unmistakable ghostliness of

Wolsey's last days. It seems likely that the ultimate destination of Wolsey's final journey was the executioner's block; when informed of the cardinal's passing, the Spanish chronicler alleges, Henry VIII remarked that "I suppose he guessed that I wanted to give him a different death."[171] As a walking dead man, Wolsey in his final days typifies the loathsome uncanniness of abjection: he was a grotesque parody of the Cardinal Wolsey who ruled the realm for nearly two decades, an evacuated shell that revealed the ultimate fragility of "identity, system, order."[172] That the chroniclers equally insist upon marking the physical decomposition of Wolsey's body suggests the material analogue to the spiritual exile occasioned by King Henry's rejection. We watch as the cardinal is gradually reduced to a corpse, the form of empty matter that entails "the utmost of abjection." Wolsey ends his life as an object of disgust—in the same manner as, for many contemporaries, he had lived it.

CHAPTER 2

The Envious Earl of Surrey

"By the Masse, now I see that the olde saied sawe is true," erupted Charles Brandon, Duke of Suffolk, as the Blackfriars divorce proceedings of 1529 crumbled before him: "there was neuer Legate nor Cardinall, that did good in Englande."[1] During his ascendancy, as we have seen, Cardinal Thomas Wolsey evoked widespread disdain in both court and country—perhaps most of all in men like Suffolk. For nearly two decades, the realm's great peers could do little but watch as their share of English governance, a formerly inalienable birthright, was increasingly consumed by the churchman's voracious political appetite.

That Suffolk himself was newly made did little to soothe this sting, and indeed, perhaps intensified it. It was only his grandfather who had managed "to emerge from the obscurity of minor merchant status," and Brandon's own elevation to the dukedom in 1514—ostensibly for service in the French campaign of the previous year, but owing primarily to his personal friendship with the king—suspiciously recalled the rise of Wolsey.[2] (The Duke of Buckingham, a man incensed by upstarts lay or clergy, was said to grumble that "the King gave fees and offices to boys, rather than to noblemen.")[3] In just three years, Suffolk had gone from master of the horse to duke of the realm—or, as Erasmus put it, the king had "made a nobleman from Dama."[4] This jab suggests the resemblance of Suffolk and the slave Dama, a horse-keeper in Persius's Fifth Satire, whose emancipation does little to elevate his innate boorishness:

> Oh you in whom truth is not even
> Conceivable, who think that you can twirl a man round once
> (Pronouncing the prescribed gibberish) and he'll be
> Free. Here, for instance, is Dama: two cents' worth of hired man,
> Woozy with flat booze and happy to perjure himself
> For a handful of wheat. This one his master accords
> The ceremonious whirl and, abracadabra, he

> Comes out of the spin a free man, with a first name: he's
> *Marcus* Dama now![5]

From the stables to a ducal spread, or from a dung cart to Hampton Court? "Le *second Roy,*" as Brandon was deemed in 1513 (even before his ennobling), or the infamous *alter rex*?[6] To some, Suffolk and Wolsey were of a similar feather. This was certainly true, as we saw in the last chapter, for one Anthony Irby, who in 1516 condemned the pair for their mutual corruption of the young King Henry: "It is a wonder to see the kyng, how he is ordered now a days: For the Cardynall & the duke of Suffolk, which the kyng haith brought vpp of noughte, do rewle hym in all thynges as they lyst; whedr it be by Negramancy, wytchecrafte, or pollycy no mann knoweth."[7]

In affective terms, the disgust that Wolsey evokes in Suffolk—or that Suffolk evokes in Buckingham and Erasmus, or that both Wolsey and Suffolk evoke in Irby—returns us to Mary Douglas's notion of "matter out of place": in the universe of the Henrician court, these social particles are askew, a misalignment threatening to wreak havoc on the system at large.[8] But it is not simply the threat of contamination that prompts this response, but also that of displacement: in its disruption, the offending matter has usurped a place *from* something else, an object exiled from its native domain. In the zero-sum court of Henrician England, an ambitious social move risked knocking others out of bounds—a maddening, inevitable fact for those who could not help but watch the game unfold around them. For every Wolsey, there was a Suffolk, and for every Suffolk, a Buckingham; entitlement was an easy thing to have, but harder to hold.

But if a disgust response, as we saw in chapter 1, is one affective manifestation of social conflict in the courtly sphere—an external performance, directed at the offending, usurping object—it often occurs in conjunction with another emotional reply, far less apt to be publicized, but still vitally shaping to the psychic world in which it manifests: the *envy* that is also evoked by the successful courtly rival, the venom that churns in the guts of the disgusted, displaced observer. A natural (though by no means inevitable) affective companion to disgust, envy is contamination by the social maneuvers of another: the rival's engagement with the external world occasions a reciprocal disruption in the internal world of the envier, a reminder of the extent to which their mutual affective fates are entwined. It is no wonder, then, that envy and the related *jealousy* have been called the "rivalrous emotions," a designation that indicates their inherent connection to the world of social combat.[9] The early modern court was nothing if not rivalrous—and understanding the workings of envy, it follows, is central to the task of mapping its affective terrain more generally.

It would be possible to organize such a study around a figure like Wolsey, by considering how an object of obvious disgust and resentment inspired envy in the social superiors who were threatened by his advancement. But while certainly valuable, this approach risks obscuring the full range of the rivalrous emotions. Feelings like envy are not only evoked by the triumphs of our sworn social enemies; the flames of rivalry can be fanned by the good fortune of strangers, or—it is sometimes difficult to admit—by the success of friends and allies, whose victories, even as we celebrate them, still inflict their own wounds upon us. To demonstrate such situational complexity, this chapter considers *envy* as an affective touchstone in the life and work of perhaps the realm's most infamously haughty young man: Henry Howard, the poet Earl of Surrey. The son of England's senior peer, Surrey was, to be sure, incensed by the upstarts and newly made men with whom he waged social war—but his experience in the Henrician court, I argue, was equally shaped by a rivalrous, envious orientation towards even those closest to him.

To consider envy thusly finds it lurking in some potentially unexpected places—such as, for example, the structure of an early modern elegy. The envy of others is treated explicitly in Surrey's famed elegies to his friend and poetic mentor Sir Thomas Wyatt; in "W. resteth here, that quick could never rest," "Dyvers thy death doo dyverslye bemone," and "In the rude age when science was not so rife," Surrey affirms his own relationship to Wyatt by denouncing the envious hearts of false mourners.[10] But the elegiac poet, I argue, was not immune to envy himself. The first half of this chapter thus considers the rivalrous emotions in "So crewell prison" (c. 1537), Surrey's haunting memorial to his boyhood friend Henry Fitzroy, Duke of Richmond—better known to history as the illegitimate son of King Henry VIII, deceased suddenly in his late teens. After even a cursory reading of "So crewell prison," it is difficult to remain unmoved by the tenderness of Surrey's commemoration: cast as a reflection on the experience of shared adolescence, the elegy offers an astonishingly intimate glance into the formative years of two of Henrician England's most powerful young men. But despite this intimacy, idealization, and even latent eroticism—aspects that have occupied the elegy's previous commentators—I suggest that the poem's primary emotional subtext registers a different kind of impulse.[11] Composed during a period of personal turmoil for Surrey—after an act of violence at court, he had been imprisoned in the same grounds where as a youth he lived with Richmond—the poem reveals, like much of Surrey's work, the poet's profound ambivalence toward the Henrician political world that inscribed his identity, and his profound ambivalence toward the friend and symbolic kinsman whose unexpected death left him to negotiate its corridors alone.

Moving forward in Surrey's life, the chapter's second half tracks the rivalrous dynamics that shaped the earl's spectacular and sudden demise: one that would cost him his head at barely the age of thirty, charged with a treasonous plot to seize the English crown. The documentary record surrounding Surrey's downfall is flush with the affective register of envy, as the earl becomes symbolically locked in a tortured, ambivalent relationship with the nine-year-old Prince Edward—half-brother to his departed friend Richmond, and a boy whose future reign Surrey had particular interest in shaping. The mechanics of envy and jealousy, as they are understood both by modern researchers and their early modern counterparts, underpin not only Surrey's fall, but the emotional atmosphere of the dying king's court.

A model of these (inherently ambivalent) rivalrous emotions offers a framing context for the key events of Surrey's life—and a framing context for the courtly crisis occasioned by the end of King Henry's four-decade reign, in which England's most powerful men grasped and clawed for their share of the country's future.

Surrey's "Noble Fere": The Life and Death of Henry Fitzroy

As readers have long observed, "So crewell prison" offers a moving depiction of Surrey and Richmond's personal friendship. At the remove of some 400 years, however, what is not as apparent is Richmond's identity as a figure of national consequence in Henrician England. Despite his illegitimacy, Henry Fitzroy was the only surviving royal son in the first half of King Henry's reign, and the details of his brief life are accordingly chronicled in the dispatches of ambassadors, councilors, and courtiers.[12] Fitzroy's symbolic importance to English politics provides the civic context for Surrey's personal grief, and the action of the elegy variously engages both the private and the public consequences of his friend's untimely death. But Richmond remains relatively obscure to many modern readers of "So crewell prison," whose engagement with the young duke seldom exceeds the bounds of his traditional resting place, the brief explanatory footnote. To appreciate fully the force of Surrey's elegy, it is necessary first to excavate the historical Richmond, in order to gauge his significance both to Surrey and to the English body politic.

As the sexual appetite of Henry VIII is a cornerstone of modern lore about the king, it is a bit surprising to find that Henry Fitzroy was the only illegitimate child to be recognized during his long stay on the English throne. Despite his son's bastardy, King Henry wasted little time in grooming him for a future place in English politics: after his birth in 1519, Fitzroy's arrangements were immediately undertaken by his godfather Wolsey, and the boy was only six when his elevation to the dukedoms of Richmond and Somerset in 1525 made him England's most decorated peer. As the nominal head of the crown's revived attempt to establish conciliar management in the north, Richmond spent his early years among his own household at Sheriff Hutton, where he was immersed in both humanist learning and the aristocratic arts—an educational regime apt for a boy many already thought could one day rule the realm. In 1529 he served a short term as nominal lord lieutenant of Ireland, and in the same year, the ten-year-old boy was summoned to the first sessions of what would come to be known as the Reformation Parliament.

It was also in 1529 that Richmond entered the orbit of the Howard family: after Wolsey's demise his care was transferred to Thomas Howard, Duke of Norfolk, uncle of the increasingly influential Anne Boleyn and father to the then thirteen-year-old Earl of Surrey. Almost immediately, Norfolk took steps to forge a bond between the promising royal child and his own precocious son—who was, according to the imperial ambassador Eustace Chapuys, already writing letters in "very good Latin."[13] At a private meeting in December 1529, Norfolk informed Chapuys of this "project which he had":

> The King has entrusted to me the education of his bastard son, the duke of Richmond, of whom my own son may become in time preceptor and tutor, that he may attain both knowledge and virtue, so that a friendship thus cemented promises fair to be very strong and firm.

Though the future Queen Anne, a Howard relation, was already sharing the king's bedchamber, this was not enough for Norfolk, ever the patriarch; it was by means of Surrey and Richmond's projected friendship that he hoped to secure a place for the Howards in England's long-term, post-Henrician future.

In April 1530 Richmond left Sheriff Hutton for his new residence at Windsor, where he and Surrey spent several years leading the life recalled in "So crewell prison." Their growing friendship took the boys beyond Windsor's walls, and in the autumn of 1532 Richmond and Surrey joined the royal train to Calais on its diplomatic mission to secure French support for King Henry's ongoing divorce proceedings. After Henry returned to England in November, Richmond and Surrey remained with the French court, as pledge of the pending Franco-English treaty; entertained by the French princes, the boys wintered in Paris, enjoyed spring at the magnificent Palace of Fontainebleau, and spent the summer touring the southern provinces on progress with King Francis. Recalled to England in August 1533, they became further entwined when Richmond was wed to Surrey's sister Mary that November (though the couple's youth prevented the union from being consummated). Fitzroy's death in July 1536 was sudden: Chapuys reports on the 8th of that month that Richmond had been judged "consumptive, and incurable," and on the 18th Lord Lisle in Calais was similarly informed that "my lorde of Rychemonde [is] very syck."[14] King Henry, who had both a personal and political stake in his son's health, was especially distraught, and Chapuys wrote to his superiors that Henry had "no hope that the duke of Richmond can live long, whom he certainly intended to make his successor, and but for his illness, would have got him declared so by parliament."[15]

On July 22, Wriothesley records, the seventeen-year-old Richmond "departed out of this transitorie lief at the Kinges place in Sainct James."[16] His son's death could not have come at a more politically volatile time for Henry: just months earlier, the king had executed his second wife and married his third, and it was only days before Fitzroy's death that Parliament had finalized its attempt to give shape to the now-muddled succession. Though details remain unclear, it seems that Henry did not want the distraction and stress of a public funeral for Richmond: on August 3, Chapuys reported that the body had "been secretly carried in a wagon, covered with straw, without any company except two persons clothed in green, who followed at a distance, into Norfolk, where the Duke his father-in-law will have him buried."[17] Unfortunately for Norfolk, however, the job was apparently bungled, and the duke soon found himself a victim of Henry's famous temper. With a hand "full full full of color and agonye," Norfolk attempted to defend his performance to Thomas Cromwell, the king's principal secretary:

> This nyght at viij a cloke came dyuers lettres to me from my frendes and seruantes abowtes london, all agreing in one tale, not a litle to my sorow, that the kynges highnes shuld be in gret displesure with me because my lord of richmond was not carried honorably and so buryed: my lord I dout not ye know the kynges plesure was that his body shuld be conveyed secretly in a close cart vnto thedford

> and at my sewte thider and there so buryed; and accordyng to the same I sent order with both the cottons and commanded them that his body shall haue be wrapped in lede and a close cart provyded for hym, whose body was neyther put in lede nor no close cart provyded for him nor yet conveyed veray secretly.[18]

Fortunately for Norfolk, the matter was soon forgotten by the king—but not, we must imagine, by Surrey, whose virtuoso poetic commemoration in "So crewell prison" is a natural counterpoint to Richmond's unexpectedly humble burial. At the very least, we do know that the earl remained devastated by his friend's death; months later, Norfolk reported that Surrey had been sick with grief for "a great parte of the last yere," and he was still "very weke, his nature ronnyng from hym habundauntlie . . . for thought of my lord of Richemond."[19]

But unfortunately for the earl, there would be little time to grieve in the immediate wake of Richmond's death. October 1536 marked the beginning of the popular religious uprisings known as the Pilgrimage of Grace, and both Norfolk and Surrey played strategic roles in their eventual suppression.[20] In early 1537 order was finally reestablished after a confused campaign, and in the conflict's aftermath Surrey remained away from court on account of illness.[21] When he rejoined the court in July, the specter of the Pilgrimage brought with it disastrous consequences: in an infamous episode, Surrey seems to have struck another courtier (traditionally said to be Edward Seymour, brother of the pregnant queen) to defy the treasonous charge that the Howards had secretly sympathized with the Catholic rebels.[22] Though respect for Surrey's rank spared the loss of his hand (the routine penalty for acts of violence within the bounds of court), the twenty-year-old earl was nonetheless reprimanded and confined to Windsor in July 1537—a palace still haunted by the memory of Richmond, who had been dead for only a year.[23] "So crewell prison," written during his stay, is the product of both this period of custody and Surrey's grief—grief that would remain with the earl until the end of his short life.

Surrey, to be sure, was greatly moved by the loss of his closest companion; though destined to outlive his friend by only a decade, he never in his adult life seems to have matched the *amicitia perfecta* he enjoyed with Richmond. Yet to understand the full complexity of this bond, it is necessary to say another word about Surrey's emotional profile. Surrey enacted—and indeed, perhaps helped inaugurate—a social archetype that would become increasingly prevalent throughout the sixteenth century.

I mean the angry young man of privilege, who found his way of comprehending the world—one defined by warfare, neo-chivalric cults of honor, and a masculine investment in the aristocratic arts—perilously threatened by a changing social order, in which kings and queens were happy to raise an army of bureaucrats and middlemen to administer their increasingly centralized realms.[24] Though noblemen such as Surrey continued to serve a crucial function in England's political hierarchy, they found less room to actualize their own ambitions, and some, at least, developed a temperament marked by frustration, impulsivity, and recklessness—especially toward the hated social upstarts (such as Seymour), whom they saw as usurping the nobility's God-given role as monarchal advisers. Surrey exemplified this brand of sixteenth-century man; as we will see in later chapters, Sir Philip Sidney was something of this type, as certainly was the infamous Robert Devereux, Earl of Essex at the end of Elizabeth's reign. And though these flames burned bright, they also burned quickly: Sidney died in war at thirty-one years of age, while Surrey and Essex died by the axe at thirty and thirty-five respectively. In his short life, Surrey was imprisoned at least three times for unsanctioned violence—though, because of his social standing (as we saw above), his punishments were perfunctory. As Surrey was supremely aware, the distant blood of royalty was in his veins—and in the tense, final months of King Henry's reign, it was alleged that he had plotted to seize the crown himself from the young Prince Edward. Though these charges did not stick, Surrey was finally deemed guilty of quartering in his badge the ancient arms of Edward the Confessor—an implicit claim of royalty, so it was said, and thus an implicit threat to the king's prerogative. This heraldic crime was enough for Surrey to lose his head in January 1547, the last person executed in Henry's long, bloody reign.[25]

Surrey's sensitivity to matters of precedence, honor, and social standing ultimately cost him his life. When reading "So crewell prison," it is thus important to consider what else, besides grief, he may have felt toward Richmond, both before and after his death. It is possible to speculate, especially when we reframe the question: what else did Surrey, at the ages of both thirteen and twenty, feel toward the best friend who was younger, but of a higher rank; who was illegitimate, but was a royal son; and who was, by many accounts, being groomed to rule the realm? How did a young man of Surrey's volatile temperament respond to this unique playmate, perhaps the only adolescent in the realm whose standing surpassed his own?

Though any answers must be tentative, we can grid what we know of Surrey into the larger social matrix that underpinned Henrician aristocratic culture. This task must take its bearing in the familial interplay of Howard and Tudor—a relationship of enormous psychological complexity, perhaps most of all to Surrey. To put it another way, what did it mean to Surrey that he was a Howard, what did it mean that he was *not* a Tudor, and how did the answers to such questions inflect his friendship with Richmond? Buried in the Howard family's ancestral tomb, Richmond was something of an honorary Howard; for his own part, we will see below, Surrey often indulged in fantasies that seem to efface the distinction between Howard and Tudor. But such fantasies were just that. Surrey was not a Tudor, and his increasingly flagrant insistence on the Howard family's ancestral royalty suggests the envy and aggression inherent in such projective identifications. There are many reasons to suspect that Surrey's response to Richmond's death was profoundly ambivalent, underpinned by the long-fought competition of two powerful feelings: the idyllic fantasy of sameness, in which he and Richmond lived and ruled the realm together as brothers, and the agonizing reality of difference, that cold-blooded cultural logic assuring finally that Surrey and Richmond were not the same, and that Howard was not Tudor.

When reading the poem, this is the question I'd like us to keep in mind: is it reasonable to believe that a man like Surrey, whose concern with matters of honor and precedence was arguably pathological, would have felt no envy, no resentment, and no anger at the superior fortune of his friend? I think the answer is convincingly no, and that the manifest grief of "So crewell prison" is undercut throughout by a darker affective register. More specifically, I detect in the poem a node comprised of the rivalrous emotions I introduced above: envy, jealousy, and latent aggression. In "So crewell prison," it is possible to explore the poem's contestatory energy across these distinct, yet affiliated emotions; their collective operation, I suggest, fuels the ambivalence that ultimately shapes the expression of Surrey's grief.

The Experience of Envy

For the reasons discussed above, envy seems to have been a core component of Surrey's emotional profile.[26] But what, precisely, characterizes the phenomenon of envy? Despite its apparent universality—recent scholars note that nearly "all cultures have a word meaning something close to envy, even though words for other common social phenomena may be absent"—defining the sentiment is deceptively difficult.[27] In contemporary English, this confusion arises largely from a lexical imprecision: in common usage, the word "envy" is often exchanged freely with overlapping terms like "jealousy" or "resentment." Yet both philosophical and empirical research insists upon the importance of distinguishing envy from the related rivalrous emotions, a taxonomy that will be central to my subsequent discussion of "So crewell prison."

In literary studies of the early modern period, *envy* most obviously features in René Girard's notion of "mimetic desire," the process through which one party's desire inflames that of another.[28] This concept alone, however, does not account fully for the variety of contexts in which this rivalrous sentiment emerges—envious desire is not always mimetic—and it is thus important to supplement our understanding with the insights of alternate research traditions. Most basically, of course, scholars characterize envy as the discomfort we feel at another's good fortune, the pain that accompanies the recognition of "another's superior quality, achievement, or possession."[29] To experience envy, however, is to experience any number of concurrent feelings, and the variegated nature of its pain suggests that envy is a compound emotion: as Maria Miceli and Cristiano Castelfranchi note, envy can be theorized across a variety of affective spectra, including *longing-greed-covetousness, admiration-emulation, anger-resentment-sense of injustice,* and *depression-despair-inferiority*.[30] Like many emotions, a degree of cognitive appraisal is crucial in the envious subject, but it is the specifically *comparative* nature of envy—the awareness of one's own lack and another's intolerable gain—that distinguishes it from non-differentiated hostility or antagonism. As this unfavorable comparison becomes embedded in feelings of social inferiority, the subject's self-respect is accordingly threatened; this affective mechanism proves especially intense for a man like Surrey, for whom social standing is paramount.[31] This is because envy (as well as jealousy) is most powerful when a rival threatens some domain that we have deemed central to our sense of self:

> The critical variable that determines whether the successes of close others make us feel good about ourselves (reflection) or have the opposite effect (comparison) is the *relevance* of the other's success or personal qualities to our self-definition. Reflection results when the other's performance is in an unimportant domain. We are motivated to maintain high self-evaluation, so we bask in the reflected glory of our friends' unimportant (to us) successes because they are not threatening to us. But when personal relevance (i.e., domain importance) is high, we are likely to experience envy or jealousy.[32]

Richmond was a rival that could trigger Surrey like no other. As this passage suggests more generally, however, the envier's precise attitude vis-à-vis the rival (and thus the coveted advantage) is contextually dependent, leading to an affective field that is often contested; this dynamic reflects the ambivalence that I detect in "So crewell prison." Recent research suggests that there are at least two distinct forms of envy, unique in their associated thoughts and actions: the *malicious* (or *true*) envier longs to destroy the rival's advantage, whereas the *benign* envier (free of venom, but not frustration) aspires to join the rival in the desired position.[33] Envy is an amorphous emotion, capable of evoking a multitude of concurrent responses: the envier is tortured both by an attraction to the unfulfilled, desired object and by the venom occasioned by its distance.

In early Tudor England, envy was an equally vexed concept.[34] The English word "envy" ultimately derives from the Latin *invidia*/*invidere*, to look upon (*in* + *videre*) with malice, scorn, or rivalry; the basic sense of malicious envy was thus actively used in the period, as Renaissance thinkers inherited a classical and medieval Christian framework that denounced *invidia* among the deadliest of sins.[35] In Thomas Wilson's *A Christian Dictionarie*, "enuie" is neatly defined as that "affection which makes men grieue & fret at the good and prosperity of others," and the "enuious" soul is defined as one "who repineth and grutcheth at the welfare and happinesse of others."[36] In the Renaissance emblem tradition, the conventional iconography of *invidia* (popularized by Ovid) portrays Envy as a gaunt, haggard woman, who is imagined "fast gnawing on the flesh / Of Snakes and Todes, the filthie foode that keepes hir vices fresh."[37] Whitney's collection offers a typical example in its commentary:

> This, Enuie is: leane, pale, and full of yeares,
> Who with the blisse of other pines awaie.
> And what declares, her eating vipers broode?
> That poysoned thoughtes, bee euermore her foode.[38]

In *The Faerie Queene*, Spenser adapts this trope in his famous portrayal of Envie:

> inwardly he chawed his owne maw
> At neibors welth, that made him euer sad;
> For death it was, when any good he saw,
> And wept, that cause of weeping none he had,
> But when he heard of harme, he wexed wondrous glad.[39]

Closer to Surrey's time, Alexander Barclay's *Ship of Fools* (a translation/adaptation of Sebastian Brant's late fifteenth-century *Das Narrenschiff*) offers a similar depiction of those "whiche greatly them delyte / In others losse":

> If one haue plenty of treasour and ryches
> Or by his merytis obteyne great dignyte
> These folys enuyous that of the same haue les
> Enuy by malyce, the others hye degre
> And if another of honour haue plente
> They it enuy and wysshe that they myght sterue . . .
> These folys desyre agaynst both lawe and right
> Anoters good if they may get the same
> If they may nat by flaterynge nor by myght
> Than by fals malyce they hym enuy and blame.[40]

In its basic configuration—the painful desire to level another's advantage—the sense of malicious envy in early modern English was quite similar to the modern definitions we have seen above.

Yet Renaissance thinkers also utilized a concept of benign envy, even if no such lexical category existed. Consider, for example, the reaction of Sir William Cornwallis to the heroes of the ancient world:

> When I heare of any famous Action of our time . . . it takes away my sleepe, not with Enuie, but with an honest Emulation. I desire to robbe no man of his Glory, but to participate with Experience: well it pleaseth not my Destiny, I hope it will do, that's my Comfort: In the meane time I will see Battailes in Imagination, and reade them, since I may not be in them.[41]

As Cornwallis makes clear, this desire to emulate is not predicated on robbing another of his glory, or destroying the object of envy. Yet the feeling that disturbs his sleep seems hardly pleasant, and is therefore distinct from the less agitative positions of admiration or reverence. Despite his protestation, Cornwallis describes the emotional configuration of benign envy, even though the term was not linguistically native to the early modern period.

In fact, Cornwallis's professed distinction between envy and emulation reveals another contour to the early modern understanding of envy. Despite the common impulse to keep both terms distinct—such as in the late sixteenth-century treatise that distinguishes "countentious enuies" from "honest emulations"—the word "envy" was nonetheless also used in the period to signify an emotionally neutral, or even admirable, form of emulation.[42] This lexical overlap was certainly native to Surrey's period: in *The Image of Gouernance* (1541), Sir Thomas Elyot describes how a counselor of high merit will "ingender in noble men an honest enuy, eyther to excede hym in vertue, or at the leste to be iudged equall vnto hym," while John Palsgrave (incidentally, Richmond's former tutor) imagines that his translation of a neo-Latin classroom drama will move "some lyttell grayne of honeste and vertuous enuye" in the hearts of King Henry's subjects.[43] In fact, some modern studies of envy have also argued for the emotional specificity of emulation, an orientation in which "there is no ill will towards the advantaged party," an innocuous rival perceived merely "as an example to follow (and possibly surpass)."[44] Though it is not necessary here to enumerate the precise differences between benign envy and emulative envy (a subject on which scholars disagree), it is important to note that there is a category of emotional response (often labeled "envy" in modern *and* early modern speech) that entails not pain, but genuine feelings of admiration and inspiration at another's advantage. Whether or not we deem such feelings a species of envy, the larger point remains: notions of envy and emulation are entwined, suggesting the ambivalence so often evoked by another's social superiority.

With these dynamics of envy in mind, I'll now turn to the poem itself. Despite its obvious elegiac action, "So crewell prison" is also inundated with the emotional investments I have outlined above in my taxonomy of envy: a tangled network of malice, desire, admiration, emulation, and (above all) ambivalence.

The Envious Elegy: "So Crewell Prison"

At Windsor Castle in the summer of 1537, Surrey found a ready circumstance to conjure the memory of his childhood friend. Though a meditation on the poet's past, "So crewell prison" takes its bearing from this contextualized present, and it is in this manner that Surrey compounds the generic action of elegy by dramatizing the act of memory that inspires the elegy itself. A foundational motif throughout Surrey's work, memory thematically governs such poems as "When ragyng love with extreme payne" and "Dyvers thy death doo dyverslye bemone," as well as (and perhaps most prominently) his translation of the *Aeneid*.[45] In "So crewell prison," however, the mechanics of memory are uniquely doubled: the poem recalls both a person and a place, and it reveals how such memories necessarily overlap.

Though Henry Fitzroy becomes the eventual subject of "So crewell prison," the poem begins with an address to Windsor itself:

> So crewell prison howe could betyde, alas,
> As prowde Wyndsour, where I in lust and joye
> With a kinges soon my childishe yeres did passe,
> In greater feast then Priams sonnes of Troye.[46]

By outlining the poem's topographical and temporal scope, this apostrophe introduces the atmosphere of ambiguity that underpins "So crewell prison." The tangled syntax of the first two lines, which collapses "prison" into "Wyndsour," reflects the poet's disorienting confinement within a familiar setting, while Surrey analogously disrupts the poem's temporal frame by invoking complementary images from both the personal and the (mytho-)historical past. As a site of memory, Windsor becomes conflicted ground: its celebration of Richmond is occasioned only by his death, while Surrey's return to this generative site comes under rather unpleasant circumstances. The hostile Windsor of 1537, tortured by this paradox, becomes the natural analogue to the prelapsarian Windsor of Surrey's youth—until, that is, the poem reveals that even this memory of Windsor is subject, in more subtle form, to the emotional complexity that characterizes the poet's description of his present state.

If it is hard to square the Windsor of the past with the Windsor of the present, Surrey's celebratory comparison of Windsor and Troy is also troubled. In the most basic sense, the image is tempered by the reader's knowledge of Troy's ultimate collapse—a fact that casts a shadow over Surrey's recollection, and that prefigures the conceptual fall of Windsor in the wake of Richmond's death. But the precise terms in which Surrey frames this association are suggestive. In one sense, yoking Troy and Windsor has an obvious attraction; as Candice Lines notes, with this image Surrey effectively "writes himself into the royal family, as Richmond's brother and a king's son himself."[47] Yet despite this idealization, a set of darker associations also lurks in the margins of this metaphor. If Surrey and Richmond stand as the Trojan royal sons, Henry VIII must figure as King Priam—a particularly ominous identity for Henry, when considered next to the brutal rendition of Priam's death (by the hand of Pyrrhus) that Surrey would later translate in the *Aeneid*:

> At the altar him trembling gan he draw
> Wallowing through the blodshed of his son;
> And his left hand all clasped in his heare,

> With his right arme drewe fourth his shining sword,
> Which in his side he thrust up to the hilts.[48]

Furthermore, the very association of Henry and Priam has an inherently ironic currency, as the symbolically fecund Priam (with his fifty sons) stands as the crushing inverse to Henry's own generative difficulties. The image has a final twist when we recall that Pyrrhus *also* slaughtered several of Priam's sons. Polites, the most notable case, is gruesomely described by Surrey as

> fleing fourth till he came now in sight
> Of his parentes, before their face fell down,
> Yelding the ghost, with flowing streames of blood.[49]

Unpacked fully, the logic of the metaphor suggests a latent aggression not only toward King Henry, but also toward Richmond, and even toward himself—the poet casts himself explicitly as a Trojan prince, and implicitly as a Trojan-slaughterer.[50] Though Surrey had probably not yet come to translate his *Aeneid* in 1537, he was undoubtedly aware of the metaphor's implications: by beginning his elegy with the comparison of Windsor to Troy, he introduces an emotional ambivalence that will increasingly preoccupy the poem.[51] Surrey's status as a son of Troy is a site of both idealization and aggression, conflicting emotional responses that come to define the poet's attitude to his lost friend.

It should also be clear how the double logic of the opening stanza replicates the emotional architecture I have associated with envy. By effacing the hereditary distinction between Surrey and Richmond, and by insisting instead on their symbolic equivalency as Trojan princes, the poem enacts the behavioral profile associated with benign envy: it eliminates the social disparity by elevating Surrey to a position coequal to the rival's advantage. Yet, given the ominous history of Troy, the metaphor equally contains a violent, malicious fantasy, culminating in the destruction of both the rival and his advantage: a textbook enactment of "true" envy. "Upward social comparison," observes Richard H. Smith and his colleagues, "often represents an unattainable, frustrated desire, invidiously personified in the advantaged person."[52] And, as further research suggests, the pain and frustration of such upward social comparison is amplified enormously when the envied party's advantage seems to be absolute: as with, for example, the cultural logic that assured social preference for the younger Richmond, despite his youth and bastardy.[53] Given this context, I suggest that Surrey harbored no small amount of this social envy, and the opening lines of "So crewell prison" reveal the poet vacillating between an emulous love for his symbolic brother and a malicious aggression toward his social superior.

As the poem continues, Surrey depicts a variety of scenes which similarly enact this ambivalence, and which trigger the emotional configurations of envy. Masculine contests are a primary occasion in which Richmond is remembered—and though these activities certainly depict the tender act of adolescent bonding, they also introduce to the poem a more explicit dynamic of rivalry, standing as a narrative analogue to Surrey's emotional ambivalence. Athletic competition was a cornerstone of Surrey and Richmond's boyhood training in the aristocratic arts; such contests form a central motif of Surrey's recollection, animating much of the poem's charm and pathos. These bouts, however, carry a sense of both contention and intimacy, and the aggression they entail may be thought to channel Surrey's envious, emulous relationship to his friend. Surrey's description of mock combat offers an explicit example: "On fomynge horse, with swordes and frendlye hertes / With chere as thoughe the one should overwhelme, / Where we have fought and chased oft with dartes."[54] The stark contrast of "sordes" and "frendlye" suggests the proximity of combat and camaraderie within their role-play, their antagonistic "chere" (Middle English, "countenance") confirming that the feigned pretense of mutual aggression is an integral part of their combative drama. Though the combat may be fictionalized, the rewards of athletic triumph inspire the genuine exchange of violent energies; this ambivalence is native to the ritual altogether, which serves as preparation for the bloody transactions of real combat in the future.

In the stanza devoted to hunting, we find a series of equally pregnant associations, latent with the material of envious rivalry:

> The wyld forest, the clothed holtes with grene,
> With raynes avald and swift ybrethed horse,
> With crye of houndes and mery blastes bitwen,
> Where we did chase the fearfull hart a force.[55]

It is certainly true that such lines can be read in terms of eroticism: the classical exempla of Adonis and Hippolytus provide a model for associating the hunt with the repression and sublimation of sexual desire, and Wyatt's famed "Whoso List to Hunt" may have offered Surrey an immediate precedent for the metaphor.[56] But the passage also depicts the process through which the adolescent boys were socialized as members of the warring class: presumably accompanied by adult men, Surrey and

Richmond here learned to generate and regulate the same violence that underpinned the aristocracy's crucial sociopolitical identity as an instrument of controlled force. Such depictions of the symbolic, regulated violence of adolescent bonding suggest the more naked hostility that is latent in Surrey's emotional response to Richmond's memory. And crucially for boys like Surrey and Richmond, jousting and hunting were not socially neutral acts: they were imbued with the dynamics of age, identity, and birthright. Accordingly, because they activate the mechanism of social competition, they are also implicated in the ambivalent trajectory of identification and envy I have located elsewhere. Surrey both did and did not want to become one with his friend, just as he both did and did not want to overtake him symbolically—an emotional state, I think, that manifests remarkably in the quasi-aggression of Surrey's grieving memories.

The Experience of Jealousy

Of course, aggression and rivalry in "So crewell prison" are not limited to such boyhood exercises. Though much time at Windsor was conducted under the sign of Mars, an important share was also governed by Venus, and the poem's wistful memories of the erotic hunt naturally compliment the boys' adventures in the woods and lists. To this end, it is important to expand our discussion of envy by considering a distinct but intimately related phenomenon: the rivalrous dynamics of jealousy.

As is the case with envy, it is no easy task to arrive at a working definition of "jealousy"; though the emotion contains its own affective mechanism, in common speech "jealousy" routinely stands in for the affiliated "envy." Because of this confusion, scholars have devoted no small time to parsing the two emotions, and both theoretical and empirical research suggests that each has a set of unique characteristics.[57] More precisely, "envy" and "jealousy" have something of an opposite valence: whereas the envier suffers on behalf of some current lack—the coveted advantage, just out of reach—the jealous subject cannot tolerate the threat to something he or she already possesses (or thinks to possess)—and the anticipation of its loss, whether reasonable or unreasonable, fuels the subsequent agitation. In most situations, the threat is occasioned by a specific rival; hence, jealousy is most often thought in terms of a three-party relationship, as in the familiar case of romantic jealousy.[58] Yet, despite these differences of orientation, envy and jealousy often co-occur (as is clear from ordinary experience), and their affective domains overlap. At the categorical level, envy and jealousy tend to prompt similar reactions: "both can involve some form of hostility (envy may produce resentment and rancor; jealousy may produce anger over betrayal), and both can involve some form of lowered self-esteem and sadness (envy because of inferiority and longing and jealousy because of rejection and loss)."[59] Though distinct, these emotions are clearly linked in our common experience, and it is no surprise that both emerge in the affective subtext of "So crewell prison."

It is equally unsurprising that "jealousy," like "envy," was a quite flexible term in early modern English. Renaissance usage often entailed the basic configuration of three-party rivalry, as shown in this verse "description of Iealousie":

> It is the death of ioy, twixt man and wife,
> Where loue is too much loaden with mistrust:
> It makes the maide to feare the married life,
> Least firmest faith should fall to be vniust:
> It beats the braine and grindes the wit to dust,
> It makes the wise a foole, the wealthie poore,
> And her that wold kepe house, to ope the dore.[60]

Then, as now, jealousy was a common condition of wedded life. A similar sentiment is repeated in an advice manual of 1540:

> Wedded persons may thus passe ouer theyr lyues quietly and without complaynynges, yf the husbande become deafe, and the wyfe blynde. Signifyenge, that womankynde is much subiecte to the sycknes of gelousie, wherof vndoubtedly springeth greate variaunce & playntes. . . . [She'd thus avoid] the suspicion to be made Cokequen [a female cuckold], yf she wanted her eye syghte.[61]

And I needn't spend more time showing that romantic jealousy was an active concept in the early modern period: Shakespeare, after all, provided us with its most enduring epithet.

But like "envy," the term "jealousy" also encompassed a broader register. Descended from the Greek *zelos*, jealousy in the Renaissance was intimately connected to the notion of *zeal*; as such, it too participated in a much larger semantic network, of contextually fluid association. Jealousy, like zeal, entails the intense activation of emotional energy—and like zeal, its ethical valence is shaped by the particular whims of the speaker. This ambivalence is well reflected in early modern usage. While Thomas Wilson, for example, defines jealousy in the sense of triangulated (romantic) rivalry—"Griefe, for suspition of dishonesty in married yoake-fellowes,

Husbands or Wiues"—he also offers a positive sense of the term: "One which loueth others truely, not for lucre and glory to him-selfe, but for the benefit of the persons loued. . . . Heere Iealous is taken in good part."[62] Furthermore, jealousy (like envy) also had a close association with the act of emulation. Indeed, in ancient Greek, *zelos* can refer to honorable emulation, as in Aristotle's *Rhetoric*: "Emulation [*zelos*] . . . is therefore virtuous and characteristic of virtuous men, whereas envy [*phthonos*] is base and characteristic of base men."[63] In the early modern period, the amorphous boundary between these terms is illustrated splendidly by an annotation in the Geneva Bible, which describes the Apostles' persecutors as "ful of blinde zeale, emulation and ielousie."[64] As with envy, the experience of jealousy is varied, involving ambivalent feelings of rivalry, aggression, and emulation, often simultaneously.

In "So crewell prison," notions of jealousy offer a valuable guide for considering the specifically eroticized competition latent in the poem—that is, when a third party becomes implicated in Surrey and Richmond's combative play. Windsor's "ladyes bright of hewe" provide this source of libidinal competition for the boys, whose attempts at teenage love are often imbued with rivalrous energy.[65] This dynamic can be detected in the passage describing their love-struck banter:

> The secret groves, which ofte we made resound
> Of pleasaunt playnt and of our ladyes prayes,
> Recording soft what grace eche one had found,
> What hope of spede, what dred of long delayes.[66]

Within the pastoral world of Surrey's idealized Windsor, such ostensibly erotic (and homoerotic) expression must also be read as contentious—the kind of rustic sparring Surrey may have encountered in his own reading of the pastoral mode, and that Spenser would go on to portray so notably in *The Shepheardes Calendar*. Though ostensibly good-natured, such poetic contests serve as a further analogue to the physical rivalry of masculine play.

But more notably, Surrey himself reveals the thematic proximity of jealousy and eroticized rivalry in the stanza devoted to a sporting event with Richmond:

> The palme playe, where, dispoyled for the game,
> With dased eyes oft we by gleames of love
> Have mist the ball and got sight of our dame
> To bayte her eyes which kept the leddes above.[67]

In his memory of the disrupted game, Surrey recalls both the envious rivalry of physical competition and the jealous rivalry of erotic competition. On one hand, the match is another example of direct engagement between Surrey and Richmond, an extension of the various war games described elsewhere in the poem. In this sense, vying for both skill and advantage entails envy and emulation: as Kenneth Burke elegantly notes, "what we call 'competition' is better described as men's attempt to *out-imitate* one another."[68] Yet on the other, Surrey suggests that the true source of the boys' contention lies not in the action on the court, but in their battle to attract the female spectators: here, the three-term configuration of jealousy rules the day, governing Surrey and Richmond's development as both aristocrats and as sexually mature men.

As a concrete site in which eroticism and rivalry converge, the sporting of "So crewell prison" suggests the larger way in which the celebration of Richmond's life is fraught with impulses that are often competing; in Surrey's recollection, formative moments of both adolescent bonding and adolescent sexuality are framed within an oppositional context, bubbling with latent energy of both jealousy and envy. This emulative combat is a crucial counterweight to the more obvious dynamic of "So crewell prison," in which Surrey comes to identify with his lost companion: as Lines has demonstrated, the poem systematically "erases any distinction of identity between the two friends," while the increasingly intimate description of their shared bedchamber ("The voyd walles eke, that harbourd us eche night . . . wherwith we past the winter nightes awaye") suggests the extent to which Surrey and his "noble fere" finally become indistinguishable.[69] Throughout the poem, Surrey works with one hand to efface the distinction between Howard and Tudor, even as he cannot help but affirm it with the other. Such confusion of intersubjective boundaries is a key dynamic of the rivalrous emotions, and it is one that ultimately underpins the poem's concluding movement.

We have seen how the bulk of "So crewell prison" is an architectural catalog, in which the castle's various locales trigger memories from Surrey and Richmond's shared past. In the poem's conclusion, however, Surrey comments directly on his grief, seeking desperately to make sense of both Richmond's loss and his own imprisonment. With "sobbing sighes," Surrey rails against Windsor itself, asking for some account of his friend's absence:

> 'O place of blisse, renewer of my woos,
> Geve me accompt wher is my noble fere,

> Whome in thy walles thow didest eche night enclose,
> To other lief, but unto me most dere.'[70]

Though consistent with the poem's larger mode of address—"So crewell prison" is, of course, an apostrophe—Surrey's accusation here begins a series of displacements and confusions that overwhelm the final lines. Unsurprisingly, Windsor provides no satisfactory answer:

> Eache stone, alas, that dothe my sorowe rewe,
> Retournes therto a hollowe sound of playnt.[71]

This echo exemplifies the erosion of boundaries that has been steadily enacted by the poem; it is a ghostly utterance that both does and does not emanate from Surrey's own mouth. Because it is an act of reflexive speech, Surrey is implicated in his own allegation: though he may charge Windsor with his sorrow, Windsor charges him right back. To compound the confusion a final degree, there is even a sense in which the speech belongs to Richmond, the figure who has from the elegy's opening moments haunted the castle.

We need not embrace a fully psychoanalytic reading of the poem to acknowledge the emotional displacement at play in these passages. In simplest terms, Surrey's fixation on Richmond's absence provides an attractive safeguard from the events that have resulted in his imprisonment: by immersing himself in the loss of his friend, Surrey sidesteps the need to confront his own erratic behavior. (He also avoids the unenviable task of condemning those responsible for his sentence, including King Henry.) In this sense, the intensity and quality of Surrey's grief suggest that his lamentation for Richmond is in many ways a displacement of the sorrow he feels for himself: grief for the friend, in other words, is substituted for the narcissistic mourning of Surrey's own wretched state.[72]

Yet at the same time, when Surrey does explicitly address his own misfortunes, we may also detect some attendant aggression toward Richmond: the friend who, by virtue of his unexpected death, has abandoned the poet and condemned him to unhappiness. This sentiment emerges in the elegy's final lines, when Surrey finds means to express the hostility and resentment that lurks beneath his grief:

> Thus I alone, where all my fredome grew,
> In pryson pyne with bondage and restraynt,
> And with remembraunce of the greater greif,
> To bannishe the lesse I fynde my chief releif.[73]

Like Jonathan Crewe, I find it difficult to read this concluding moment without detecting some animosity toward the friend who has left the poet in his time of need.[74] A logical extension of the poem's latent rivalry motif, this aggression is a counterpoint to the larger elegiac action—but, given the reality of Richmond's death, Surrey seems to feel no small guilt at his own ambivalence. The logical conclusion of rivalry is a fantasy of the other's destruction: it is this thought that Surrey cannot tolerate, and he must accordingly divert its attendant aggression toward himself and his own misfortune. Insofar as Surrey feels abandoned by Richmond, he develops an anger that must be subsequently repressed; insofar as he has also become identified with this lost friend, the anger directed outward must be also directed toward himself. This ambivalence forcefully emerges in the final couplet—in which, despite the ostensible agenda of the elegiac occasion, it is difficult to ultimately know what part of Surrey's grief is the greater.

The properties of the rivalrous emotions help account for the position in which "So crewell prison" leaves its grieving poet: as R. Horacio Etchegoyen and Clara R. Nemas put it, envy entails "the paradox that the same faculty that allows [the envier] to appreciate the good qualities of the object is at the same time the source of unbearable pain."[75] In this view, envy is grounded upon "an unconscious projective identification with the envied person, who represents the image of whom the envying person would want to be in the ideal sense . . . [but] because feelings of inferiority partly motivate such identification, this idealization is blended with resentment and derogation."[76] Surrey and Richmond certainly enjoyed a close relation, as symbolic brothers of the highest social order—but as experience often confirms, we are most quick to envy "those who are close to us in terms of time, space, age and reputation."[77] This feature of social life was not obscure to Renaissance thinkers:

> Lastly, near kinsfolks, and fellows in office, and those that have been bred together, are more apt to envy their equals when they are raised. For it doth upbraid unto them their own fortunes, and pointeth at them, and cometh oftener into their remembrance, and incurreth likewise more into the note of others; and envy ever redoubleth from speech and fame.[78]

Such proximity, and the co-mingling of social identities it entails, ultimately confound Surrey's attempt to console himself with his verse, in which he finds it impossible to clearly delineate the object of his grief.

Despite its resounding success as a poetic performance, "So crewell prison" thus fails as a tool of grief. If, as Peter Sacks has argued, the conventional elegy guides its speaker through the "work of mourning," then Surrey's poem to Richmond must be recognized for the way it rejects consolation: there is no vision of renewal, no sublimation of the lost object, no affirmation of the speaker's willingness to endure.[79] In this sense, the poem has surprising affinities with the modern elegy, which has been characterized by a tendency toward "unresolved, violent, and ambivalent" forms of mourning.[80] Though "So crewell prison" can express, it cannot finally escape the act of memory that entwines Surrey's present fate with the idealized vision of his friend. At the poem's end, Surrey is left with only the choice between two kinds of grief—and though the lesser may be banished, it is only by reference to the larger shadow that still hangs over both Windsor and the speaker. "So crewell prison," it turns out, is an unexpectedly angry poem: the troubled comparisons to Troy, the simmering displays of adolescent aggression, and the severity of the poet's melancholy suggest a well of emotional energy too often ignored by scholars. The poem registers the concurrent loss of an ideal companion, of a pastoral youth, of face at court, of a promised future: it accordingly reflects, in its emotional tenor, the profound entanglement of tenderness, melancholy, and aggression. As a core emotional response of courtly combat, envy installs the affective network through which these varied feelings flow.

Like Surrogate Father, Like Surrogate Son

Though deprived of Richmond, Surrey was restored to court in the fall of 1537—where (as Susan Brigden puts it) "he assumed the role of guardian of honour and defender of true nobility, and began to be notorious for the extremity of his pride."[81] He was a principle mourner at the November funeral of Queen Jane, who died only days after giving birth to Henry's long-sought legitimate male heir; in the next three years, Surrey was appointed to a number of local posts in Norfolk, and in 1541 was made a Knight of the Garter. (And as that year turned over, he also attended the trial and execution of his infamous cousin Katherine, the second Howard queen to share Henry's bed and die by his will.) But Surrey, by his own admission, was still fueled by "the fury of rechless youth," and before long he was jailed for a second and third time. In the first incident of 1542, he was imprisoned in the Fleet Prison after challenging an adversary to a duel over a private matter.[82] In the second, his notorious Lenten romp of 1543, he and a posse of friends were charged with terrorizing London "in the night abowght the stretes and breaking wyth stonebowes off certeyne wyndowes"; this incarceration inspired one of Surrey's best-known lyrics, the scathing jeremiad "London, hast thow accused me."[83]

But despite these disruptions, in the years that immediately followed—what would be the final years of his life—Surrey became quite happily entwined in the emulous, envious rivalry of another: that of Richmond's father. Now in his sixth decade of life, the ailing King Henry renewed his war with Francis I of France in 1543, backed by the (ostensible) support of imperial forces. This was to be, reflects David Potter in his magisterial account of the conflict, a war between "two ageing warhorses . . . prematurely aged by illness," whose "relations since 1515 had been marked by alternating phases of competition in war and diplomatic/cultural display."[84] Childs similarly notes that the action found fuel in the long-simmering, "intense personal rivalry" between the princes, with Henry making "no secret of his desire to emulate his ancestors, especially Henry V, and revive the ancient English claim to suzeranity over France."[85] The psychodrama here seems to reflect Henry's grasping attempt to reclaim long-expired years for both his body politic and body natural—fanning, in the words of Polydore Vergil, his long-simmering desire "not merely to equal but indeed to exceed the glorious deeds of his ancestors."[86]

It is perhaps unsurprising, then, that in his declining years, Henry had fantasies of recapturing his former glory, three decades exactly after winning his spurs on French soil at Thérouanne and Tournai. Yes, the spirits of both his royal ancestors and his younger self would be revived—and King Henry was "determined to heave his huge body into armour" and don those spurs again.[87] But, as Potter outlines, this was something of a large issue: for Henry to personally lead English forces was "like conveying an ungainly and threatening totem into the midst of the war; there was no doubt his presence was an encouragement but it also had its penalties."[88] It was a delicate point indeed, and one that occasioned considerable logistical attention; English councilors were reluctant to voice their concerns, while Chapuys, noting that Henry possessed "the worst legs in the world," observed that troops would be forced "to march much more slowly because of the weight and illness of the said lord King."[89] Eventually, a diplomatic calculus thankfully proved that both princes might forgo direct forward command with no loss of honor—but King Henry, who "night and day thought of nothing else" but military glory, would still eventually taste war on French soil, suited in a massive coat of armor preserved today at the Metropolitan Museum of Art.[90]

It was ultimately the young Surrey, not much older in 1543 than Henry had been in 1513, who would become the king's own avatar in the field, a linkage through which cross-generational fantasies of honor and conquest might be shared between the earl and the father of his closest friend. We see hints of this dynamic early in the conflict, when Surrey was allowed to cross the Channel and observe the Anglo-imperial siege of Landrecy in 1543; King Henry recommended him personally to the emperor, whom he asked "to order the captains and lieutenants of [his] army to help and assist in all things in which the said Earl may advance and improve his knowledge of military affairs."[91] (Though even here Surrey couldn't stay out of trouble: according to Chapuys, Henry was not pleased by "a certain foolish letter written by the earl of Surrey," who was consequently ordered "to abstain in future from making such reports.")[92] When English troops were deployed the following year, "the Duke of Norffolk" and "therle of Surrey" were appointed leaders of "the vantgards"; Surrey was named lord marshall of the army, and soon he and his father began (an ultimately untenable) siege of the port town of Montreuil.[93]

In July 1544 King Henry had made the journey to Calais; rather than fortifying Surrey and Norfolk's siege, he and his old friend Suffolk embarked upon a concurrent assault on Boulogne, which surrendered to great fanfare in September. Surrey, who had come to witness the siege personally, arrived just in time: a "Trayne of Powder was set to the Castell" on the 11th of that month, and "the *Kinges Majestie*, accompanied with the said *Erle of Surrey* . . . went to his Standing to see the Castell fall."[94] The surrender, which Sessions deems "the most spectacular military triumph of Henry VIII's career," offered cause for immediate celebration, and the king's victorious entry into the city was "carefully dramatized to make the decaying Henry VIII appear like Henry V on the nearby field of Agincourt."[95] His honor appropriately puffed, Henry soon returned to England, eventually appointing Suffolk to defend his prize—but, in August 1545, the duke died before he could assume his post. This was great luck for Surrey, who was weeks later named "Lieutenant, and Captain General, Commander-in-chief and Governor" of Boulogne.[96]

With this appointment, Surrey was now, undisputedly, Henry's proxy in the field. And in fact, there emerged a triangular dynamic in which Surrey, inhabiting the symbolic position of his lost friend, appears to actively dismiss the guidance of his own father in favor of the surrogate Henry.[97] The keeping of Boulogne—"the one tangible fruit of [the king's] campaigns in France," and the nexus of Surrey and Henry's twin chivalric fantasy—was a money-pit for a realm already sinking in debt, and consensus in the king's council urged for a speedy withdrawal.[98] In a letter from Windsor that September, Norfolk explicitly warned his son to "anymate not the kyng to moche for the kepyng of boleyne, for who so doth at length shalt get small thank" among those at court.[99] But this, and similar advice that he should be "maid werye . . . of Bowleine," did little to deter Surrey, who relished his lieutenancy, and who would in the coming months continue to construct elaborate plans for its fortification and victualing.[100] "In conversation," an imperial ambassador reported, King Henry had "called Boulogne 'his daughter'"—and Surrey, in turn, stuck up admirably for his symbolic sister.[101]

In early November 1545, the earl received a scathing letter from Norfolk's secretary, which did little to hide his real father's displeasure:

> I see my lordes grace somewhat offended by your priuate letteres to the Kynges Majestie of such vehemency as towching the animatynge of the King's Majesty for the kepynge of Bowlleyn and in especial considering his dyuers letteres adressed to you lordschype to the whiche as he thinketh ye haue gevyn simple credence for what his grace and the rest of the Cownsell worketh in for the renndre of Bowleyne [and] the conclewdyng of a pease.[102]

Despite Norfolk's explicit instruction to the contrary, Surrey had continued to inflame the king's desire for a hopeless cause; in fact, in a personal letter to the increasingly invalid Henry, Surrey boasted of his search for "the grounde of most advauntage for your majesties campe if it shuld be your pleasure to come to the felde the next yere."[103] To the great annoyance of the royal advisors, the earl's dispatches had a special gravity: what the "Cownsell worketh . . . in vi daies," Surrey was warned, "ye with your letters sett bake in sixe owres, sutche importans be your letters in the kinges oppinion at this tymme."[104] But that "every cownsellor saithe away with it" mattered little to Henry Howard or Henry Tudor, united in equal vehemence for Boulogne as an English holding.[105] Given the familial symbolics inherent to this affair, the precise manifestation of Norfolk's anger and betrayal seems particularly apt: "I herde my lordship [Norfolk] saye," Surrey was told, "that he had rathre burie yow & the reste of his childrene befoure he shulde geffe his consent to the rwyne of the realme."[106]

But things went bad for Surrey, and they went bad quickly. On January 7, 1546, only two days after dispatching an elaborate stratagem for Henry's forces in the region, Surrey suffered the first defeat of his military career, when French troops overwhelmed his army at St. Etienne, slaying nearly two dozen English captains and forcing the (hungry and destitute) common-file to a mutinous retreat.[107] This "shame of St. Etienne," Sessions suggests, "mark[ed] the first stage of Surrey's downfall," and the earl himself was instantly affected—in the midst of the English retreat, so records one contemporary account, Surrey had apparently "begged Sir John Bridges and some of the gentlemen who were with him to stick their swords through his guts and make him forget the day."[108] In their account of the disaster, Surrey and his command scrambled to emphasize the positive—there was "mo of their parte slayne then of oures," they reported, and (more importantly) assured that "ther was no defaulte in the Rulers nor lacke of courage to be geven them"—but an unreceptive audience awaited in London; only days after the battle, the imperial ambassador François van der Delft concluded his dispatch on the matter by observing that Surrey "has consequently lost greatly in reputation, and there is considerable discontent at these heavy losses."[109] (Surrey was also a victim of the early modern post: while his own debriefing was still in transit home, he was sent a scathing letter from the Privy Council, who, having learned of the defeat, could "nott butt marvyll very much thatt in so many dayes [Surrey had] aduertysed hither no part of that mater.")[110]

The defeat of St. Etienne shattered Henry's faith in his chivalric surrogate, and Surrey's attempts at damage control "did so little satisfie our King (who lov'd no noyse but of Victory) that he ever after disaffected him."[111] The immediate cost was the earl's lieutenancy, which was transferred to his old rival Edward Seymour, a man much advanced since 1537: now earl of Hertford, Seymour had (as Sessions puts it) "not only distinguished himself as the leading military figure of England, both in Scotland and in France, but had also represented the king in almost every major diplomatic initiative."[112] (He was also, not unnotably, uncle to the young male heir of a moribund king—a fact that becomes quite relevant to Surrey's ultimate demise.)[113] With considerable frankness, Secretary Paget (another "new man") urged the earl to "passe the thing over in silence" and accept a lesser command, lest a retreat home further tarnish his reputation:

> Being hitherto noted, as you ar, a man of a noble courrage and of a desyre to shewe the same to the face of your ennemies, if you shuld now tarye at home within a wall, havyng I doubt a pece of your authorite toched, it woold be thought abrode, I feare, that either you wer desyrous to tary in a sure place of rest, oreles that the credit of your courrage and forwardnes to serve wer diminished, and that you wer taken here for a man of non activite or service.[114]

It seems safe to say that such sentiments, from such a source, must have especially stung the earl—and indeed, when on trial a few months later, Surrey (so says one account) would command Paget to "hold thy tongue, for the kingdom has never been well since the King put mean creatures like thee into the government."[115] But Surrey was a man who, in his own words, couldn't "dare kepe silence," and continued to advocate for himself, despite pending demotion to captain of the rearward—and that March, as Hertford assumed his new command, the Privy Council summoned Surrey home to account for a variety of issues related to his former governance, including some "aduertisementes . . . of treasons that ar conspired specially touching the victuails & munintions."[116] A diplomatic missive of the 28th suggests his welcome, noting that "the Earl of Surrey, formerly captain of Boulogne, arrived at Court yesterday, but was coldly received and did not have access to the King."[117] It seems the consequence of his defeat was not lost upon the earl: "after the ouerthrow of the grete skyrmoche at St Etiuens," a witness later reported, "I hard hym saye he had the kinges majestes dyspleashor or disfavour, [to which] he hath taken greate thought."[118]

In ten months, the earl would be headless. But it was not St. Etienne that signaled Surrey's doom—and in fact, Henry would soon thaw, bestowing on him several honors for his French service in April and May. Rather, Surrey had to die because Henry soon would. "His Majestie was sickly," all were aware as 1546 ticked on, "and could not long endure," leaving the nation to wonder just who would steady the ship of state as a nine-year-old prince became a nine-year-old king.[119] This, the realm's most pressing political dilemma, choked the dying Henry's court, now dually anchored by Surrey's primary rival Hertford—who would, as future duke of Somerset, serve as lord protector for the first half of his nephew's imminent reign—and lesser rival Lord Admiral John Dudley—who would, as future duke of Northumberland, himself unseat Somerset and orchestrate the remaining years of Edward's short kingship.[120] It was with grave consequence that Surrey lost his own bid to govern the young prince.

Prince Envy? The Death of Surrey and Prince Edward's Legacy

In some seventy years of life, the Duke of Norfolk had established himself as one of the sixteenth century's premier political survivors—and he predictably spent the final months of King Henry's reign attempting to ensure that the Howards, a pillar of ancient English nobility, had a place among those who would rule the boy king. Unencumbered by Surrey's intractable sense of ancestral purity—and by this time, apparently growing weary of (what he called) "my foolish son's demeanour"—he concocted a plan in the summer of 1546 to intimately enhance his family's affinity with the emerging Seymour regime:

> I brake unto his Majesty most humbly beseeching him to help that a marriage might be had between my daughter [Richmond's widow] and Sir Thomas Seymour [Hertford's infamous brother]; and whereas my son of Surrey hath a son, and divers daughters, that with his favour, a cross marriage might have be made between my Lord Great Chamberlain [Hertford] and them: and also where my son Thomas hath a son . . . that he might be in like wise married to one of my said Lord's daughters. [121]

In 1538 Norfolk had made earlier efforts (with apparent royal support) to bestow "his doughter, the Duchesse of Rychmonde . . . uppon the saide Sir Thomas Seymour." [122] His renewed attempt, however, would similarly come to naught—owing in no small part, we'll see, to his son's obstinacy.

In 1546 Surrey too considered, with grave concern, his place in England's future—but he did so in a manner that fixed his gaze firmly on the past. This is exemplified in Surrey's famed "Arundel portrait," an iconographic spectacle prepared by William Scrots, successor to Holbein as England's royal painter. (See figure 2.) In the painting, which has been analyzed in great detail, a full-length Surrey emerges triumphantly from a centered arch, to an interior space flush with marble statues and decorative icons in a classical mode.[123] Most prominent in this frame is the pair of figures flanking Surrey, each holding a shield: a man, to the viewer's left, displays the paternal arms of Surrey's ancestral link to Edward I, while a corresponding woman advertises the earl's maternal inheritance from Edward III. There is little subtle about this announcement of the subject's royal blood. But of even greater interest, given the focus of this chapter, is the composition of the earl's right arm, which leans against a broken pillar emblazoned in gold: in Surrey's original design, the column's anchor was to feature a "tablet wher my lord off Richmondes pictuire shuld stand."[124] For reasons that remain obscure, Surrey abandoned the plan in the final months of his life, and the column's base instead features the motto *SAT SVPER EST*—"enough survives." But it is striking that, nearly a decade later, Surrey's "noble fere" remained important enough to have been featured in so provocative a portrait—and indeed, it has been suggested that its inherent provocativeness may have ultimately occasioned Richmond's absence, lest the envelope be pushed a bit too far.[125] For it seems at least partly clear, as Sessions (and others) have thoroughly detailed, that the Arundel portrait looks forward to the coming

Fig. 2. *Henry Howard, Earl of Surrey*, NPG 5291. By courtesy of the National Portrait Gallery, London.

succession, despite its obvious reverence for the Howard past. In boasting a "genealogy worthy [of] a possible king," the painting argues that its subject "possessed a right to be Protector to the young Prince Edward"—and the canceled image of Richmond, Edward's half-brother, would have powerfully reminded that Surrey had already once nursed the blossoming of a Tudor royal son.[126] At the time of Surrey's trial, we will see below, similar images of genealogical interest were seized from the Howard residence at Kenninghall—where they served, we must presume, not as external envoy of Surrey's credentials, but rather as an identity-affirming mirror of their subject, mired in the most difficult (and final) year of his young life. The form of that identity, emerging from the insistent, inextricable proximity of Surrey's Howard blood to the Tudor throne, replicates much of the symbolic dynamics embedded in "So crewell prison."

And that proximity would eventually kill him. The powers that be, including the dying king, wanted him dead, so they found a way to make it so—and, to be sure, Surrey did little to make things difficult for them. Though many official records are now lost, a narrative of Surrey's ultimate downfall emerges from a variety of sources. He was arrested on December 2, 1546, when Richard Southwell, a cousin to Surrey, revealed that "he knew certain things of the earl, that touched his fidelity to the king"; after an initial confinement at Lord Chancellor Wriothesley's house, on the 12th he was "sent to the Towre of London" via a humiliating march through the streets of London.[127] (Norfolk was arrested the same day for undisclosed reasons.) In the weeks that followed, royal agents scoured for "report off suche" Howard doings that "myght in any wyys towche the kynges hyghnes & hys posteryte," eventually compiling a litany of possible charges by which Surrey, and for good measure his father, might be destroyed.[128]

Surrey's conduct was scrutinized on a variety of fronts. Specific inquiries, for example, were made about the earl's governance in France—whether (quite ridiculously) he had plotted the "selling or yelding vp of Bulleyn"—while agents equally considered more nebulous matters like "my lord of S dissembling" and "my lord of Surreys pryde and his gowne of gold."[129] But in the month of investigation, three major themes emerged in the crown's discovery, and each tellingly engages the central focus of this chapter: Surrey's ambivalent, envious affinity with the royal family, a dynamic first apparent in his complex friendship with the lost Richmond.

The first concerned Surrey's relationship with Richmond's half-brother, the nine-year-old Prince Edward. Earlier that year, it was alleged, Surrey had initiated a discussion of "who were meetist to haue the rule and governmennt of the prynce," arguing that "his father was the meetist personage to be deputed to that roome as well in respecte of the good seryvce that he had donn as also for his estate."[130] Sensing a potential whiff of treason, the authorities raised the issue directly with men like Hugh Ellis, the earl's servant, who was asked "whether you haue hard the said Erle at any tyme speake of the sycknes or deceasse of the kinges majestie and who shuld . . . haue the rule and gouernment of the prince?"[131] Further depositions similarly suggested that Surrey openly "thought noe man soe mete to have the governance of the Prince as my Lord his Father," and issues relating to this notion are featured prominently in the interrogatories prepared for Surrey himself:

- yf the King shuld dye my Lord prince being of young and tendre age whether you haue at any tyme diused who shuld haue the rule and gouernance of him
- whithr you have at any tyme sayd that if the King shuld die my lord prince being of tender age you or your father would haue the rule & gouernance of him

- what meanes and wayes have you at any tyme devised and doon wherby you might rule the King in his owne tyme or the prince if god shuld dispose of his Majestie[132]

In other words, Surrey was accused of thinking exactly what the Arundel portrait seems to suggest he may have thought: that the Howards, through both birthright and service, were natural guardians of a royal minor, a role they had played in the past. Given the fantasies of the Richmond elegy, Surrey's particular focus on the meritorious claim of Norfolk is telling: if, a decade after presiding over Richmond, the duke could reprise his role as surrogate father to Edward, Surrey would again find himself the symbolic brother of a Tudor heir. And if the power ultimately fell to Surrey himself—as would seem likely, given Norfolk's age, and as the Arundel portrait seems to argue—the earl further collapses the distinction between Howard and Tudor, reiterating the affective implications of "So crewell prison."

The second point of contention returns us to Norfolk's marriage plot of that summer—a plan (it seems) largely foiled by Surrey, who was "so much incensed" against Hertford.[133] (Though it presumably counted for less, it was also said that Lady Richmond's "Fantezy would not serve to marry with" Admiral Thomas.)[134] But, with a little revision, there was one part of the scheme that Surrey could endorse:

> She should dissemble the matter, and he would finde the means that the Kings Majestie should speake with her himselfe, but that she should in noe wise utterly make refusall of him, but that she should leave the matter soe diffusedly that the Kings Majestie should take occasion to speake with her againe, and thus by length of time, it is possible that the King should take such a fantezey to ye that ye shall be able to govern like unto Madame Distamps, which should not only be a means to halpe her selfe but all her freinds should receive a commodyte by the same.

The mistress of Francis I for some two decades, Anne, Duchess of Étampes wielded profound influence in the French court: in other words, Surrey thought to bawd his sister, the beloved Richmond's widow, to the rotting body of her former father-in-law. (Lady Richmond, it was reported, said "she would Cutt her own Troate rather then she would consent to such a villany.") According to the crown's further investigation, "therle of Surrey" did indeed "wishe or deuise that his sister of Richemond might rule about the king," hinging on the possibility that Henry "might caste some Love vnto her wherby in processe she shuld leave as greate a stroke aboute him as Madamme Destampz doth abowte the Frenche king."[135] When Surrey was questioned, the issue was likely broached both indirectly and explicitly. Besides wondering "whithr you have at any tyme procured any person to dissemble . . . for the better compassing of your purposes"—and asking for his hypothetical opinion on a man who, "cumpassing hymself to gouerne the realme [and] rule the kynge," did "for that purpose aduise his daughter or sister to becom an harlot"—Surrey's interrogators were also slated to ask directly "whethr euer he made his father pryvey to the mater of my Lady of Richemondes."[136] (In one query list, a canceled item wonders if Surrey had "procured [his] sister or any othr woman to be the kinges concubyne"; a version of the question was perhaps asked anyway.)[137]

In fact, according to one account, Lady Richmond informed investigators herself that Surrey had advised her to "lay herself out to please the king"; at the trial, when "shown a certain writing in the hand of his said sister in which she made this charge against him," an exasperated Surrey exclaimed "Must I, then, be condemned on the words of a wretched woman?"[138] The precise force of Surrey's plan has long been debated; as Childs observes, apologists have traditionally been forced to "bend over backwards to exonerate Surrey in this affair," suggesting that the earl's words had been "distorted by his malicious sister and her evangelical friends," or that Mary had perhaps "genuinely and guilelessly mistook her brother's sarcasm for literalism."[139] But I see no reason why an increasingly desperate Surrey, having already seen two kinswomen share the king's bed, could not have stooped to such a suggestion with seriousness. Ironic or not, the very notion again activates the convergence of Howard and Tudor that governed the thematics of "So Crewell prison"; it is yet another permutation by which Surrey symbolically insinuates himself into the Tudor line.

The final major focus of the crown's investigation was the one that actually secured the earl's destruction. In an insignia at Kenninghall, it was said, Surrey had "usurped the royal arms of England" by displaying the heraldry of King Edward the Confessor—and to the crown, records a (skeptical) Spanish chronicler, this "was evident proof that he desired to make himself king."[140] Peter R. Moore, who offers extensive analysis of this deadly charge, concludes that any "argument that Surrey aimed at the throne as the heir to Edward the Confessor . . . verges on the theatre of the absurd"—but the era's treason trials so often staged such theater, and it was enough to doom both Surrey and his father.[141] ("I have concealed high Treason," Norfolk confessed in desperate attempt at self-preservation, "in keeping secret the false and traiterous Act, most presumptuously committed by my Son *Henry Howard* Earl of *Surrey*, [of] putting and using the Arms of St. *Edward* the Confessor.")[142] It did not matter that the Howards had long asserted a right to these arms; the family claimed legendary descent from the Saxon warrior Hereward the Wake, a contemporary of St. Edward who resisted Norman rule, while (more concretely) Richard II had bestowed them upon Thomas Mowbray, the first Duke of Norfolk.[143] It also did not matter that Surrey had earlier consulted with the realm's garter king of arms about his ancestral rights, and left understanding "that he had the opinion of Heralds therein."[144]

What only mattered was that, unlike some of the flashier charges, Surrey could and would not deny this infraction—so when his enemies, with the king's blessing, dubbed it treason, the die was cast. "For what intent and purpose you put tharmes of St Edward in your cote, armmore, or scochen," Surrey was asked, and "nowe beare the sayd armes at this tyme more then you or your father have doon at any other tymes before"?[145] Furthermore, this heraldic crime was of particular interest to Henry. With only weeks left to live, the king personally revised a list of interrogatories that begins as follows:

> If a man cumming of the colaterall lyne to the heyre off the crown who ought not to beare tharmes of England but in the seconde quarter with the difference of theyer auncestre doo presume to change his ryght place and beare them in the first quarter, leaving out the true difference of thaunsestre, and in the lieu therof vse only the very plase of the heire masle apparent, how thys mans intent is to be iudgyd and whether thys importe any daunger peril or slandre to the title of the Prince or very heire apparent and howe it wayeth in our lawes.[146]

Bearing arms in the first or second quarter of his shield—the vital difference between Howard and Tudor, the crux by which Surrey so often seemed confounded, made a matter of geometry. At the residence at Kenninghall, the formal bill of indictment read, Surrey "dared to be fashioned and painted beside his own arms, together with the emblems of Henry Howard himself, the said arms and the said emblems now belonging to our Lord the King," thus "falsely, maliciously, and treasonously hoping, wishing, and desiring to deprive the most illustrious and serenest Lord our King of the laws, merit, titles, and names of his royal state," with the purpose of "disrupting our most excellent Lord and disinheriting the said Prince Edward of his true and indubitable title concerning the aforementioned crown."[147] At the bar, Surrey vigorously defended his ancestral rights—and defended himself against the many charges that were not included in the indictment, but that nonetheless were presented at trial. The jury—which, humiliatingly, was "a common Inquest, not of the Peers, because the Earl was not a Parliament Lord"—condemned him to the axe, and on the "nynetenth daie of Januarie the Erle of Surrey was lead out of the Towre to the skaffolde at the Towre Hill and their he was beheaded."[148] As for Norfolk, "it was thought that the Duke would hardly escape, had not the King's death, following shortly after, reserved him to more mercifull times."[149] A survivor to the end, he would outlive Henry's heir, dying an octogenarian in 1554.

Though Henry's agents would loudly decry "the moste execrable and moste abominable entent and entreprise of the said Erle of Surrey and his Father the Duke of Norffolke," not all observers were convinced: Van Der Delft, for example, duly informed the emperor of the alleged Howard plot to "usurp authority by means of the murder of all the members of the Council, and [gain] control of the prince by them alone," but equally noted that because "the Earl of Hertford and the Lord Admiral . . . have obtained such influence over the King as to lead him according to their fancy," it was suspected that "the misfortunes that have befallen the house of Norfolk may well have come from the same quarter."[150] (When told the news, Francis I of France was said to have "wondred moche, and sayed that he knewe the Duke of Norffolke for he had been with hym, and . . . wolde never haue thought enye syche thynge yn hym.")[151] Indeed, it seems that Hertford and the lord admiral, backed by a court party full of similar "new men," found it convenient that the highest pillar of the English nobility should crumble in the weeks before Henry gave up the ghost, and before a new regime would be installed to guide the boy king. (That the Howards were also associated with the old faith did little to endear them to this largely reformist clique, despite Surrey's own apparent evangelical leanings.) As we have seen, Surrey's struggle to parse his own aristocratic identity had long been intensified by the advancement of such men, and his antipathy helped further underpin his fall; "the Earle of Surrey," one deposition reports, fumed that "those men which are made by the Kings Majestie of vile birth hath been the distraction of all the Nobilitie of this Realme," while Lady Richmond similarly informed investigators that "her Brother hated them all since his being in custody in *Windsor* Castle."[152] At Windsor he had sought the ghost of Richmond, robbed of him too soon; now, in his final time on earth, he found himself robbed not only of his own life, but of reaffirming and realizing his role as preceptor and tutor to the Tudor heir, in the form of Richmond's half-brother.

On January 19, 1547, nine days before King Henry VIII himself would die, the Earl of Surrey became the final broken pillar that would adorn the ruins of Henrician England. (His father's life was spared only by the loss of the king's own.) This classical image is a fitting enough one for the man whose translation of Virgil would forever turn the course of English poetry, and whose lifelong commitment to the betterment of his nation, so argues his biographer, emulates "Aeneas' epic quest, at least in intention if not achievement."[153] It is thus also fitting, I think, to conclude this chapter with three remarks upon the earl written in Latin.

The first is a letter composed by Surrey's children in the spring of 1546, with the guiding hand of their Latin tutor, to welcome their father home on his unhappy return from France. Though formal in tone and construction, there is nonetheless, as Childs notes, "a child-like sweetness to the letter and a touching reverence undiminished by recent events."[154] (That is, the defeat at St. Etienne and the disgrace of his recall.) What interests me the most is the children's concluding statement, which expands the epistle's scope considerably:

> We also congratulate the whole Kingdom, because, resting as it does on the shoulders of Henry, our invincible and greatest King, and defended by his arms, it appears to have won a most illustrious name among foreign nations thanks to the efforts of you, a second Henry, whilst leaving nothing for the French except envy, lamentation, and a dread of yourself.[155]

Alterius Henrici. In his brief life, Surrey so often was—and so often wanted to be—a second Henry; a second Henry Fitzroy, a second Henry Tudor. And while perhaps Surrey did inspire *invidiam* among his French adversaries, his maddening status as a second Henry, we have seen throughout, occasioned no small envy in himself.

The second is an excerpt from Sir Thomas Chaloner's *De Republica Anglorum Instauranda*, a ten-book Latin epic on English themes published in 1579. Although perhaps best remembered today as the first English translator of Erasmus's *The Praise of Folly*, Chaloner was (like Norfolk) a notable survivor of his tumultuous age, variously serving as soldier, diplomat, and courtier in the reigns of Henry, Edward, Mary, and Elizabeth.[156] Named clerk of the Privy Council in December 1545, he had close affinity with the men who would destroy Surrey—and when reflecting upon that act from the safety of Elizabeth's reign, could not help but mourn the life cut too short. In the midst of an encomium on the "venerable race of Norfolk"—described as "great in learning, greater in arms, and greatest in faithful counsel"—Chaloner bestows particular praise on the poet earl, framing his downfall in a telling way:

> There was one hero, but alas he was taken by cruel fates!
> Surrey could have been placed first before all others
> If wild Lachesis had not stripped away his mounting honors,
> Envy harming (him) with a sideways ax and heedless deeds.[157]

With "two envious hands," he continues, "jealous Nemesis extracted punishments with blood not long ago."[158] Surrey was struck down by the fates, envious of his virtue—and though not a novel trope, we nonetheless again find envy and Surrey connected in the elegiac context. But Chaloner goes further when addressing Envy more precisely, declaring it "so often fatal to the British court": "are you not able," he continues, "to pluck the nation's hoped for fruits before they are ripe?" [159] In this recollection, the whims of fate become coequal with the whims of the men (like Hertford) who wielded Henry's axe—each poisoned with an envious breast. But through Chaloner's pen, the nobility that Surrey embodies becomes the founding verse of a new, corrective prophecy: "it would be worthy," he prays, "that an emulative nation spring forth with appropriate zeal, to lead them in imitating their noble heroes in action."[160] Envy, emulation, and imitation—the affective nodes so active in Surrey's memory of Richmond, here helping to define his own legacy.

I lied about the third. It was not originally composed in Latin, and is not a reflection specifically about the earl—but given what we've seen in this chapter, it might as well have been. "Above all," Francis Bacon suggests, "those are most subject to envy, which carry the greatness of their fortunes in an insolent and proud manner."[161] Bacon here explicitly describes those who elicit envy—but the splendid ambiguity of *subject* cuts both ways. Despite his bloody end, fortune shone on Henry Howard from birth—and it should come as no surprise that in 1539, only two years after Richmond's death, the 22-year-old earl was famously described as "the most folish prowde boye that ys in England."[162]

CHAPTER 3

The Rejected Earl of Leicester, the Rejected Sir Philip Sidney

In the final movement of book V of *The Faerie Queene*, Artegall, the knight of justice—who, aided by the war-machine Talus, had already extended his cold and brutal mandate to the far reaches of Faerie Land—liberates the island commonwealth of fair Irena from the arch-tyrant Grantorto, in an episode refracting the cankered plight of historical Ireland, a long-festering wound in the side of Elizabethan political culture. Having toppled the head of the insurgency, Artegell sets out to cleanse the isle of Grantorto's stain, hunting down rebels and collaborators while working to restore the authority of its rightful sovereign. Yet before Artegall can fully "reforme that ragged common-weale," he finds himself recalled to Faerie Court, his virtuous tasks obscured at home by the shade of "enuies cloud."[1] In answering the summons, he is beset by the dual hags Enuie and Detraction—who, with their monstrous pet the Blatant Beast, do "barke and bay / With bitter rage and fell contention," befouling the honorable knight with words "most shamefull, most vnrighteous, most vntrew."[2] In chapter 2 we saw the power of envy in the courtly sphere, and Artegall proves no match for its barbs and bites: he must yield the stage to Calidore, a knight whose courtly arsenal will, in the poem's final proper book, prove at least a bit more apt than sword or flail. Bruised and battered from his long endeavors, and smarting from slander's sting, Artegall trudges forth to Gloriana's court, "returning yet halfe sad."[3]

This is hardly a notable end for a rather notable knight, and it is easy to appreciate why his return is a doleful one. But why, we may stop and wonder, does the poem describe this disgraced hero as *half* sad? Why is Artegall's sadness only partial, and what comprises this alternate, conflicting response? What does this emotional state tell us about Artegall, and what does it reveal more generally about the Elizabethan courtly experience?

This chapter is an attempt to imagine what these mixed feelings might be, and how they might emerge from the particular nature of Artegall's career of royal service. My focus, however, lies not with Artegall's struggles in the fictive court of faerie, but rather with those of the courtly makers themselves: a group also tasked with negotiating the emotional intricacies of life at court, and whose varied fortune as servants to Queen Elizabeth would find complex expression in figures like Spenser's knight of justice. In my analysis, this contested affective terrain is situated in an equally contested social context: the political experience of the late 1570s, a period crucial in shaping the climate of Elizabeth's subsequent rule. My interest in this chapter surrounds two key players on this stage: Robert Dudley, Earl of Leicester (the famed courtly favorite) and his nephew and protégé Sir Philip Sidney (the famed courtly poet).

The most notable courtier of the Elizabethan period, Leicester was the central node of a vast network of courtly patronage and influence; this amorphous collective, which I will (informally) refer to throughout as the Leicester party, found common ground in a series of broad ideological commitments, such as an interventionist outlook on the affairs of Europe and an inclination to the reformed faith. Yet despite Leicester's unequaled mastery of the courtly game, the actualities of Elizabethan policy routinely brought disappointment and frustration to those of his political persuasion—and despite their overriding personal loyalty to the queen, men like Leicester and Sidney had to brave the persistent sting of waylaid plans, neglected proposals, and personal slights.[4] To begin charting the affective consequence of this position, I will in this chapter consider how the Leicester party contended with courtly *rejection*: the affective response occasioned by the blockage, deferment, or disruption of one's political goals, and (as in the case of Artegall) by the failure to have one's political value actualized and appreciated within the court's social world.[5]

Recent research has shown that rejection hurts, both psychically and physically.[6] It is not pleasant to have one's ambitions thwarted—and that pain is exacerbated, we must imagine, when those ambitions are weighed on a geopolitical (and even cosmic) scale. But there is also, I argue in this chapter, a silver lining to this affective cloud of courtly frustration. Such ostensible failures also have a shadow life as *productive* social moments, generating new modes of personal identity and new forms of political collectivity: a conciliatory affect comprising the other half of Artegall's sadness. Rejection, I suggest, could be powerfully constitutive to Elizabethan courtiers like Leicester and Sidney, insofar as it sanctions a reciprocal ethos of protest and opposition: an ostensible failure, when salvaged and repackaged as heroic or ennobling, can become a striking announcement of one's refusal to be fully integrated into the symbolic universe of Elizabeth's court, and of one's willingness to break script from its enabling fictions. But what starts as a posture of individual bravado (or heroism, or narcissism, or recklessness) is soon transformed, through the channels of performance, to an intersubjective act: by broadcasting his own alienation, the courtier offers an alliance to the similarly minded, inviting them to join him in an alternate social order. This community of disaffection—galvanized both by a concurrent set of political and social goals, and by the ongoing opposition to those goals—assumes the role of a courtly subculture, founded and sustained by the affinity of negative affect.

In the uncertain courtly climate of the late 1570s, such a recuperative model of rejection was particularly valuable for Leicester and Sidney; it finds particular expression, I suggest, in the pageantry that they sponsored in this period. In the second half of the decade, the Leicester party treated Elizabeth to an elaborate series of multimedia events—such as the queen's progresses to Kenilworth and Woodstock, and Sidney's pageant *The Lady of May*—in which all manner of suits, appeals, and advertisements were couched in the splendor and spectacle of nominal royal delight. But despite their primary (and genuine) commitment to the task of royal ingratiation, these literary performances, I argue, nonetheless seem to anticipate and account for the possibility of their own failure. Leicester and his proxies embed within these texts certain discursive contingency plans, in which spoiled or frustrated attempts at flattery and insinuation might be retroactively claimed as a symbolic, collective victory by the ostensibly slighted party. As we will see, and as Leicester and Sidney were well aware, even the stock tropes of royal performance housed a latent source of entropic and oppositional energy, waiting to redeem a would-be failure. In the 1570s, when Elizabeth's grip on England's symbolic and political order was not yet fully realized, it was a particularly valuable time to squeeze royal lemons into courtly lemonade.

Why So Rejected?

The precise manifestation of Leicester and Sidney's courtly rejection in the 1570s emerged from two primary nodes of social contestation.

The first entailed Leicester's long-simmering ambition to secure Elizabeth's hand in marriage—an extended affair that had lingered, albeit faintly, for nearly two decades.[7] It was shortly after her accession in 1558 that Elizabeth developed her affection for the young Robert Dudley; as master of the horse, he enjoyed close and frequent contact with the queen, and within less than a year their intimacy was the subject of rumor and innuendo on both sides of the Channel.[8] Perceptions worsened in September 1560, when Dudley's wife Amy Robsart was found dead of a broken neck, apparently after "falling downe a paier of stayres."[9] Though cleared of wrongdoing by the coroner's inquest, Dudley was plagued for decades by rumors of a domestic conspiracy—a theory infamously expounded in the so-called *Leicester's Commonwealth* (1584), a Catholic polemic that has been called "the most notorious of Elizabethan political libels."[10] Yet despite this bad publicity, Elizabeth wavered little in her affection for Dudley, and within only weeks of Robsart's death, reports circulated that "hyr Hygness shoolde marry hym" before too long.[11]

There was no doubt that England longed for a royal wedding; in the first Parliament of the reign (only weeks after her coronation), the queen was petitioned with a formal request to find the realm a suitable king, in whom its future hopes might be secured.[12] But Elizabeth could not, as unvalued persons do, carve this matter for herself—and whatever the inclinations of her heart, Dudley was not an especially apt choice for such a royal match. The queen's young court, already swirling with envy and resentment at his being favored, would hardly be settled by such a choice, and by embracing her own subject (a fraternization usually thought beneath a prince's dignity), Elizabeth equally threatened to tarnish her reputation abroad, all the while foreclosing the possibilities of matrimonial diplomacy. Throughout 1561, Dudley scrambled to make himself a more appealing candidate, even entreating the Spanish powers to agitate on his behalf—but the support he had secured was not enough to sustain him in the coming months. By 1563, Susan Doran argues, Elizabeth was left with "apparently little desire and certainly no intention of taking Dudley as her husband."[13] The moment had passed for Dudley, who was no longer a plausible romantic contender; "the queen will never choose to marry me," a Spanish ambassador reported him to say, "because she is determined to marry some great Prince."[14] In the years to come, Dudley (now ennobled as the Earl of Leicester) would devote no small energy to undercutting, or outright sabotaging, the foreign suitors that vied for Elizabeth's hand—and while this opposition cannot be attributed merely to spite, there is nonetheless no small hint of cumulative rejection in the affective cloud surrounding it.[15] Although Elizabeth would never marry Leicester or any great prince, there were certainly times when the latter seemed close to happening: especially, as I will touch upon later, in the final years of the 1570s. Leicester's marriage suit was an early casualty of Elizabeth's reign, but proved remarkably resilient in clinging onto life.

The rejection of this possibility, we will see, is reimagined and rechanneled in the courtly performances that he sponsored.

The second cause of agitation in the 1570s—more immediate, more intense, and more dispersed among Leicester's party—concerned the religious strife that ravaged the nations of Europe, and the extent to which England should and could enter the fray. Leicester, Sidney, and a group of similarly minded men at court (including Secretary of State Francis Walsingham and William Davison, English ambassador to the Low Countries) persistently pushed for direct English military intervention in the late 1570s; their overriding agenda concerned the ongoing revolt in the Netherlands, and how England might best help this Dutch resistance overthrow the yoke of Spanish tyranny. Leicester envisioned himself commanding an army, with Sidney at his side, to overthrow the forces of Continental papistry—and on many occasions during this period, he was assured by the queen that his plan would be enacted. Yet, as so often was the case with Elizabeth, such plans changed swiftly, and in the 1570s both Leicester and Sidney were consistently frustrated in these long-sought ambitions. Their fantasies would not be realized for nearly a decade, in the final years of both their lives.

Some context is necessary. In the second half of the 1560s, inhabitants of the so-called Low Countries—a complex patchwork of distinct, though geopolitically related provinces, corresponding largely to the modern nations of Belgium, Luxembourg, and the Netherlands—took up arms against their collective Habsburg sovereign, in attempts to liberate themselves from King Philip II and escape the flames of his inquisitors.[16] It was no easy thing to rule the Low Countries, an amorphous political conglomeration that boasted its own hereditary aristocracy, and Philip II (who was not, like his father, born in the Low Countries) was willing to make the necessary concessions, granting members of the Dutch nobility a nominal stake in their own governance.[17] On matters of religion, however, Philip would not budge, and his refusal to accommodate the growing pockets of Calvinism in his territories—combined with more endemic frustrations over taxation and centralization efforts—sparked outbursts of iconoclastic resistance in 1566.[18] Yet this initial push would meet a hasty end: the Calvinist forces of William (the Silent) of Orange, the charismatic rebel-prince whose name would become synonymous with the struggle for Dutch independence, were no match for the counterinsurgency of the Duke of Alba, whose Spanish troops restored a brutal order to the land and secured the governorship for their general.[19] With Philip's blessing, Alba installed a blood tribunal to exterminate whatever traces of resistance might be uncovered, and in the wake of his entry into the Low Countries, over 60,000 people are said to have fled the region.[20] Orange, however, would not be deterred, and the rebellion simmered over the next decade, variously engaging the Spanish with waves of violence and uneasy truces.

For Leicester and his fellow reformers, the situation in the Netherlands activated a number of personal motivators, both sacred and profane: delivering the Dutch their independence would liberate a valuable economic center from French and Spanish control and strike a blow at the heart of Continental Catholicism. A letter to Walsingham of 1571 reveals the intensity of Leicester's commitment to immediate intervention on the Dutch behalf:

> I think her Majestie shall be advised not to lose all these good advantages offered her, specially when they tend both to the setting up of Gods true Religion, and establishing of her own surety, with augmentation of her Crown. For my part, I never found cause since her Reign, that moveth me more to further it; and be you assured, I will do all that is possible that somewhat may come thereof.[21]

But while no friend of the papal authority—whose bull of excommunication had, only a year earlier, essentially entailed a contract on her life—the queen was even more loath to sponsor insurrection against an anointed king; this was especially true after her own harrowing experience in the Northern Rebellion of 1569.[22] And though the infamous massacre of St. Bartholomew's Day in 1572 (witnessed firsthand by Sidney and Walsingham) would fortify the resolve of England's interventionist reformers, it ultimately helped to mend relations between England and Spain, who formalized their amity with the Treaty of Bristol in 1574.[23] In the years that followed, Leicester and his allies on the council continued to agitate for intervention, with little success.

The tide seemed to turn in the fall of 1576, when a swarm of mutinous Spanish troops "putt to sacke" the city of Antwerp, unleashing "a petyffull slavghter & a mysarable spoyle" on that city's unfortunate citizens.[24] Like the sack of Rome (1527) and the Massacre (1572), the siege of Antwerp (or "the Spanish Fury") would become another iconic moment in the sixteenth century's long history of religious violence. The galvanized Dutch States (often fractured by matters of policy and religion) formed a united coalition of resistance, and Queen Elizabeth, now receptive to her council's pleas, tentatively authorized financial and military support to the cause. But despite the waves of optimism that swept through the Leicester party, their hopes would prove agonizingly hollow: the two years that followed were plagued with difficulties and deferrals, and Leicester could do little but wait for a command that would not materialize, as did the many on the Continent who sought his coming. The decision was finalized in March 1578, when Elizabeth reached a compromise: rather than deploying the promised English forces, which threatened to antagonize Spain and France, she would instead sponsor the German reformer Count John Casimir, whose mercenary army would protect the interests of the Dutch States.[25] After months of negotiations and assurances, the sudden shift in policy—from direct military intervention (through the states themselves) to indirect financial intervention (through the proxy Casimir)—was a grave disappointment to the gung-ho counselors.

To understand the quality of this rejection, it is necessary to recognize the vast energies (social, psychic, and intellectual) that Leicester had invested in his promised generalship. In the second half of the 1570s, correspondence on both sides of the Channel buzzed with anticipation of the earl and his forces—a collective excitement that made Elizabeth's eventual decision devastating. "My Lord of Leicester," it was first reported in the English diplomatic community, "is the moste deseirowse to goe the chiefe of this Iorney that ever yowe herd of, and dothe labor that bothe by his owen policy, and by the favor of all his freindes."[26] This deployment seemed inevitable—and "yf ther be cause to send ayd," Leicester himself would later ensure, "her majestie doth promys my self shale have the Chardge."[27] According to one report, in fact, the earl had made up his mind before Elizabeth:

> My Lord of Leicester commeth over generall of all the men which her majestie shall send in the lowe Countries. This is his full determynation, but yet vnknowen vnto her highnes, nether shall she be acquainted with it, vntill she be fully resolued to send.[28]

In this conviction, Leicester was encouraged by a network of hopefuls on the Continent—including, he was told, the Prince of Orange himself, who "dailye insist vppon the callinge ouer of your Lordship, aswell to satisfie his longinge desyre to see and honour youe in person, as for the common wealhes sake, which he is owt of dowbt shalbe singularlye relieued by your transportation."[29] As Leicester was reminded, he was essential to the Dutch cause, both as a political supporter and as a general:

> I fynd the Prince the most desyrous man in the worlde of your Lordships comminge ouer, and yt ys the strenge he daylye harpes on, but as one carefull, I thinke, aboue all men, of your Honors welfare.

> He hath considered and discoursed with me at large of all the difficulties, one of the greatest whereof might be your longe absence from court, which might perhappes breede as greate preiudice one waye as proffit another, knowinge how by your credytt and presence there, all their causes haue the better speede and successe.[30]

This fondness, in fact, extended to those of his party: when discussing with Orange "persons to supplye your Lordships roome," the English ambassador William Davison made the welcome suggestion of "my good Lord of Warwick, your Lordships brother, or, if that might not be, Master Phillip Sidney, both men so agreable to his Excellencie, as in a world I could not haue made a choyce to his better contentment, for the honorable opinion he hath both of the one and other."[31]

Because of this intense expectation, Elizabeth's sudden change of policy in March 1578 was crushing. Only days later, Leicester reveals his despair in a heart-wrenching letter to Davison:

> I know you thinke much in me that I have wrytten so syldome to you of late, but truly I have byn so trowbled to se the alteracions of our resolucions as I nether had mynd to wryte, or doe any thing.[32]

For Leicester, it was impossible not to take the news as a personal failing, and thus as an implicit insult to his honor:

> And ageyn, for my owne parte, hit can not but greve me, putting my self so farr forward as I dyd, & the matter in so great shewe of my going as yt was, to imagyn what want may be thought in me that so great a chaunge ys happened, spetyally being a mynister, as I have been, in the cause, & holding the place I doe. But I take god to record I have donne my best & vtter most to sett hit forward as I thought hit most safe & honorable for her majestie, and he knoweth best also how lytle I sowght therin any iote of my owne partyculer.

In language bordering on the apocalyptic, Leicester's anxiety for the realm's safety has a clear theological bent, a feature which suggests the extent to which his intervention was framed as a divine mandate:

> Well I can say no more, but I pray god we be all as we ought & that her majestie & this Realme fynd no dangerous lacke of this alteracion. . . . I had rather a 1,000 tymes hassard my lyffe in seking to

> preuent so great daungers as everye way ar lyke to happen to vs & our frendes, than lyve in the greatest fellycyty or securytye for my owne personne that may be wyshed. But our good god hath found vs, I fear, to vnworthie [of] his former blessinges. Hit ys he alone nowe that can help vs, I meane myraculously, seing the apparaunt ordinary courses ar so overslipt.

But perhaps most of all, Leicester could not but feel that he had failed Orange personally:

> I have almost nether face, nor countenance to wryte to the prince, his expectacion being so greatly deceaued, but I hope you wyll lett him faythfully knowe how yt greveth me, & that he wyll think I am a subiect & seruant, but that loveth him as much as any mann that lyveth, who soever he be, and wysheth his prosperytye as greatly, and so shuld he have found, yf god had byn pleasyd that I had come this voyage or that yet hit may please him that so hit may fall out hearafter.

For those of Leicester's party, this was all a bitter pill to swallow. After years of hopeful expectation, they had missed their chance to seize the reins of Christendom—and this failure, combined with that of Leicester's marriage suit, would greatly shape their affective world in the immediate future.

The Nature of Rejection

In the late 1570s a cluster of very powerful men at court were bound by a mutual dissatisfaction with the queen's proceedings, which often seemed (to them) overtly contemptuous of her advisors' counsel, her realm's well-being, and her own personal safety at large. When exploring the emotional resonance of this configuration, one fact is paramount: by rejecting the aims of men like Leicester and Sidney, Elizabeth inflicted no small violence on their very identity as English subjects. For a prominent peer like Leicester, the queen's policy of deferment could be experienced as a direct ontological injury; by denying Leicester his army, she barred him from actualizing the active political selfhood for which he was, according to the culture's logic, natively designed.[33] Sidney shared with his uncle this neo-chivalric outlook on the nature of service and autonomy—but like Surrey, with whom he shared a general affective disposition, Sidney would never fulfill the promise of his upbringing, and his courtly career was even more plagued with frustrations and disappointments.

Rejection is a difficult thing to study, insofar as the word often serves as an umbrella term for concepts such as "rejection, ostracism, abandonment, and exclusion"—but it is a topic of enormous interest in social psychology and related disciplines, where scholars have been tracking, among other things, the cognitive and emotional consequences of interpersonal rebuffs.[34] It is further difficult to consider the consequences of rejection for men like Sidney and Leicester, some of the most privileged subjects in the English realm—hardly those social actors apt to garner the most sympathy. But it is crucial to remember as we proceed that the affective consequences of the Leicester party's political fortunes were formed by *relative* expectations, in the sense that attendance at court can be thought of as a "status-organizing process": that is, one "in which evaluations of and beliefs about the characteristics of actors become the basis of observable inequalities in face-to-face social interaction," and where participants are thus "differentially evaluated in terms of honor, esteem, or desirability, each of which is associated with distinct moral and performance expectations."[35] Because "people pursue status as an (emotional) goal in itself," devaluation at court had significant affective consequence, even for the most well-heeled of Elizabeth's subjects.[36]

Indeed, in the last decade "dozens of studies in different nations have revealed that socioeconomic status only weakly predicts an individual's subjective well-being," while "research on the cognitive, emotional, and interpersonal consequences of being rejected shows that people's perceptions of acceptance and rejection do not always map onto how accepted or rejected they objectively are."[37] In other words, scholars now argue that "hierarchy can be conceptualized as objective social status (e.g., education level) or subjective social status (i.e. one's own judgment of one's status)"—and, it turns out, "subjective social status [is] more consistently and strongly related to psychological functioning" than more traditional markers of class and cultural rank.[38] Recent research speaks of a "local-ladder effect," in which "an increased sense of power and a sense of social acceptance" relative to peers leads to higher subjective well-being (with the opposite, of course, also being true).[39] Despite their objective, material advantages, men like Leicester and Sidney were thus still positioned to be deeply affected by such rejection, especially within the status-amplifying boundaries of the courtly sphere. This is because what has traditionally been thought of as self-esteem may be more accurately called "social esteem"—and, "threats to self-esteem," in turn, can be conceived of as "events that make the possibility of social exclusion salient."[40] Arguing that "the self-esteem system evolved as a monitor of social acceptance, and that the so-called self-esteem motive functions not to maintain self-esteem per se but rather to avoid social devaluation and rejection," theorists like Mark R. Leary and his colleagues argue that humans innately possess a "sociometer": that is, a "subjective monitor or gauge of the degree to which the individual is being included and accepted versus excluded and rejected by other people," tasked with scanning "the social environment (often at a nonconscious or preattentive level) for cues connoting exclusion, rejection, and ostracism and alert[ing] the individual by means of negative affect."[41] Subjective self-esteem is "simply an indicator of the quality of one's social relations vis-à-vis inclusion and exclusion"—making it of particular consequence to those, perched atop the social hierarchy, who were dispositionally inclined to puff their feathers.[42]

I have suggested that feelings of social rejection among the Leicester party—that is, dips in the sociometer—led to the creation of a temporary community of disaffection, in which members actively performed their opposition to the direction of Elizabethan courtly policy. To understand the affective mechanics of this manuever, it is useful to consider the literature on the social psychology of schism. In simplest terms, a schism occurs when a splinter population, feeling rejected by its in-group, turns the tables and initiates its own process of rejection.[43] When a subpopulation feels "marginalised and discriminated against, rather than valued and respected," schismatic action "is seen ultimately as a way of escaping [the] undesired identity and emotional distress" caused by intra-group dissonance.[44] Precipitating the schism, Fabio Sani observes, is the fundamental belief among dissident members that mainstream "group identity has been subverted"; this response, in turn, "will prompt negative emotions (i.e. dejection and agitation) and decrease both group identification and perceived group entitativity (i.e. cohesion, oneness)."[45] When a courtly subpopulation like the Leicester party becomes "dissonant both with what they wish the group to become (the ideal group) and with what the group has the obligation to be (the ought group)," members must contend with "important cognitive and affective consequences . . . [that] generate a mixture of both *dejection*-related emotions (disappointment, sadness) and *agitation*-related emotions (apprehension, uneasiness)."[46] Unsurprisingly, the splintering can work to reassert and reaffirm new in-group cohesion, aligning it with affective and cognitive processes of group dynamics more generally: "group devaluation leads to higher identification with the devalued in-group," while "increased in-group identification after (perceived or actual) group devaluation is an assertion of a (preexisting) positive social identity that counters the negative social identity implied in societal devaluation."[47]

Aggrieved by the queen's rejection of their aims, the Leicester party enacted—or at least enacted the fantasy of—such in-group schism, becoming what we might term a courtly *subculture*: "an enclave, a cult, or a distraction of antithetical values that are expressions of either frustrations with or interventions into the dominant structure of legitimization and control within society."[48] And as it signaled a temporary disruption of the orthodox courtly social order, we can equally label this subculture (and the literary texts it created) as delinquent. Because antisociality is "a way of communicating one's disdain of the system and hence claiming membership among like-minded others"—and because "acts of exclusion from the formal social order are signals of eligibility for inclusion in groups that oppose the social order"—delinquent action is "perhaps the clearest possible way of indicating that you see authority as opposed to you and hence that you are opposed to authority."[49] The openness of such opposition is a key feature, making it of particular value in the hypersurveilled world of the court:

> Delinquent acts are primarily conducted as part of a group activity and a public activity. Delinquents are keenly aware of their audience and seek to manage their reputation, and part of that reputation involves establishing distance from a key outgroup—the system. Thus, delinquency is characterized not only by exclusion from the mainstream, but by inclusion in a group defined in terms of opposition to authority.[50]

From atop the Elizabethan social order, men like Leicester and Sidney performed their discontent in such delinquent play, an affective countermeasure to the frustration and blockage occasioned by their courtly rejection.

To speak of delinquency is appropriate, I think, given the intense connection between interpersonal rejection and aggression.[51] The motives for "antisocial reactions to rejection" are manifold, but have obvious connection to social slight; "anger," it has been argued, "has two important facets, namely, venting frustration and displaying dominance."[52] Indeed, in many cultures, to display anger is to assert a privilege either already possessed or actively desired—a clearly attractive reparative technique for a frustrated courtier looking to reassert a wounded ego.[53] Here the objective, ontological status of men like Sidney and Leicester once again becomes salient, because it "appears that people who are emotionally invested in grandiose self-views are the most aggressive, particularly in response to an esteem threat": it is those tending toward the narcissistic that respond in this way to devaluation, and "the link between threatened egotism (i.e., inflated self-views) and aggression has been extensively documented across a range of situations."[54] I don't think it is overreaching to suggest that enhanced egotism was part of the psychic equipment of any elite Elizabethan courtier—and indeed, the biographies of Sidney and Leicester (to say nothing of Surrey, or, as we'll see, Essex) are flush with examples of rampant self-regard.

To the Elizabethan courtier, it mattered little that such social aggression was often self-defeating: the "fundamental motivation to protect the perceived worth and integrity of the self," research suggests, can have "maladaptive consequences," while "reaffirming a threatened domain can have the effect of exacerbating dissonance."[55] (Or, as a recent book chapter nakedly announces in its title: "Social Exclusion Increases Aggression and Self-Defeating Behavior While Reducing Intelligent Thought and Prosocial Behavior.")[56] This particular response to goal-blockage and exclusion leads to the fundamental paradox of the aggression/rejection response: why on earth do people (or groups) so often respond to rejection with behavior that cannot help but demand further rejection?[57] "One possibility," suggest Kipling D. Williams and Cassandra L. Govan, "is that the need for belonging and self-esteem may pull toward inclusionary reactions and the need for control and meaningful existence may pull toward antisocial reactions"; another "is that both reactions are triggered in the individual: anger and retaliation at an implicit level, and hopes for reinclusion at the explicit level."[58] Whatever the case, it is my argument that the rejected Elizabethan courtier was forced to negotiate this precarious position: knowing that reintegration into the orthodox order was an eventual necessity, but needing still to engage in affective repair, their antisocial aggression required being bold but not too bold. This paradox, I think, helps explain the many aspects of the Tudor courtly experience that seem immediately self-defeating, or that defy strict logic: courtiers like Leicester and Sidney routinely engaged in behavior that was perhaps politically maladaptive, but affectively energizing.

Political rejection threatened to be emotionally crippling, and men like Leicester and Sidney necessarily developed strategies to manage it. One such technique can be detected in the literary performances with which they were associated. To repair the psychic wounds of political frustration and disappointment, those of the Leicester party drew collective strength from a series of textual and performative moments designed to reassert their own autonomy, by announcing themselves incompatible with the larger symbolic matrix that governed Elizabethan monarchal representation. Such moments are not simply "subversive," in the sense of suggesting a challenge to the dominant discourse; rather, they exist to publicize a challenge that has *already* taken place, and to remind the royal powers of who is making it. The mode is less immediately combative than it is confessional—though the confession, to be sure, is of the malcontent's willingness (and happiness) to engage in courtly combat. For the disaffected courtier, I suggest, such disruption could generate a heroic moment of existential autonomy—an assertion of wicked will that demonstrates, like the example of Camus's Sisyphus, that "there is no fate that cannot be surmounted by scorn."[59] Leicester and Sidney's entertainments have been primed to produce such moments: even as they celebrate Elizabeth's glory, they nonetheless have been armed with a series of embedded countermeasures, textual features that might be activated at a moment's notice to unleash an unsuspecting attack or cloak a hasty retreat. A history of failure sows anticipation of a failing future—a crippling truth, unless that possibility is co-opted in advance.

After decades of New Historicist scholarship, it is no surprise to find that courtiers and their proxies found means to thread strands of discontent and opposition within the larger, conventional framework of monarchal celebration.[60] But my point is not to observe that the pageants of the 1570s contained moments of subversion, but rather to emphasize how these texts anticipate their own failing, and how these failures can engender productive forms of collective identification.[61] Such a strategic display of disaffection is doubly fortifying to the courtier's sense of personal autonomy: it frees them from the burden of masking negative affect (and thus diverting the costly "emotional work" of such dissimulation) and flaunts, through a naked breach of decorum, that his force of will is not such that will be deterred by fear of reprisal.[62] When this technique is deployed across a network of discontent (such as that formed by Leicester, Sidney, and the similarly minded), the result is to forge an alternate model of community—an oppositional anti-court, defined by its attempt to refashion, through an act of affective reversal, negative social meaning into the stuff of identity confirmation and alternative political action.

So how did they do it? By turning to the woods.

Into the Wild

In the middle of May 1578, when riding through the woods of Leicester's estate at Wanstead, Queen Elizabeth found herself suddenly starring in

Philip Sidney's earliest surviving literary composition. During her regular summer "progresses"—in which the royal court, fully mobilized, would tear its way through the houses and manors of its nobility—Elizabeth was routinely entertained by elaborate spectacles and performances; in this particular pageant, known now as *The Lady of May*, Sidney had cast the queen as mediator in a rustic debate that had spontaneously erupted before her. A country girl, lately on the cusp of "that notable matter" of matrimony, finds herself equally inclined to the suits of Espilus—a wealthy shepherd, offering a life of ease and comfort—and Therion—a lusty forester, promising a life of activity and exhilaration. As the drama unfolds, both sides debate the merits of the lovers and their professions, before the queen is finally called upon to adjudicate.[63]

Given Therion's virile, vital associations with the active life, modern readers have tended to agree that he is *some* kind of literary figuration of the Sidney/Leicester agenda—and this is with good reason, as we will see.[64] Yet at the same time, if Sidney wanted to assure a victory for the forester, there are a few details he might have spared: when not off "stealing me venison out of these forests," the lady admits, Therion often "grows to such rages, that sometimes he strikes me, sometimes he rails at me."[65] This rather naked assertion certainly troubles Therion's representational status, and is enough for some to disqualify any association with Sidney altogether: "on a literal level," Katherine Duncan-Jones wonders, "could he have expected the Queen to reward a violent poacher?"[66]

My analysis of *The Lady of May* will conclude this chapter. Yet Duncan-Jones's reasonable question demands an answer now, and the thrust of it has implications for a more general reading of the Leicester party's literary ethos—because yes, she's fundamentally right, it does seem unlikely that Sidney would expect the queen to unequivocally reward such renegade behavior. But the very notion, as Duncan-Jones frames it, is premised on the assumption that Sidney's absolute and overriding interest *was* securing the reward for his proxy—and this supposition (and the spirit that animates it) risks limiting our understanding of courtly dynamics, especially as they inflect and are inflected by the courtier's subjective experience. As demonstrated by the literature on rejection reviewed above, there were very good affective reasons why a frustrated courtier might construe himself so unsuitably, however imprudent as a matter of immediate policy.[67]

And indeed, there were good reasons why Sidney and Leicester might want to align themselves specifically with the forester Therion, the figure whose native domain was the depths of the wild, liberated from the softening touch of art and culture, and from the order and degree of the monarch's court. By virtue of their standing, the average Elizabethan aristocrat had a functional relationship with the natural world: nobles often joined the queen in her favorite pastime of hunting, and their newly built estates, elaborately stylized with gardens, parks, and other artificial landscapes, drew much of their significance via contrast with the surrounding woodland.[68] Yet there was also a more substantial way that England's wild proved a site of identity management for Elizabeth's nobility. Concepts of the wild were a vital counterbalance in the long development of European courtesy, as a site of contestatory energy that threatened to disrupt the symbolic order of civil discourse, and that threatened to disrupt the principles of governance itself.

That wildness was thought antithetical to authority is suggested by a representative document of early 1538, in which a northern prior denounces the recent religious risings against Henry VIII:

> And as touchinge all other persones of what sorte of menn so euer theye bee, kynne or frende, or other, that shall fortune to vtter their stomakkes agaynst the kinges highnes, or to be accused of the same, I for my parte shall bere them less favour then I wold do to turkes: for turkes, albeyt they be infideles, yeat they be of the same nature, menn as we bee—and those that do rebell agaynst their naturall prince, whome by goddes lawe and mans lawe they ought to defende, be to be reputed as no menn, but as serpentes and wyelde beestes.[69]

In the ordered world of a monarch's realm, there was little room for such savageness. Yet this protestation, an orthodox Renaissance commonplace, obscures a central paradox about the nature of the wild: that, as it works to strip a man bare, wildness necessarily exposes the raw human stuff that had been fettered by his social clothes. This untapped vein of power, autonomy, and (as in the emerging "noble savage" trope) even virtue could fuel a shadow-self, an alternate guise that might, by giving the lie to the social world that cloaked it, enable a mode of intense actualization. There is perhaps no purer form of virility than the one experienced on the descent to join those "reputed as no menn." For this reason, I suggest, the wild was a site of valuable fantasy for the disaffected Elizabethan aristocrat, who saw in it a symbolic opportunity to perform the recuperative and compensatory affective measures I have described above.

Fundamentally, of course, *The Lady of May* is a pastoral literary exercise, and both foresters and wildness can be generally related to the larger discourse of pastoralism, the Elizabethan courtier's conventional mode of literary critique.[70] The social dynamics of pastoralism have been elucidated by the work of New Historicist scholars like Louis Adrian Montrose, who suggests that pastoral forms served "to mediate differential relationships of power, prestige, and wealth in a variety of social situations."[71] Rather than a mere "longing after innocence and happiness," the pastoral genre's "fundamental self-contradictoriness" made it a powerful vehicle of indirect argument, as suggested by a much-cited passage of George Puttenham:

> The poet devised the eclogue . . . not of purpose to counterfeit or represent the rustical manner of loves and communication, but under the veil of homely persons and in rude speeches to insinuate and glance at greater matters, and such as perchance had not been safe to have been disclosed in any other sort.[72]

It seems clear that pastoralism was the "appropriate medium in which living princes may be obliquely criticised or instructed," and that "its properties of dissimulation and insinuation make it apt to embody any motive that it might be impolitic, graceless, or dangerous to advance openly in the predatory environment of a Renaissance court."[73] But, as the fundamental contest of *The Lady of May* reveals, the discourse of wildness—even as it is embedded within the pastoral mode—enables a related critique which is *not* appropriate, and which *is* impolitic, graceless, or dangerous—and that sometimes this friction was to be preferred, especially as an affective resource. This association with wildness was especially valuable during the first half of Elizabeth's reign, when the political and representational modes that defined her were still pliable, and when discourse (oppositional or otherwise) was not yet inflected by the cult of Gloriana, the structure of symbolic orthodoxy that governed courtly expression in the 1580s and 1590s.[74]

Though the pageants of the 1570s were a reification of the Elizabethan symbolic order, Leicester and Sidney routinely found means within to introduce a node of chaos, by aligning themselves with this energy of the wild—a maneuver enabled by the natural setting in which they occurred. While there has been some discussion about the political nature of wildness in this period, I think that the range and significance of its affective valence has not yet been understood.[75] In the sixteenth-century imagination, notions of wildness conjured a complex tapestry of associations, telling all manner of tales about the men and beasts that inhabited the natural world. In this folk tradition, a variety of archetypes soon emerged—though it is not easy to delineate them precisely. Writing nearly a century ago, Robert Withington observed the challenge of sorting out this cast of characters:

> The relation between wild-men, green-men, foresters, Robin Hood, the Moors and the devil is very difficult to clear up. A great many cross-influences must exist; and it seems obvious that all these figures are connected.[76]

Because these stock types share an associative range, it is not necessary to profile them completely—but by sketching the broad parameters of their thematic domain, it becomes clear that they collectively activate an affective suite of aggression, virility, and opposition.

Remaining with Therion, we can begin with the figure of the forester: the man who, with trap and axe, bravely seeks his fortunes in the wild, a potent symbol and worthy champion of the active life. As Catherine Bates has recently argued, the act of hunting has long been vital to notions of "heroic masculinity" in the Western literary tradition; in the Renaissance, she importantly demonstrates, varieties of hunting motifs signaled ongoing negotiations of "wealth, status, prestige."[77] Though the forester motif figured widely in the sixteenth-century literary imagination, it seems to have been a particular favorite of Elizabeth's father—the king who, armed with his majestic codpiece, actively mythologized himself as the font of virility. As such, the forester made regular appearances in the entertainments of Henry VIII's reign, and the records of his pageants are flush with receipts for "foresters' coates and hoods" and "hunters' jackets."[78] (In fact, the forester featured in King Henry's coronation revelries, in a spectacle recorded by Hall.)[79] Furthermore, a cluster of forester songs are recorded in British Library Additional MS 31922, the "Henry VIII Manuscript," a songbook in which the work of composers like William Cornish and Robert Cooper is preserved alongside King Henry's own literary and musical compositions.[80] Though the forester/hunter figure assumes several different roles in this collection, it nonetheless harmonizes around two central assertions: that the wild is a site of both violent and erotic opportunity, and that the forester is the man best poised to activate it. Exploiting the commonplace trope of the erotic hunt, the foresters of these songs deploy an arsenal of horns, spears, and arrows to celebrate (or mourn the decline of) the masculine lustiness with which they are naturally endowed. The opening verse, for example, of Cornish's "Blow thi hornne hunter" entails an almost ritualistic invocation of the phallus:

Blow thi hornne hunter
& blow thi horne on hye
ther ys a do in yonder wode
in faith she woll not dy
now blow thi hornne hunter
& blow thi hornne ioly hunter.[81]

In general, the forester figure in this collection accrues a thematic cluster: notions of erotic abundance, implicit and explicit violence, and masculine, homosocial autonomy. Though the forester is the least savage (and least subversive) denizen of the natural world, he nonetheless stands on the threshold of wildness—and as such, he begins to introduce, in regulated form, the energies of wanton violence, sexual aggression, and unfettered autonomy that only intensify as we proceed further into its depths.

Leicester and Sidney may have especially admired one particular forester of the "wilde Countries": the infamous Robin Hood.[82] As "chiefe gouernoure" of the wild, Robin Hood presided over an outlaw court of his merry men, a political subculture bound by the affective affinity of mutual alienation.[83] He enjoyed a robust presence in the folklore of late medieval and early modern England—and we know he appealed to the Sidney family, who staged a Robin Hood performance during their spring festivities in 1574. (There's reason to think that Leicester, Elizabeth's own "sweet Robin," may have also identified with this alternate namesake.)[84] Embodying a "permanent state of resistance to governmental authority," the Robin Hood figure of the late Middle Ages was inherently "chaotic, centrifugal, even subversive."[85] Born to a "Forester [who] shot in a lusty long Bow," Robin is routinely described as a "gode yeman" in the ballad tradition; for reason of this humble start, he was a star of folk traditions (like the May Day festivals) that upended the conventional social hierarchy.[86] But in the early modern period, Robin Hood underwent an enormous social change, and it was one that made him even more meaningful to men like Leicester and Sidney. For reasons still not entirely clear, the sixteenth century witnessed a "gentrification" of the Robin Hood legend, in which the outlaw became increasingly imagined not as a working-class hero, but as a displaced, disaffected, or exiled aristocrat.[87] In the early decades of the century, he was already a figure notable in court fiction (in 1510, for example, Henry VIII and his friends took the guise of "Robyn Hodes men" to perform before Queen Catherine), and as the era progressed, Robin would become a natural denizen of the courtly universe—though one fundamentally opposed, in his kingdom of the wild, to the site of court proper.[88] Thus, in the second half of the sixteenth century, as Leicester and Sidney were rehearsing their grievances in the imaginative space of the wild, the Robin Hood of medieval lore was simultaneously adopting a form in which they might increasingly recognize themselves. In this new order, it has been said, "May games [were] now war games" and "the politics of Robin Hood [were] revolutionary"—features that, by lending a stately gravity to the tale's folk origins, aligned it with the affective mode the Leicester party.[89] Blending antiauthoritarian aggression with moral righteousness, the merry men were an apt model for a community of frustrated courtiers.

But if the forester is one step removed from the site of court and culture, there are many figures even more natively suited to the wilderness. The most prominent is the *wild* (or *savage*) *man*, the half-beast who embodied the primordial condition, untamed yet by the civilizing process. Though known by many names (wild man, savage man, green man, woodwose), he is familiar to readers of Elizabethan literature; he appears on stage, for example, as Bremo in *Mucedorus*, while his image is refracted in many personae in *The Faerie Queene*, through which Spenser explores the contours of human nature.[90] "Depicted in deliberately grotesque terms," he was "covered with a thick coat of hair, or with moss and ivy, and carrying an uprooted tree or club"; he is thus a presocial form of the forester, who (with culture's guiding hand) replaced a coat of natural hair with the cured hides of his quarry, and who traded the phallic brawn of his club for the phallic finesse of an arrow.[91] As such, the wild man equally evoked associations of violence, sexuality, and raw freedom—but as a creature immune from the laws and mores of society, he amplified them to a potentially terrifying degree.[92] From this native state, the wild man thus "implied everything that eluded Christian norms and the established framework of Christian society"—that which "was uncanny, unruly, raw, unpredictable, foreign, uncultured, and uncultivated."[93] Because the monarch's court was the epicenter of rule and culture, the wild man thus stood as a perfect inversion of the courtier: a position that might prove enormously productive for those, like Leicester and Sidney, who had temperament to inhabit it. (That wild figures were often motivated by "a case of rejected love" furthers the association for Leicester.)[94] Though the wild man existed in many forms throughout the early modern period, he was, at his core, antithetical to the principles of sovereignty; this fact prescribed his orthodox role in Elizabethan pageants, to be tamed by the queen's presence.[95] He was thus an apt vessel, even more than the forester figure, for courtly fantasies of subversion, opposition, and autonomy.[96]

The wild man was featured regularly in shows of the 1570s, in a variety of permutations. In addition to the Leicester-sponsored events discussed below, he figured in the New Year's revels of 1574, a pageant in July of the same year, and in George Whetstone's 1578 comedy *Promos and Cassandra*.[97] (Like the forester, the wild man was also a favorite of Henry VIII: the folk figure of hypermasculine abundance found reflection in one of England's most hypermasculine, patriarchal, and phallic kings.)[98] The raw vitality of the wild man figure, and a further indication of his potential suitability as a site of identification, is similarly confirmed by his linkage to characters of the divine, or legendary, variety. In many instances, the wild man is associated with a pair of related figures from antiquity: Sylvanus, spirit of the forest and countryside, and Silenus, spirit of the wild.[99] Like the wild man, both can be seen wielding uprooted trees—and Silenus, as companion to the satyrs and foster father to Dionysus, was especially prone to fits of frenzy.[100] Along with such classical contributions, the wild man's symbolic meaning was inflected by local custom. Though the wild man is a stock character of European folklore, his particular manifestation in England is indebted to the "green man" of Celtic mythology, an analogous native of the natural world—and for this reason, the savage man of the English forest is often clothed not in hides and hair, but in vines and ivy.[101] The wild man also had a curious affinity with Saint George, England's patron saint and ur-champion: for example, the "St. George plays" of the medieval and early modern period often employed "leaves or green branches" in their costuming.[102] Both the classical and native English traditions expanded the wild man's symbolic range by allowing his inherent linkage with strength, virility, and autonomy to manifest within the cosmic register of heroes, legends, champions, and divines.

And indeed, there is one such association that demands particular note. In *The Individual and the Cosmos in Renaissance Philosophy*, Ernst Cassirer importantly argues that Hercules is a principal icon of early modern autonomy: in defeating his allegorical nemesis Fortune, Hercules asserts the supremacy of truth, judgment, and freedom, epitomizing the supreme notion of valor (*fortezza*). (That is, the "strength of virility itself, the strength of the human will which becomes the tamer of destiny, the *domitrice della fortuna*.")[103] Embodying the proximity of man and god, Hercules was a particularly apt hero of the early modern period, and it is not surprising that he enjoyed a rich career as a symbol of Renaissance virtue.[104] Yet, because of his traditional signification in art and literature—armed with a club, and draped in the skin of the Nemean lion—Hercules would also develop an association with the wild man topos of European folk culture. In the Middle Ages, there grew an increasing correspondence between "a man clad in fur, and one endowed with it by nature," and for obvious reasons, many "attributes of the strong Hercules . . . coalesced into those of the conventional wild man."[105] In some cases, the association was quite explicit: for example, a fourteenth-century illustration of Seneca's *Hercules Furens* depicts Hercules as unmistakably wild, a club-wielding, anthropomorphized lion-man marked by both human hands and feline paws and tail.[106] As Michael Wintroub notes, this version of Hercules—which extends the god-man permutation to god-man-savage—reveals that the wild man equally encompasses "a discursive field in which the normative values of elites could be negotiated and/or contested."[107] The addition of Hercules further thickens the associative texture of Leicester and Sidney's interest in the wild man topos: to the unrestrained, dangerous, and audacious power of the savage man, the classical hero added notions of nobility, governance, and even humanist eloquence, all without yielding the fundamental core of volatility that makes savagery so seductive in the first place.

Virility, aggression, autonomy, rebellion, violence, lust, subversion, phallicism, patriarchy, heroism, primitivism, naturalism, frenzy, audacity, degeneration, and virtue: the discourse of wildness evoked many things in the sixteenth-century English imagination. Some were commendable, even honorable. But many still were chaotic, posing an inherent danger to the core principles of governance and social order—or, perhaps worse still, in the case of many of the gendered terms, announcing a specific challenge to the authority of a (virgin) queen. Insofar as identification with wildness entails a kind of style, this symbolic range may be thought to entail what Sarah Thornton (adopting Bourdieu) calls "subcultural capital," the "subspecies of capital operating within . . . less privileged domains" of mainstream culture.[108] The discourse of wildness was a thing of endless productivity for a cadre of disaffected men in Elizabeth's court, in which they could find a thematic and formal vocabulary to perform affective states of rejection, discontent, and antisociality—and indeed, to dismantle, however temporarily, the very notions of courtship.

With the previous discussion in mind, I will now consider how the oppositional thematics of wildness are deployed by the Leicester/Sidney circle in three entertainments of the late 1570s: the pageants at Kenilworth and Woodstock in 1575—which begin to employ the disaffected poetics I have been describing—and Sidney's *The Lady of May* in 1578—which, in response to three additional years of rejection, is even more explicit in promoting the discontent of its sponsors. In each performance, elements from the lexicon of the wild are strategically exploited in the service of an antisocial undersong, sounding notes of negative affect even within the celebratory mode of the entertainment proper. Such songs would soon enough become the official soundtrack of the pasture—but in the 1570s, they emerged from a considerably more frenetic place, and were invested with fantasies of a wilder nature.

Leicester and Sidney, Entertainers

Kenilworth, 1575

In July 1575 Leicester hosted an entertainment for the roving queen at his magnificent castle of Kenilworth. Present during the nineteen-day celebration was the young Philip Sidney, freshly returned from his two-year finishing tour of Europe; the primary poetic architect, however, was the well-known writer (and grizzled soldier) George Gascoigne, who seems to have guided much of the festivities.[109] The events were recorded in two contemporary accounts: Robert Laneham's eyewitness report, published in 1575 as *A Letter Whearin Part of the Entertainment Vntoo the Queenz Maiesty at Killingwoorth Castl in Warwik Sheer in This Soomerz Progress 1575 Iz Signified*, and Gascoigne's pseudo-official version, published (anonymously) a year later as *The Princelye Pleasures, at the Courte of Kenelwoorth*.[110] As these texts reveal, the queen was honored with such panoply of spectacle—song and dance, playlets, combat, pyrotechnics, and special effects—that it has been often claimed that the events entailed a de facto marriage proposal on Leicester's behalf.[111] Yet, in spite of this motive—or, perhaps more rightly, because of it—there also exist moments of oppositional energy, in which Leicester and his proxies anticipate the likely failure of this very proposition. In doing so, they find means to assert their own wild autonomy, by promoting the suitor's fundamental inability to be integrated in (and thus reduced to) the symbolic universe of his beloved.

At the outset of her stay, Elizabeth was lavishly celebrated even before she reached the grounds of Kenilworth proper: "there met her on the way, somewhat neere the Castle, *Sybilla*, who prophecied vnto her Highnes, the prosperous raigne that she should continue, according to the happy beginning of the same" (2:290). With this happy ambush, Elizabeth was treated to a welcome verse, promising a peaceful future for herself, her subjects, and her realm.

Yet even within this conventional welcome, the Sybil—"placed in an arbor in the parke neere the high way where the *Queenes maiestie* came" (ibid.)—finds subtle means to establish a demarcation between the feminine source of the queen's authority and the masculine consensus by which it is enabled. This tension is detected even within her ostensibly benign prayer for a peaceful realm:

> You shalbe called the Prince of peace,
> and peace shalbe your shield,
> So that your eyes shal neuer see
> the broyls of bloody field. (2:291)

Though apparently unremarkable, these lines acknowledge a literal fact of no small importance: Elizabeth's eyes *won't* ever see the field of war, and this is precisely the feature that separates her from martial subjects like Leicester, Sidney, and Gascoigne. Though Elizabeth may preside over the fictive combats of the pageant world, the Sybil reminds her that she, unlike her mighty father, was a monarch barred from the theater of war. Elizabeth's engagement with the realm of blood and steel was restricted to the kind of martial role-playing we see before Tilbury—a justly celebrated gesture, but one whose rhetorical power is ultimately premised on the queen's fundamental incompatibility with the realm of genuine combat.

But while Elizabeth may have been excluded, the site of war was nonetheless a key domain for the formation and management of aristocratic identity, in which men like Leicester and Sidney strove to "vindicate their honor and authority" through exploits in the field.[112] The same neo-chivalric spirit that inspired their flair for martial pageantry assured that the symbolic combats they staged were an inadequate substitute for the thing itself: the real place for affirming their aristocratic ontology was in battle, and this was the birthright that Elizabeth insistently denied them. Indeed, when the opportunity was finally presented, many would ruthlessly seize it: the queen's command was routinely disobeyed in times of war, when her generals found means to subordinate her will to their own. (As we will see in the next chapter, this was a tactic of the Earl of Essex.) These social dynamics are being negotiated even within the celebratory mode of the pageant—and, for all its orthodoxy, the observation that Elizabeth's "eyes shall neuer see / the broyls of bloody field" cannot help but activate alternate ways to read the mock-combats that will be subsequently staged for her entertainment.

After the confirmation that Elizabeth's reign would be marked by tranquility, she encountered a bellicose dumb show that suggested the opposite:

> Her Majesty passing on to the first gate, there stode in the Leades and Battlementes thereof, sixe Trumpetters hugelie advaunced,

> much exceeding the common stature of men in this age, who had likewise huge and monstrous Trumpettes counterfetted, wherein they seemed to sound: and behind them were placed certaine Trumpetters, who sounded in deede at her majesties entrie. And by this dum shew it was ment, that in the daies and Reigne of K. *Arthure*, men were of that stature. So that the Castle of *Kenelworth* should seeme stil to be kept by *Arthurs* heires and their seruants. (2:291–92)

The trumpeters, with their exaggerated height, physical prowess, and "huge and monstrous" phallic devices, signal the potent virility of Leicester's world, recalling the brawn of the savage man archetype. It is thus not surprising that they announce the earl as a figure of Arthur: the font of British chivalry, a heroic warrior, a defender of the faith, and (above all) a king.[113]

It is difficult to think that this is not, on some level, a challenge to Elizabeth's authority: she is being welcomed as a *subject* to an alternate realm, an artifact of England's heroic past, in which Leicester rules as warrior-king. Indeed, though Leicester took extensive steps to modernize the grounds, Kenilworth was still an "ancient military fortress," recalling the domains of the overmighty peers that Elizabeth's father and grandfather struggled so endlessly to undo.[114] In the 1570s Leicester continued to fortify and expand his arsenal at Kenilworth, from which he commanded a nearly unthinkable reserve of potential power:

> Not for over half a century had a subject possessed such formidable military resources. If only he could have ensured the loyalty of his men, Leicester was in a position to defy all comers, even perhaps his sovereign. He was the last of his kind in English history.[115]

Though the arsenal wasn't merely for show, its primary force is symbolic, transforming Kenilworth into a counterculture monument to the force of Leicester's exceptional magnificence—though one devoted officially, of course, to eliciting her majesty's pleasure.[116] When we recall that Henry VIII was invested in the mythos of Arthur, whose ancient authority would premise his world-shattering claims of religious prerogative,[117] it becomes clear that the symbolic world of Kenilworth provides an alternate court to Elizabeth's own, grounded in the patriarchal principles of a hypothetical Dudleian rule.[118] Given this investment in virility, it is not surprising who Leicester elected as the champion of his heroic, masculine realm: "when her maiestie entred the gate, there stoode *Hercules* for Porter"

(2:292). For the interventionalist Leicester party, who ached to don spurs on behalf of the Low Countries, such fantasies of a militaristic empire were an obvious affective well, counteracting the threat to aristocratic ontology posed by Elizabeth's continual reluctance to engage.[119]

As the festivities continued, the pageant's engagements with the discourse of wildness became further explicit. Later in the week, for example, Elizabeth encountered an "*Hombre Saluagio*, with an Oken plant pluct vp by the roots in hiz hande, him self forgrone all in moss and Iuy" (2:250). Initially unaware of the queen's presence, the savage man has been stirred by the disruption of his domain, and seeks someone to explain "why all these worthy Lords and Peeres, / are here assembled so" (2:297). In a comic exchange with Echo, the wild man (who seems to have been played by Gascoigne) is led through a brief précis of the pageant's proceedings to date—a recapitulation that serves to emphasize the extraordinary efforts of "O *Dudley*," who "gaue him selfe and all, / A worthy gift to be received, / and so I trust it shall" (2:301). He finally spots Elizabeth herself, the guest of honor; he falls to his knees, begging that she might accept the service of such a "wilde and sauadge man" (2:302).

Unlike many of the playlets during the progress, the saga of the Savage Man is left puzzlingly unresolved; despite his promise (and willingness) to yield, there is no catharsis, no transformation, and no integration into the social order. The texts give no hint of Elizabeth's response, and the terms of his submission are accordingly unclear. Indeed, his final words to the queen contain a barely concealed challenge—"And take in worth the wilde mans words, / for else you do him wrong"—and his concluding remarks, as Gascoigne tells it, invoke rejection and despair:

> let me go seeke some death,
> Since I may see this Queene no more,
> good greefe nowe stop my breath. (2:303–4)

An odd way, it seems, to conclude the sequence, which is notable in itself for suspending the conventions of the wild man transformation trope.

But the reason for this abrupt ending may be indicated by an event that is omitted in Gascoigne's text. As Laneham tells it, another incident had actually concluded the wild man episode:

> Az thiz Sauage for the more submission brake his tree a sunder, kest the top from him, it had allmost light vpon her highness hors hed: whereat he startld and the gentleman mooch dismayd. See the benignittee of the Prins, az the foot men lookt well too the hors, and

> hee of generozitee soon callmd of him self, no hurt, no hurt quoth her highnes. Which woords I promis yoo wee wear all glad to heeer, and took them too be the best part of the play. (2:251)

Though merely an accident, it is suggestive that the savage man brings near-disaster to the queen, via the very act that is intended to signal his submission: her courtiers might sublimate much of their desires, but there is nonetheless a potential cost to the civilizing process of Elizabeth's court. In fact, according to a contemporary Spanish dispatch, the wild man episode wasn't the only occasion at Kenilworth that presented danger to the queen:

> The queen majesty, as I write, is far away from here, at my Lord of Leicester's castle, called Kenilworth, where the earl has treated her to many festivities. It is said that one day, while going to hunt, a traitor (whom they then seized) shot at her with an arrow—though others say he was just shooting at the deer, and meant no harm. The bolt passed by the queen without hurting her, thank God.[120]

Was there a Robin Hood lurking in the woods of Leicester's Kenilworth? The queen, it seems, didn't have much luck with clubs or arrows on this visit—the phallic signifiers of the wild proved a too-real reminder of the dangerous virility that stood in symbolic defiance of her order.

As we have seen, the Kenilworth festivities were punctuated by an oppositional undersong, in which Leicester and his agents embedded themes that strategically cut against the spirit of the celebration proper. This is perhaps no better exemplified than by the events surrounding the so-called Masque of Zabeta, a sequence in which the organizers seem to deploy, but at the same time anticipate the failure of, a coded marriage proposal to the queen. Apparently intended as a centerpiece of the queen's visit, the masque reveals how the nymph Zabeta, a former disciple of Diana, is encouraged to join Juno and her cult of matrimony.[121] (Continuing the prevalent motif, the performance also features "a man cladde all in Mosse," who announces himself as "the wylde mans sonne" [2:309].) But though the show was "*prepared and redy (euery Actor in his garment) two or three dayes together*," it never was realized—and while allegedly postponed for "*lack of opportunitie and seasonable weather*," it has in fact "long been suggested (and is generally accepted) that the real reason for the cancellation of Gascoigne's marriage masque was the sensitivity of its overt call for Queens to wed" (2:322; ibid. footnote 556). By printing the playlet's text in his 1576 account, Gascoigne scores a minor revenge, ensuring that the nixed performance would still have life in the public record: the volume's preface, in fact, explicitly signals the inclusion of "one Moral and gallant Deuyce, which neuer came to execution, although it were often in a readinesse" (2:289). In not addressing "the real source of the queen's displeasure," Susan Frye observes, this maneuver "subtly undercut[s] her and protect[s] the participants by pretending that her actions are unfounded."[122]

But even more important is the fact that, while this particular show was canceled, Leicester seemed determined that Elizabeth would hear the tale of Zabeta, one way or the other. Days later, in the final moments before "her departure from thence, the Earle commanded master *Gascoigne* to deuise some Farewel worth the presenting"—and to do so, the poet clad himself "like vnto *Syluanus*, God of the Woods" (2:322). Of the dozens of allegorical figures that had appeared throughout the week, Gascoigne selects the lord of "these woods and wildernes" to engage Elizabeth for a final time; he follows alongside the queen as she rides, delivering a series of speeches designed to entice an extension of her visit (ibid.). As Sylvanus explains it, the "late alteration in the skyes" should be attributed to the "flowing teares" of the gods, grieved at her imminent departure, and the anticipation of which reverberates throughout the natural world:

> Not onely the skies scowled, the windes raged, the waues rored and tossed, but also the Fishes in the waters turned vp their bellies, the Deere in the woods went drowping, the grasse was wery of growing, the Trees shooke off their leaues, and all the Beastes of the Forrest stoode amazed. (2:324–25)

But Sylvanus next turns to the show that had been allegedly ruined by this meteorological upheaval: in lieu of the canceled performance, Gascoigne himself unfolds the "strange and pitifull adventures" of Zabeta—the nymph "surpassing all the rest for singuler gifts and graces"—and her unlucky suitors—"whome shee hath turned and conuerted into most monstrous shapes and proportions" (2:326). As they proceed throughout the forest, Sylvanus narrates this gallery of wretched souls (such as "Constance," turned to "this Oke," or "inconstancie," to "yonder Popler"), forcing the queen to gaze upon the casualties of her displaced erotic obstinacy (2:326–27). Of particular interest is the fate of "Ambition":

> She dyd by good right condemne hym into this braunch of Iuy, the which can neuer clyme on hygh nor florysh without the helpe of some other plant or tree, and yet commonly what tree soeuer it ryse

> by, it neuer leaueth to wynde about it, and strayghtly to infolde it, vntyll it haue smowldred and killed it. (2:327)

Though a normal enough indictment of the courtly rat race—and of the clawing upstarts that so aggrieved men like Sidney and Leicester—ivy is also the essential signifier of the English wild man, an association that substantially thickens the moment's symbolic importance. On one hand, the wild man is a living monument to the deleterious effects of unchecked courtly ambition: covered in ivy, he offers visual witness to the process of predation that Sylvanus describes, and which slowly erodes the bedrock of aristocratic ontology. Yet on the other, the wild man is not simply covered in ivy, but is made *of* it: in this sense, he is ambition animated, with the seizing of autonomy it entails, and with the threat of destruction to those who might impinge it. Following an increasingly familiar pattern, this slick maneuver embraces the alluring threat of courtly ambition even as it righteously condemns it.

But the centerpiece of Sylvanus's catalog is the figure of "Deepe desire," who was turned into "this *Holy bush* . . . now furnished on euery side with sharpe pricking leaues, to proue the restlesse prickes of his priuie thoughts" (2:328).[123] Unlike Zabeta's other victims, desire is given the opportunity to speak for himself—but his attention is fixed not on his tormentor, but on Elizabeth. He returns to the queen's meteorological significance, reviewing how these "great floods of mone" have disrupted the natural order, before imploring her to

> commaunde againe,
> This Castle and the Knight,
> which keepes the same for you:
> These woods, these waues, these foules, these fishes
> these deere which are your dew. (2:329–30)

Such a pledge, he assures, will redeem his natural form. Sylvanus equally craves, in his final words, "that you would either be a suter for him vnto the heauenly powers, or else but onely to giue your gracious consent that hee may be restored to his prystinate estate" (2:331).

Like the earlier savage man episode, the princely pleasures of Kenilworth end indeterminately, at least as it appears in the textual record. Elizabeth's response is not recorded, but the progress proceeded as expected: an implicit rejection of desire, as it is framed by this final encounter. But why, to conclude these weeks of extravagance and expense, was Elizabeth even given this final opportunity to reject her host?

Did Leicester and Gascoigne really expect the queen to embrace the offer?

The answer, I think, is that this rejection has been anticipated, and written into the text itself, via the contestatory forms that Leicester inhabits: forms that, in effect, underwrite the failure of their own rhetorical aims. The very shape of Leicester's transmuted desire (the consequence of his enforced submission to the Elizabeth-figure Zabeta) flaunts its aggression, threatening to prick those who encroach upon its space. The threat of violence is specifically phallic, as when Sylvanus quips on the differences of "he *Holly*" and "she *Holly*": "Nowe some will say that the she *Holly* hath no prickes, but thereof I entermeddle not" (2:328). But the "prystinate estate" of Leicester's desire—that is, the desire that *would* be unleashed by Elizabeth's favor, and to which she herself would submit—is more threatening still in the sheer magnitude of its force:

> I am that wretch *Desire*,
> whom neither death could daunt;
> Nor dole decay, nor dread delay,
> Nor fayned cheere inchant.
> Whom neither care could quench,
> nor fancie force to change. (2:328)

It is only Zabeta's rejection that has capped the bottle of desire—and it is hard to imagine why Elizabeth would want to uncork it.

In 1575, it would have been exceptionally unlikely for Elizabeth to give her hand to the Earl of Leicester. I find it hard to believe that any of his associates expected that she would.[124] While this certainly does not mean that Leicester would have rebuffed the opportunity to become an Arthurian king of England, it does suggest that he was aware of his suit's near impossibility—and accordingly, that he and his agents knowingly constructed a fictive world that was ultimately destined to memorialize its failure. In anticipation of this inevitable end, Leicester populates this world (and associates himself with) a cast of wild figures that are adversarial, threatening, and fundamentally unsuitable for engaging the queen: a maneuver that, when considered retrospectively, co-opts the autonomy of Elizabeth's choice, and reconfigures her rejection as a confirmation of his own fundamental power. This consolation is grounded upon the performance of opposition and contention; in the texts of the Kenilworth shows, the discourse of wildness functions as an escape clause, drafted ahead to absorb and refashion the sting of frustrated desire. It is no accident that Leicester's guise of the holy bush so resembles Zabeta's lover

Contention, who was transformed to a “bramble Bryer” armed to “catch and snach at . . . garments, and euery other thing that passeth by it” (2:327).

In a perceptive chapter—which tellingly begins with the heading “Gascoigne’s Wilderness Years”—R.W. Maslen notes that “George Gascoigne specialized in the fiction of failure”; this tendency is perhaps best exemplified in “Gascoignes Wodmanship,” his most famous lyric, which recounts a woeful hunter who “shootes awrie almost at every marke.”[125] Emerging from the discourse of the wild, I suggest, the Kenilworth festivities reflect Gascoigne’s deep commitment to failure—but it is failure pointedly deployed in the affective interests of Leicester and his allies.

Woodstock, 1575

Not long after the events at Kenilworth, Elizabeth was treated to another such round of festivities at her manor of Woodstock, organized by its keeper (and Leicester client) Sir Henry Lee—the man who would go on, as the queen’s official champion, to become the guardian of the Elizabethan neo-chivalric cult of honor.[126] Though surviving records don’t account fully for her month-long stay, we do know that she witnessed, with apparent delight, an intricate pageant of interlocking, star-crossed lovers in the romantic mode; its centerpiece is the two-part drama of Gaudina and Contarenus, a rousing tale in which love is ultimately sacrificed for public service.[127] Though readings diverge wildly, there is near-universal agreement that the entertainment must, in some way, be read in conjunction with Kenilworth; some, for example, find it a “response or riposte” to the pro-matrimony slant of the previous event, while others have “argued that there are close similarities in their respective agendas” regarding “Leicester’s ambitions as defender of the Protestant cause in the Low Countries.”[128] And though there is consensus that she was pleased by the proceedings—part of which, at least, she commanded “should be brought her in writing”—I still think there is a way in which the masculine prerogative of the Leicester party is embedded within the surviving text: the saga of Gaudina and Contarenus again offers the opportunity to transform royal rejection into a badge of empowered alienation.[129]

As in many such entertainments, the host of this sequence is a denizen of the wild. The story is unfolded by the unfortunate Hemetes, a blind hermit who presides over an isolated bower “couered with greene Iuie, and seates made of earthe with sweete smelling hearbes” (2:374). Recalling Zabeta’s victims at Kenilworth, he is defined primarily as a casualty of erotic violence, the terms of which are twisted into the larger narrative.[130]

Once a strapping knight, Hemetes fell for a coy enchantress ("most deynty to be dealt with"); to rebuff his advances, she "putt on the shape of a Tigresse so terrible to behould" that he was convinced (prophetically) to "neuer more sett eyeon her" (2:377).[131] His vow became literalized, however, when he was "sodenly striken blynde" by Venus, as punishment for his rejection of love (2:378). (His sight, unsurprisingly, is eventually restored by Elizabeth's presence.) This hermit figure is a central framing device, which situates the narrative within the realm of wildness—and the symbolic freight of enforced hermitage will stand in sharp contrast to the position of self-imposed exile that the story's Leicester figure will eventually occupy.

In the pageant, Leicester ultimately seems to occupy the role of Contarenus, "a knight (of estate but meane but of value very great)," whose love for Princess Gaudina has been frustrated by her father (a "mighty duke" of Cambria), at whose behest he was magically exiled for a term of seven years (2:375, 374). In the first sequence of the pageant, Hemetes recounts how Gaudina, fleeing her father's court, is finally reunited with her champion; in her journey, she becomes the chaste companion of Loricus, another knight jilted in love, who serves as her protector until Contarenus's arrival.[132] In the second half of the entertainment, a playlet works to undo the forward progress of the first. In its action, "this haughty Duke" elects to "leaue his Princely states" in search of his daughter—and though not the most sympathetic figure, he now assumes the role of the questing knight, "whom fortune doth constraine, / with fruitlesse toyle to trauel stil in vaine" (2:414, 413, 414). A Queen of Faerie (before the figure was synonymous with Elizabeth) moderates their eventual encounter, in which the Duke begs her, on behalf of "countries good," to "neglect, / The Loue of him which led you so astray" (2:423); the Faerie Queen similarly urges Gaudina to suppress her love for the public good. Despite rigorous debate on the nature of civic duty, Gaudina will not budge: as a last resort, the Duke turns to Contarenus himself, "to see if his desire might be delaide" for the sake of the commonwealth (2:427).

It is thus by his own will that Contarenus, after hearing further deliberations, reluctantly forsakes his long-sought beloved, agreeing to "yeeld to Countries good / the thing which to possesse so neere he stood" (2:430). With good reason, this is often taken as the swan song to Leicester's kingly ambitions; Berry, for instance, argues that here the earl offers "explicit" acknowledgment that "his service could not be rewarded with marriage."[133] But the larger point, I think, is the extent to which the Leicester-figure assumes complete mastery over his beloved; it is Contarenus who takes possession of Gaudina, and it is Contarenus who agrees to dissolve their love—in an act, what's more, that only serves to glorify his civic virtue. If the Kenilworth entertainment is underwritten by a bond of interpretive insurance, in which rejection is anticipated and accounted for in advance, here there is hardly need for such safeguards: the Woodstock pageant dismisses Elizabeth before she has any chance to say otherwise.

Such a posture is reflected in Contarenus's refusal to be reintegrated into the newly harmonized Cambrian court. Though the Duke welcomes him home, and vows to reward him handsomely for his loyalty, Contarenus views his exile as final:

> My Lord, what you haue done, your state maintains,
> exiling me that did offend your eye,
> My life must be in course of restlesse paines,
> for her whom care of countrey doth denye.
> Good hap light on the land where I was borne,
> though I doe liue in wretched state forlorne. (2:430)

The extent of his sacrifice is magnified by this oppositional mode; by construing himself as a political martyr, Contarenus only serves to amplify his own stoic resolve. The knight leaves once again as a man apart, a hero cast out from his own brood, but one whose unimpeachable virtue is now free to serve a master who might better appreciate its value. Alienated from the courtly world, he is left to roam "where so aduentures hard shal carry"—that is, throughout the wilds and frontiers of unknown lands (2:434). What's more, Contarenus explicitly declares that this antisocial impulse will, in fact, ultimately forge new channels of affinity:

> And tel my Lady deere that I intend,
> henceforth to seeke if I may meet her friend,
> Loricus whom the Hermit did commend,
> Ile bid him thinke and hope one day to find
> Reward for that his faithful seruice long,
> til when we both may plaine of fortunes wrong. (2:434)

Like Leicester and Sidney, the disappointed knights Contarenus and Loricus are conjoined in a community of discontent.[134] Even in absence, the socio-spatial valence of this community is suggested by the de facto member Hemetes, the third such jilted knight: this is a collective of the wild, united by the mutual affective experience of frustration, and bonded by the mutual social experience of courtly alienation.

Perhaps, as is often suggested, the Woodstock pageant does entail Leicester's vow to renounce his erotic claim to Elizabeth, if he is only given leave to pursue his fortunes elsewhere—like in the Low Countries, backed by an army of her soldiers.[135] But even so, the affective essence here seems to be one of relative positionality, in which Leicester announces the productiveness of rejection, and his readiness to "retire and draw [him] selfe apart" (2:431). This force of will, and the streak of latent sadism that accompanies it, is finally etched in the princess herself, in a brand that marks her as forever his:

> Yet this I am assur'de her Princely heart,
> where she hath lou'd wil neuer quite forget,
> I know in her I shal haue stil apart,
> in honest sort I know she loues me yet. (2:434)

This is, I think, no small consolation—and it is one of immense empowerment for a frustrated and rejected subject. And, as Doran notes, it would have to do: "In November 1575 Elizabeth declined to accept the sovereignty of the Netherlands which had been offered to her by the States of the provinces, and over the next two years she consistently turned down their appeals for a military alliance."[136]

"If," begins the *Tale of Hemetes*, "you marke the woords with this present world, or were acquainted with the state of the deuises, you shoulde finde no lesse hidden then vttered, and no lesse vttered then shoulde deserue a double reading ouer" (2:374). Depending on who is doing the double reading, I suggest, the 1575 entertainments at Woodstock could simultaneously contain very different affective registers.

The Lady of May, 1578

I arrive finally at Philip Sidney's infamously obscure entry into the realm of literary politics: *The Lady of May*, performed at Leicester's newly purchased manor of Wanstead in mid-May 1578. The themes of opposition, virility, and audacity pervade Sidney's literary debut—a reflection of three further years of disappointment and frustration with Elizabeth and her policy. (To remind: it was only two months earlier that Elizabeth had suddenly abandoned her long-promised, long-delayed plans for direct intervention in the Low Countries, opting instead to fund the mercenary troops of Count Casimir.) There are exceptionally few things that can be settled in this odd little show—though Linda Shenk has recently offered the intriguing suggestion that it reflects the contemporary Anglo-Dutch relations discussed above—but I will here argue one main point: the affective stakes of *The Lady of May* have not yet been accounted for, because we have not yet understood the precise implications of Sidney's adversarial mode.[137]

The Lady of May begins with a spatial disruption, in which the boundaries of Wanstead's aristocratic frame are breached by a foreign presence. It was during a stroll through the manor's garden, just as Elizabeth "passed down into the grove," that

> there came suddenly among the train one apparelled like an honest man's wife of the country; where, crying out for justice, and desiring all the lords and gentlemen to speak a good word for her, she was brought to the presence of her Majesty.[138]

She falls in supplication, begging that the queen aid her in her plight. The point of contention, we've seen above, is her daughter's two very different suitors, "both loving her, both equally liked of her, both striving to deserve her" (21.19–20). But what might otherwise suggest a light interlude, we learn, has a more serious dimension:

> But now lastly (as this jealousy, forsooth, is a vile matter) each have brought their partakers with them, and are at this present, without your presence redress it, in some bloody controversy; my poor child is among them. (21.20–23)

The distraught mother points Elizabeth in the direction of the broil, praying that she might defuse the escalating tension and deliver her daughter to safety.

Though conflict is an integral part of Elizabethan pageantry, the combative elements often emerge (as we saw at Kenilworth and Woodstock) from a framework designed to contain, distance, or soften the violence—such as the overt presence of allegorical, fantastical, or historical content, or the ritualized ceremony of the tournament tradition more generally.[139] But the clash at Wanstead entails a very real breach of the social order, recalling not the mythical battles of the earlier pageants, but the "controuersie betwene . . . wilde men" that plagued administrators in Tudor Ireland.[140] Though these combatants, so apt to be allegorized and abstracted, are not realist in any modern sense, they are still of a different register than dragons, faeries, and enchantresses; as such, their conflict recalls the local feuds and personal conflicts that really did occupy the lords and justices of Elizabeth's realm, particularly in its frontiers. It is through this verisimilitude, ironically enough, that Sidney defuses much of the queen's symbolic majesty: even within the framework of monarchal deference, *The Lady of May* imagines (like the Sybil at Kenilworth) a space that is largely immune to the coercion of Elizabeth's social and symbolic authority, by creating a humble landscape that makes no attempt to soar to the aerial register of the (soon-to-be) Faerie Queen. To begin his pageant, Sidney announces Elizabeth's alienation from the playworld created in her honor, by staging a challenge to which she is (in his mind) fundamentally unsuited to respond: the symbolic body politic of Albion's warrior queen might be fit to parlay with Hercules and sylvan gods, but what could the body natural of the 44-year-old Elizabeth do to quell an outbreak of rustic gang warfare?

And the conflict is sudden: after the country lady departs, and before Elizabeth can proceed further, "there was heard in the woods a confused noise, and forthwith there came out six shepherds, with as many fosters, haling and pulling to whether side they should draw the Lady of May, who seemed inclined neither to the one nor other side" (22.15–18). (Also amidst the fray is the comic schoolmaster Rombus, an ancestor of Shakespeare's Holofernes, whose absurd commentary on the action is repaid in full with "many unlearned blows" [22.22].) The struggles are finally suspended at the sight of Elizabeth, and the young lady steps forward to unfold the opposition of Therion and Espilus. I now quote her appraisal in full:

> Espilus is the richer, but Therion the livelier. Therion doth me many pleasures, as stealing me venison out of these forests, and many other such like pretty and prettier service; but withal he grows to such rages, that sometimes he strikes me, sometimes he rails at me. This shepherd, Espilus, of a mild disposition, as his fortune hath not to do me great service, so hath he never done me any wrong; but feeding his sheep, sitting under some sweet bush, sometimes, they say, he records my name in doleful verses. (25.2–10)

Her dilemma, as posed to the queen, is "whether the many deserts and many faults of Therion, or the very small deserts and no faults of Espilus be to be preferred" (25.11–13).

Before adjudicating, Elizabeth is presented with several rounds of argument (by both the litigants and their seconds) on "whether the estate of shepherds or foresters were the more worshipful" (26.24–25). Espilus stresses both the abundance and ease of the shepherd's life, marked as it is by the "pasture rich, the wool as soft as silk"; he begs the lady to "let not wild woods so great a treasure have" (26.9; 25.34). Therion, on the other hand, stresses the wild autonomy of a life unfettered by such objects:

> Two thousand deer in wildest woods I have,
> Them can I take, but you I cannot hold:
> He is not poor, who can his freedom save,
> Bound but to you, no wealth but you I would. (26.13–16)

After these opening statements, "the shepherds and foresters grew to a great contention whether of their fellows had sung better"; the shepherd Dorcas and the forester Rixus continue the verbal skirmish, debating the relative merits of their trade for a period much longer than the primary rivals (26.23–34). As they see it, the distinctions between both suitor and vocation point to a fundamental divide in matters of temperament: Rixus is appalled that any would "liken Espilus, a shepherd, to Therion, of the noble vocation of huntsmen," while Dorcas equally refuses to "liken Therion to my boy Espilus, since one is a thievish prowler, and the other is as quiet as a lamb that new came from sucking" (27.13–14, 18–20). But while Dorcas will further extol the easy life of the shepherd (whose contemplative eye is only "busied in considering the works of nature"), Rixus suggests that the virtues of pastoralism are *already* a natural component of the active life:

> I was saying the shepherd's life had some goodness in it, because it borrowed of the country quietness something like ours. But that is not all; for ours, besides that quiet part, doth both strengthen the body, and raise up the mind with this gallant sort of activity. (28.14; 29.14–17)

With this rhetorical maneuver, the debates are brought to a close, and Elizabeth is granted the floor.

With good reason, readers of the pageant have often puzzled over Sidney's sympathies in the conflict, and virtually every possible permutation has been proposed. Some have argued that Sidney had no horse in this forensic race; Catherine Bates, for example, suggests that "the two suitors are in essence exactly the same," and that the impossibility of choosing between them signifies the "ultimate arbitrariness" of Elizabeth's power.[141] Duncan-Jones, as we have seen, sees his allegiance as more pointed, claiming the pageant's design makes it "both apt and predicable that the Queen should choose Espilus, the inoffensive shepherd, rather than Therion, the active forester."[142] But Sidney is most often thought to side with the champion of the active life, an outlook that underwrites several of the most influential readings of the pageant: Stephen Orgel, for example, argues that the gruff Therion still displays a sensitivity to the "contemplative virtues," obviating his more limited rival, while Montrose similarly finds that "Sidney harmonizes action and contemplation in the forester's life," by moving "the audience from a situation of indecision between two antithetical extremes to a realignment that shows one term to incorporate, revise, and transcend the other."[143] With Therion thus associated with the interests of Sidney, Leicester, and the more actively inclined Protestant party, he becomes, in many such readings, an advocate for the author's position on any number of topical issues, such as intervention in the Netherlands, the royal favor owed to Leicester, or Sidney's desire to take a more rigorous role in English politics.

As should be quite clear, I too associate Sidney and Leicester with the virile, aggressive, and autonomous energy of the wild forester Therion, for the reasons that have been enumerated in this chapter. But the import of this association may have a different valence than has been usually understood, and it is one that is best exemplified by how Elizabeth elected to resolve the conflict. After the conclusion of the debate, the lady begs Elizabeth to make her selection, with a final proviso that "in judging me, you judge more than me in it" (30.12). The queen's decision, however, is recorded by Sidney in a maddeningly truncated response: "This being said, it pleased her Majesty to judge that Espilus did the better deserve her; but what words, what reasons she used for it, this paper, which carrieth so base names, is not worthy to contain" (30.13–15). This outcome, unsurprisingly, has elicited even more critical puzzlement: if Sidney built the superior case for Therion, what do we make of his defeat? Some, like Orgel, have viewed the outcome as a disastrous mistake—the queen, perhaps not paying full attention to the pageant's subtleties, simply assumed that "shepherds are the heroes of pastoral"—while others, like Montrose, suggest the queen's decision was purposeful and deliberate, entailing a "conscious and pointed rejection of Sidney's pastoral paradigm for the just and temperate relationship that should obtain between freeborn English gentlemen and their sovereign."[144]

But to return at last to Duncan-Jones's central question: is it reasonable to think that Sidney would have expected his virgin queen to sentence the May Lady to an outlaw life, made only worse by regular beatings? Probably not. Yet there can be no denying, as we have seen in this chapter, that Leicester and Sidney consciously and deliberately associated themselves with the forces of wildness in the pageantry they sponsored. As Edward Berry has persuasively argued, the May Day context suggests (or perhaps insists) that Therion is the pageant's folk champion: it is he, not the gentle shepherd, who must preside over the day's celebration of virility and misrule.[145] For the traditional May King is none other than Robin Hood: a man who, like Therion, famously boasts to "*lyve by our kynges dere*."[146] As de facto ruler of Wanstead's symbolic frame, this Robin is an apt guise for he who rules its literal one: Robin Dudley, Earl of Leicester. Leicester's association with the forester figure is made further explicit by the pageant's epilogue, in which Leicester ("Master Robert of Wanstead") is ironically imagined as a "huge *catholicam*," praying to the Virgin Elizabeth on a pair of "Papistian beads" (31.23–24, 28, 31). This bizarre moment, like so many others in the pageant, is difficult to assess. It is perhaps most commonly read (though I'm not sure rightly) as "Dudley's decisive abdication from the king-game"; it is also possible to assess the image wickedly, insofar as Leicester accepting Elizabeth's rejection humbly is about as likely as him turning to the pope. But one thing is clear: it quite explicitly transforms the defeated Leicester into a hermit-figure, the malcontent of the wild. [147] This precise image is deployed by Cooper, to culminate his ode on the forester's retirement:

> Now will I take to me my bedes
> for and my santes booke.
> And pray I wyll for them that may
> for I may nowght but loke.
> yet haue I bene a foster.[148]

Leicester is a disappointed hermit, and disappointed hermits are retired foresters.[149] Given the entire network of associations, it seems impossible not to read Therion as a proxy for Leicester.

We are left, then, with granting Duncan-Jones's premise, but radically inverting the conclusion we draw from it. Therion is an unlikely winner in this contest, but this does not, in turn, mean that he lacks the author's sympathies: rather, it reveals that Sidney was willing to cast his uncle in a losing role, and accordingly dictate the terms of the inevitable rejection. This would not, in fact, be unusual for Sidney: in both poetry and prose, Bates argues, "Sidney's numerous avatars" find themselves "put into positions in which they repeatedly fail . . . to hit, hunt, or shoot properly."[150] But failure can be co-opted. As in the other pageants, *The Lady of May* insistently asserts the benefits of the forester's life, which in its wildness valorizes notions of virility, aggression, self-sufficiency, and autonomy. In the foresters, Sidney presents an antisocial community of outlaw hunters, a site of fantasy identification that could not possibly be accommodated within the Elizabethan symbolic order. As such, the (anti)sociality of the "wild fool" inherently threatens the more pliant community of the "sheepish dolt"—a community which is, as Dorcas himself reveals, simply a reconfiguration of the conventional courtly world:

> How many courtiers, think you, I have heard under our field in bushes make their woeful complaints, some of the greatness of their mistress' estate, which dazzled their eyes and yet burned their hearts . . . making our vales witnesses of their doleful agonies! So that with long lost labour, finding their thoughts bare no other wool but despair, of young courtiers they grew old shepherds. (28.18–26)

Despite attempts to differentiate between the young courtier and the despairing shepherd, they are still creatures of the same order. By embracing this form of retirement, the ex-courtier remains bound, sheep-like, to the same symbolic system that he attempts to flee; pastoral retreat is rendered harmless, a benign form of opposition that is anticipated, accommodated, and underwritten by the larger terms of the bond of courtship. As Rixus rebuts, to become truly unfettered from the courtly world, one must go off the grid entirely, by embracing the virtue and freedom of the wild:

> O sweet contentation, to see the long life of the hurtless trees; to see how in straight growing up, though never so high, they hinder not their fellows; they only enviously trouble, which are crookedly bent. What life is to be compared to ours, where the very growing things are ensamples of goodness? We have no hopes, but we may quickly go about them, and going about them, we soon obtain them; not like those that, having long followed one (in truth) most excellent chase, do now at length perceive she could never be taken. (29.18–25)

For Sidney and his party, this is a site of affective redemption, home to an antisocial community that draws collective strength from its outcast status. The very identity of this subculture is premised on rejection, which is again reimagined as a badge of honor.

Derek Alwes, in his provocative reading, suggests that "failure was *inscribed*" in *The Lady of May*—and to a point, I agree, in the sense that Sidney could hardly expect Elizabeth to choose the suitor in which his own identity was invested.[151] Yet in the larger sense, I am arguing that it was even more impossible for Sidney to lose: by choosing Therion, Elizabeth publicly endorses Sidney, and co-signs his party's temperament, and by choosing Espilus (as she did), she ascribes to them an outsider status that they have already prepared to embrace, and which they have primed as a site of psychic and social empowerment. The oppositional dynamics of wildness, quite ironically, make *The Lady of May* a very accommodating play: a fact confirmed by its baffling conclusion, a song in which the winner Espilus (possibly in duet with Therion) tells "two short tales" in praise of the wild agenda.[152] They are both worth quoting in full:

> Silvanus long in love, and long in vain,
> At length obtained the point of his desire,
> When being asked, now that he did obtain
> His wished weal, what more he could require:
> "Nothing," said he "for most I joy in this,
> That goddess mine, my blessed being sees."
>
> When wanton Pan, deceived with lion's skin,
> Came to the bed, where wound for kiss he got,
> To woe and shame the wretch did enter in,
> Till this he took, for comfort of his lot:
> "Poor Pan," he said, "although thou beaten be,
> It is no shame, since Hercules was he."

Officially, Espilus's song is said to be "tending to the greatness of his own joy, and yet to the comfort of the other side," but this can hardly be taken at face value: the first ditty tells of the forest god's erotic triumph, and the second of the shepherd god being assaulted by the wild man's legendary form. Clearly the song is meant to champion the spirit of Therion, in a way too forceful to be conciliatory—but this does not necessarily mean, as is usually claimed, that Sidney expected his forester to be crowned victor. As we have seen, there is another way that Sidney might have controlled the fortunes of his litigants. This ode to wildness was likely sung, despite Therion's defeat: anticipated by the pageant's architect, Sylvanus and Hercules are finally vindicated, even in the face of public rejection.

In the *Arcadia,* it has long been argued, Sidney displays little overt sympathy to the "Cittezens of the woodes," that dangerous rabble of common folk who upend the social order with open rebellion.[153] But as a means of aristocratic identity management, I hope to have shown, the outlaw, outsider fantasy was nonetheless an invaluable affective resource for Leicester, Sidney, and their adherents—men ostensibly rejected by the queen's maddening refusal to place their will in front of her own.

In from the Wild

If *The Lady of May* provided an affective boost for the Leicester/Sidney party, it would have been a much-needed one: the early months of 1578 did not bode well for those of their persuasion, and things would continue to degrade as the year unfolded. Interventionist fantasies of military glory remained spoiled by Elizabeth's pledge to Casimir; to make matters worse, the queen had recently reopened marriage negotiations with Francis, Duke of Anjou and Alençon, brother to the French king—a suitor who provoked widespread disdain in both court and country, but perhaps most of all to men like Leicester and Sidney. The rejection I have discussed throughout this chapter—which, refined through a community of opposition, might be called upon as a source of political strength—was hardening into despair, and resistance to the queen's will seemed increasingly futile. It is perhaps unsurprising, then, that during the queen's summer progress in 1578, the pageantry she witnessed (with which Leicester seems to have had at least some connection), took on a rather different tone. In these performances, Queen Elizabeth is praised in strikingly new terms:

> Who euer found on Earth a constant friend,
> That may compare wyth this my Virgin Queene?
> Who euer found a body and a mynde
> So free from staine, so perfect to be seene,
> Oh Heauenly hewe, that aptest is to soile,
> And yet doste liue from blot of any foyle.[154]

Just a few years earlier the nymph Zabetha was indicted for this very disposition, and the queen herself was begged to counteract the ruin it had brought to Leicester's world. But here, in a stunning reversal, Elizabeth's state of unmatched matrimony is reimagined as a reflection of her unmatched virtue.

This shift in emphasis would have drastic implications for the future of Elizabethan representation: "The Norwich entertainments of August 1578," Susan Doran argues, "were the first recorded public occasion where the appearance of the cult of the Virgin Queen can be seen."[155] This cult, it seems, emerged from a desperate attempt to thwart the undesirable match with Alençon—an attempt that was ultimately vindicated, insofar as Elizabeth was forced to concede, in 1579, that the would-be nuptials evoked too much ill will to proceed. (Talks, however, would linger for years to come.) But before long, the image of Gloriana would be ruthlessly seized upon by Elizabeth herself—who, in an ironically familiar maneuver, refined this site of opposition into a reservoir of enormous power, from which she fueled the machines of orthodoxy that would dominate her reign's second half. This system of representation, Montrose observes, "may have had its origins in symbolic resistance to the royal will"—but in its "exorbitant final phase, this resonant nexus of images was instrumental to the interests of the monarch and her increasingly authoritarian and isolated regime."[156]

To be sure, this regime did not eradicate the discourse of wilderness from Elizabethan literature; indeed, George Peele's *Araygnment of Paris* (c. 1581; pub. 1584), the first major pastoral entertainment of the 1580s, stages the woodland gods Faunus, a "hunter [with] a faune," and Siluanus, a "woodman with an oken bowe laden with acornes."[157] But in terms of oppositional spirit, Peele's offering bears little resemblance to the pageants sponsored by Sidney and Leicester in the 1570s. In this performance, as Montrose describes, Elizabeth's mastery of the fictive scene is undisputed:

> Entertainments such as those sponsored by the Earl of Leicester at Kenilworth and Wanstead in the 1570's ostensibly offered a choice to the Queen but it was one in which the options were skewed against female independence or dominion. . . . *The Araygnement of Paris* is typical of royal entertainments in its hyperbolic treatment of the royal spectator and her fictional personae. But it differs from many of the entertainments of the previous two decades in that it fully acknowledges and celebrates the Queen's own choice, her complex transcendence of the simplistic oppositions contrived by her courtiers.[158]

In light of such thematic developments, Montrose is surely correct in suggesting that pastoralism settled into "an authorized mode of discontent" in the Elizabethan court, and thus not "a critique made in terms of a consciously articulated oppositional culture."[159] But the earlier discourse of wildness, I have suggested in this chapter, *did* enable such an oppositional (counter)culture, at a time when many Elizabethan courtiers were increasingly alienated by their queen's policy—and at a time, in the 1570s, when there was still a place for such pricklier disaffection.

In the early cantos of *The Faerie Queene*'s fourth book, a grand tournament is organized by the noble Satyrane—the half-satyr hero who tamed his innate savagery to join the fraternity of virtuous knights. Throughout the tourney, Satyrane fares exceptionally well, until the arrival of an unknown figure:

Till that there entred on the other side,
A straunger knight, from whence no man could reed,
In quyent disguise, full hard to be descride.
For all his armour was like saluage weed,
With woody mosse bedight, and all his steed
With oaken leaues attrapt, that seemed fit
For saluage wight, and thereto well agreed
His word, which on his ragged shield was writ,
Saluagesse sans finesse, shewing secret wit.[160]

This savage man unleashes a frenzied attack on the other competitors, single-handedly routing the field before the awed spectators. Satyrane, who had forsaken the woods for the civil world, is defeated by a foe whose engagement with the wild is absolute.

Who is this brutal knight, who dispatched his adversaries so completely? The narrator delivers us from uncertainty:

Much wondred all men, what, or whence he came,
That did amongst the troupes so tyrannize;
And each of other gan inquire his name.
But when they could not learne it by no wize,
Most answerable to his wyld disguize
It seemed, him to terme the saluage knight.
But certes his right name was otherwize,
Though knowne to few, that *Arthegall* he hight,
The doughtiest knight that liv'd that day, and most of might.[161]

Long before he was half-sad, the knight of justice understood the attraction of savagery. Like Leicester and Sidney, he was charged with protecting the realm of the Faerie Queene—and like Leicester and Sidney, he understood that sometimes it required stepping outside of it entirely.

CHAPTER 4

The Dreading, Dreadful Earl of Essex

"Love is a thing full of anxious fear."[1] So says Ovid's grief-struck Penelope, in a phrase often poached by Renaissance humanists, as she pleads for news of her husband's long wandering fleet.[2] In the middle of July 1597, the 63-year-old Queen Elizabeth I was similarly beset with anxious fear, and similarly watched the sea for sign of her beloved. Only days before, the most worthy men of her realm had set a triumphant course for Spain, intent on relieving the arch-tyrant Philip II of both his navy and his colonial plunder; the voyage was commanded by royal favorite Robert Devereux, Earl of Essex, the man who had assumed the place in Elizabeth's heart once held by his stepfather, the great Earl of Leicester.[3] But fate was cruel to the English fleet. Shortly after its departure, both land and sea had quaked with "an extreame storme which lasted afore and after six dayes": the "leke wether at this tyme of the yere," exclaimed Admiral Thomas Howard, vice-admiral of the enterprise, "was never cene by man."[4]

The queen's love for her peers (and the soldiers they commanded) was not conjugal, and her suffering paled beside Penelope's years of grief—but this mattered little at the time, as Elizabeth anxiously awaited word of the "storme beaten fleet."[5] When it finally came, the news was better than expected: though bruised and battered, and thwarted in their aims, her ships had reached safe harbor. The queen was especially relieved to learn of Essex, whose vessel had staggered to port "in great extremetye & imminent perrill of sinkinge in the sea"; upon hearing of his return, the earl was later told, "the wattr came plentyful out of her eyes."[6] For Essex, however, there was little time to celebrate. He still had a war to wage, and a fleet to reassemble:

> Since my last I am remoued from Fawmouth to Plimmauth, a most toylesumm iorney, butt such as I cold nott forbear, because I must seeke to gather my scattered flock. I haue found Sir Walter Rawleigh,

> Sir Francis Vere, Sir George Carew, Sir William Haruy, and Captain Throgmorton, with 4 of the queens greatt shippes heere.[7]

"I mett with Sir William Brooke and Sir Ferdinando Gorge," Essex continues, "in the Drednought," as plans were hatched to set sail again.

"The rise of English naval mastery," writes Geoffrey Parker, "may be said to have started with the launch of the *Dreadnought*, the first 'all big-gun battleship,' in 1573."[8] A vessel of very "neere twenty saile" and over thirty guns, the *Dreadnought* was among the first experimental designs of master shipwright Matthew Baker, the man whose technical genius would revolutionize the warships of the Elizabethan navy.[9] As "probably the most gifted English shipwright of his age," Baker initiated a paradigm shift in nautical design; in his hands, the discipline of shipmaking (revitalized by an innovative use of blueprints and formulaic procedures) became a field of enormous imaginative dexterity, freeing the architect from the laborious task of managing adjustments at the site of construction.[10] Under his direction, English warships were equipped with an extended gundeck and sleeker design (the "race-built" style), an optimization with results that seemed fantastical: Elizabeth's navy could now carry heavier, more devastating artillery, *and* do so with greater precision and finesse. The *Dreadnought*'s relative ordinance capacity was without equal, and before long new ships were commissioned and old ships were retrofitted according to her model. It was with this technical mastery, fifteen years later, that the English captains "completely thwarted Philip II's design to invade and conquer the realm, and drove the Armada into ignominious flight back to Spain."[11] It is with good reason, then, that Parker speaks of the rise of English naval supremacy as "the *Dreadnought* Revolution of Tudor England."

But in the bone-shaking storm of July 1597, the *Dreadnought* may have had some trouble living up to its name—at least, that is, if we are to go by the accounts of her unlucky sailors. Sir William Brooke, the *Dreadnought*'s commander in the action, sent rueful report of the "distres and harmes receaued by this late tempest"; "euery one," he admitted, "complain of to be in his ship."[12] Others in the fleet were more forthcoming about the dire experience of braving the storm. As Sir Walter Raleigh describes it, the conditions on his *Warspite* were dreadful indeed:

> In my shipp it hath shaken all her beams, knees & stanches well in a sunder, in so mich as on Saterday night last wee made accompt to have yeelded our seules vp to god, for wee had no way to worke

> ether by triinge, hollinge, or drivinge that promised better hope, our men beinge wasted with labor & watchynge & our shipp so open every wher, all her bulk head rent & her verye cookrome of brike shaken down in to powder.[13]

In one of his most powerful early poems, the young John Donne similarly recalls the horrific scene:

> Lightning was all our light, and it rain'd more
> Then if the Sunne had drunke the sea before;
> Some coffin'd in their cabbins lye, 'equally
> Griev'd that they are not dead, and yet must dye.
> And as sin-burd'ned soules from graves will creepe,
> At the last day, some forth their cabbins peepe.

"Compar'd to these stormes," Donne reveals, death seemed "but a qualme," and the desperate crew could not manage "to feare away feare" in the face of oblivion.[14]

But for a man like Essex, whose sense of self was built on fantasies of martial glory, it was not even this threat of destruction that summoned feelings of dread: on the contrary, it was the intolerable thought that he would be barred from fulfilling the promise of his generalship, and that King Philip would escape a crippling defeat. When the fate of Essex was still unknown, Raleigh worried that "ether my Lord Generall hymme sealf will wrestell with the seas to his perrill, or constrayned to cum bake, be fovnd vtterly hartbroken"—despite the fact that, as all would readily admit, "it be not in the powre of man to fight agaynst ellements."[15] The earl's return confirmed the latter suspicion, as Raleigh would shortly inform the council:

> Sir I beseich yow to worke from her Maiestye summe cumfort to my Lord generall, who I know is dismayd by thes mischaunces, even to death, although ther could not be more dvn by any man vppon the yearth, God havinge turned the heavens with that fury against vs, a matter beyovnd the power or valure or witt of man to resiste.[16]

Essex was devastated by the initial setback of his command. He would quickly rally, and put to sea again, but the expedition that unfolded proved even more disastrous. This campaign, usually known today as the "islands voyage," was the final major military action of Elizabeth's reign. Less than four years later, Essex would lose his head at the queen's command.

To conclude *Emotion in the Tudor Court*, I attempt to reconstruct the emotional characteristics of the late Elizabethan courtly sphere; my focus is the Earl of Essex and his followers, who in early 1601 took to the streets of London in an infamous armed uprising. What affective state, I ask, drove Essex and his men to such a desperate action, and how did it emerge from the increasingly ruthless courtly experience of the decade that preceded it? We have seen how, in the middle years of Elizabeth's reign, a series of shared political rejections led to the creation of certain emotional communities at court; in the 1590s, as Elizabeth's death loomed and England's future hung uncertainly, the value of such alliances would only intensify, transforming court into a factional battlefield. This deep uncertainty about the future set Elizabeth's courtiers against each other, in a struggle to assert their own will in the face of oblivion.

This cultural moment, I suggest in what follows, may be best understood through the affective category of *dread*: an emotional current central to the late Elizabethan court, and central to the late Elizabethan experience more generally. Emerging from the context of religious devotion, dread may be seen as a hierarchical affect, a terror or anxiety that acknowledges the other's mastery: dread is the fearful reverence that the creation owes its creator, or that the subject owes their sovereign, or that the sailor owes the tempest, precisely because of the categorical distinction between the two. *To dread* is to fear that which is earthshaking, that which is rupturing, that which is mind-bending; it is fear, no doubt, but it is a fear that acknowledges domination, or the potentiality of being dominated.

A series of dreadful conditions marked England in the 1590s, including the aging queen's unsettled succession, persistent threats of foreign invasion, and widespread social and cultural unrest. In the courtly sphere, this general affective atmosphere led to the intensification of rivalrous, violent conflicts; the factionalism that plagued the late Elizabethan court thus gave rise to a particular form of interpersonal dread, as men like Essex and his enemies each struggled to assert their own mastery and subjugate their opponents. With the court's social hierarchy in flux, the competition was particularly grinding: courtiers and their adversaries found themselves simultaneously feared *and* fearing, each trying to dominate the other and secure the favor of their queen. It is this affective contest that defined the courtly experience of the 1590s, and that ultimately drove the Earl of Essex to his ruin.

My treatment of dread in this chapter, and my understanding of its affective dynamics, is broadly inspired by the modern psychological concept of *terror management theory*—an approach, appropriately enough for a discussion of the Elizabethan court, that situates the emotion within the context of self-esteem, culture-building, and interpersonal conflict. Emerging from the work of the cultural anthropologist Ernest Becker, terror management theory (TMT) is how a trio of psychologists in the 1980s attempted to account for a pair of bedrock questions about human behavior: "Why are people so intensely concerned with their self-esteem?" and "Why do people cling so tenaciously to their own cultural beliefs and have such a difficult time coexisting with others different than themselves?"[17] The answer to both, they discovered, owes to an existential truth.

At the core of terror management theory is humanity's awareness of its own mortality—a condition that, by virtue of our "relative helplessness and vulnerability to ultimate annihilation," presents the species with the "constant danger of being incapacitated by overwhelming terror."[18] In response, the theory suggests, we have

> solved this existential quandary by developing cultural worldviews: humanly constructed beliefs about reality shared by individuals in a group that serves to reduce the potentially overwhelming terror resulting from the awareness of death. Culture reduces anxiety by providing its constituents with a sense that they are valuable members of a meaningful universe. Meaning is derived from cultural worldviews that offer an account of the origin of the universe, prescriptions of appropriate conduct, and guarantees of safety and security to those who adhere to such instructions—in this life and beyond, in the form of symbolic and/or literal immortality.

TMT thus maintains that anxiety-buffering is contingent upon both "faith in a particular cultural drama that portrays human life as meaningful, important, and enduring" and the "belief that one plays a significant part in that drama"—and that, by "meeting or exceeding individually internalized standards of value, norms, and social roles derived from the culture," people can accordingly "maintain psychological equanimity despite their knowledge of their own mortality."[19] At the level of personal psychology, such worldviews mitigate the terror of death "primarily through the cultural mechanism of self-esteem," the system through which individuals understand themselves as a "valuable contributor to a meaningful universe."[20] It is thus through cultural participation—such as the Elizabethan aristocrat's membership in the social organization of the court, or his or her membership in the broader community of Christian faith—that "people are able to construe the self as a valuable contributor to a meaningful existence," granting them a crucial identity beyond that of a "mere material animal fated only to obliteration upon death."[21]

Because of culture's guiding role in allaying such dread, the psychodynamics of terror management are socially embedded, insofar as "people's social relationships with others play an important role in maintaining a sense of existential security."[22] From its origins, TMT "has emphasized the importance of other people to validate the individual's worldview and self-worth," arguing that "the human needs for togetherness, intimacy, attachment, and affiliation are subordinate components of the fundamental need for self-preservation."[23] Accordingly, the theory has a particular interest in intergroup dynamics, as social conflict arises naturally when anxiety-buffering worldviews clash in opposition. Because "so many of the meaning- and value-conferring aspects of the worldview are ultimately fictional," encounters with "other people with different beliefs is fundamentally threatening"—and research has thus emphasized the "critical function of the ingroup for terror management," as social units participate in "worldview defense" to ward off the existential threats posed by rivals.[24] Indeed, empirical studies suggest that reminding individuals of death's inevitability "leads to harsh punishment of those who violate values of [their] worldview . . . and more positive reactions to others who uphold values of the worldview or otherwise help validate the worldview"; in laboratory settings, for example, mortality cues "lead to increased tolerance for racism" and "to aggression directed toward people who disparage one's worldview."[25] What's more, TMT has much to say about the charismatic leaders (like Essex) who lead these conflicting social groups: studies indicate that "affection for charismatic leadership increases when terror management needs are activated," and terror management processes are thought to engender "support for charismatic leaders who share one's cherished beliefs and aggression against those who hold rival beliefs."[26] In sum, TMT reveals how a fundamental human dread guides complex behavior in the social world, as clusters of like-minded actors struggle to assert their respective worldviews in the attempt to ward off oblivion.

These, the central tenets of terror management theory, are supported by ample empirical evidence: in the last three decades: "hundreds of published studies . . . have demonstrated that mortality salience leads people to favor and defend their cultural worldview and to demonstrate that they possess socially valued attributes and skills."[27] There is little doubt,

I think, that the Elizabethan courtier invested heavily in the defense of cultural worldviews and the demonstration of social dexterity—and TMT thus offers a valuable groundwork from which to build an affective understanding of court factionalism in the dreadful 1590s, a time when threats of existential annihilation (of the monarch, of the nation, of the cosmos) seized much of public discourse, and a time when social conflict dominated the courtly sphere. In this chapter, I don't apply the prescriptions of TMT strictly—but instead, to demonstrate another way of engaging a body of extra-literary work on emotion, I use its governing insights on social conflict and affective worldview-building to launch my own treatment of courtly interaction within the emotional framework of dread. Recently, scholars have taken some initial steps in exploring the affective dimension of the Essex saga; Will Tosh, for example, observes the "highly-personalised, emotionally heightened service practised by certain members of the Essex circle," while Alexandra Gajda notes the "strikingly emotive language" of Essex's patronage correspondence.[28] To help further reconstruct the affective experience that shaped both Essex's career and the final years of the Tudor dynasty, I conclude my study of emotion in the Tudor court by considering how dreadful a place it must have been.

The Last Favorite

The man who became Queen Elizabeth's final favorite was the eldest son of Walter Devereux, first Earl of Essex (1539–1576), a royal servant whose short life (as both private investor and government agent) was consumed with the task of colonizing the intractable Irish frontier.[29] At his father's death in 1576, the young Robert Devereux inherited his earldom at the age of ten; his mother Lettice secretly married the Earl of Leicester in 1578, and after several years of travel and study Essex joined his stepfather at court in 1585. Later that year Essex followed Leicester to the Low Countries, as part of the English military effort to support continental Protestantism. Essex was granted the prestigious command of the cavalry, and he saw action at both Doesburg and Zutphen; throughout the campaign, he displayed the rash courage that would become his martial trademark. (At Zutphen, Stow records, "the earle of Essex charged with his cornet . . . threw his launce in his rest, and overthrew the first man, and with his curtelax so behaued himselfe that it was wonder.")[30] He returned to England a rising star, backed by Leicester's unequaled influence; in 1587 he was granted his stepfather's former post as master of the horse, and in the following year entered the Order of the Garter.

In 1588 Leicester's unexpected death left a vacuum at court. Though Essex would eventually inherit his stepfather's role as chief favorite, his triumph at court was not immediate, and in the final years of the decade he jockeyed for position with men like Raleigh. Around 1590 Essex married Frances Walsingham, daughter of Secretary of State Francis Walsingham and widow of Sir Philip Sidney—but did so "without acquainting the Queen therewith, who was therefore offended at it."[31] The queen's anger was only temporary, however, and in 1591 Essex was granted formal command of his first military campaign, an expedition designed to aid the French king Henri IV against encroaching Catholic forces; the action was a failure, however, and the demoralized Essex returned to court in January 1592, determined to become more involved in directing matters of state. It was at this time that he began to assemble a formidable circle of secretaries and agents, the seeds of what would become the Essex faction. Essex focused on gathering intelligence and bolstering influence on the Continent, secure in his commitment to direct military engagement with Catholic Spain.

In 1596 Essex took co-command of the English assault on the Spanish port of Cadiz, the crowning achievement of his military career. After destroying the naval defenses, Essex led a land assault on the city; with his characteristic blend of rashness and bravery, he orchestrated the daring capture of Cadiz, and soon returned home to popular acclaim. Elizabeth, however, was far less pleased with the affair, and refused to press her military advantage. Furthermore, while Essex was at war, his enemy Robert Cecil had been appointed secretary of state, and the earl now saw his influence waning with the queen; Essex, it was said, suffered a "discontent hee could not conceale, being thereupon exceedinglie dejected in countenance and bitterly passionate in speech."[32] To make matters worse, his next military command (the "islands voyage," described earlier) was an unmitigated failure. When plans to assault the Spanish port of Ferrol were spoiled, Essex diverted the remaining fleet to the Azores, with the hope of intercepting a returning transport of Spanish treasure. This gamble failed by an agonizingly narrow margin, and Essex returned to England with little to show but a damaged reputation.

Though Essex still enjoyed both favor and influence with the queen, the failed excursion of 1597 marked a turning point in his career, which would steadily decline until its end. In late 1598 he received a final chance to achieve the military glory he had so long sought: he was named lord lieutenant of the English expedition to Ireland, an army charged with suppressing the rebel chieftain Hugh O'Neill, Earl of Tyrone. In the spring of the following year, he landed in Dublin, prepared to settle matters with a quick, decisive victory—but the grim Irish terrain made a direct assault impossible, and he spent the next several months meandering through Ireland in a series of costly, minor excursions. Distanced from court, Essex became increasingly concerned about the situation at home, convinced that Cecil and his allies were actively working against his interests. In August 1599 he was tempted to lead his army back into England to confront his enemies directly, an act of treason that was prevented by his advisors. The desperate Essex met privately with Tyrone in September, where he engineered a makeshift, temporary truce with the rebel. Dismissing explicit orders to the contrary, he soon left for London, where he infamously "staied not till he came to the Queens Bed Chamber, where he found the Queen newly up, the Hare about her Face."[33]

In light of his erratic behavior and unauthorized return, Essex was soon taken into custody; for the next several months, he was confined to York House as the Privy Council debated his conduct in Ireland. His political enemies, such as Cecil, Raleigh, and Attorney General Edward Coke, worked tirelessly to prepare a case against him, which would eventually come to allege that Essex was secretly in league with Tyrone and had long desired to usurp the throne. The earl, however, maintained his popularity, and retained no small hold over Elizabeth; the queen eventually loosened the terms of his imprisonment, and spared him the ignominy of a public trial. On June 5, 1600, a special inquiry was empaneled at York House, where his performance in Ireland was denounced. Though he defended himself admirably, Essex was nonetheless stripped of all royal appointments and remained a prisoner of the queen.

Though eventually released from custody, Essex was forever banished from court, with little to show for his years of service but a mound of debt. (For their part, his enemies would continue to amass evidence in the hope of future prosecution.) In October Elizabeth revoked the earl's customary lease on sweetwine, the foundation of his income, finally dashing any hopes for recovery. As we will see, Essex and his followers grew ever more disaffected; the earl was desperate to secure both himself and his country from the enemies who, he was certain, were pushing Elizabeth and her succession closer to Spain. With the new year, Essex and his advisors fell to increasingly drastic measures: only direct action, they concluded, could free Elizabeth from the likes of Cecil and Raleigh. In the coming weeks, a plan evolved: Essex and a group of sympathetic nobles would make their way into the queen's presence, where they would (with appropriate reverence) expose her ministers for their corruption.

On Sunday, February 8, 1601, Essex and his followers were finally pushed to action, when there arrived at Essex House a delegation of councilors with a "message from her Maiestie that Robert Earle of Essex should speedily dissolue his company, and he himselfe should presently Come to the Cort, with promise that his greefs should gratiously be hard."[34] (Essex had been called to appear before the council the night before, inciting panic in his followers.) Still fearing a trap, and heeding rumors that Raleigh and Lord Cobham sought his life, Essex refused the order, as he and his confidants scrambled to put their premature plans into action; the messengers were imprisoned in Essex House, and the earl and his roughly 300 followers set off, armed but not armored. Banking on his popularity, Essex decided first to appeal to London before engaging the queen herself: his men marched through the streets, proclaiming that they came only in self-defense, intending to forestall a plot against the earl. The action, however, was a disaster. The townspeople didn't rise to his aid, and the Privy Council had preempted the mob's arrival, alerting several of London's key officials. The city gates were shut, streets were blocked, and a counterforce was deployed; Essex and his ever-shrinking company narrowly escaped by boat to Essex House, where they would surrender after a brief siege.

The fallout of the uprising was immediate. In the Star Chamber, Essex and his followers were denounced by members of the Privy Council; in London they were (by official instruction) denounced from the pulpit. On February 19 Essex and his coconspirator Henry Wriothesley, Earl of Southampton, were found guilty of treason, for open rebellion and seeking the lives of the council members. Though Southampton was spared, Essex was executed at the Tower six days later.

The Nasty Nineties

The spectacular fall of the Earl of Essex, a self-destruction underwritten by the combined operation of fear and desperation, is something of an index to the social and political atmosphere that settled over England in the final years of Elizabeth's reign. Quite apart from the courtly intrigue at the center of power, it was a precarious time for England more generally: as all Elizabethans were aware, the queen was creeping towards the grave, the realm lacked an heir, and unrest at both home and abroad threatened the very existence of their nation. In both court and country, dread was perhaps the defining affective mode of the 1590s—an era Patrick Collinson famously dubbed the "nasty nineties"—and it was in these dreadful times that Essex emerged as England's most formidable courtier.[35]

The affective significance of dread begins with the word itself. Despite today's more casual usage, "dread" in the early modern period was not simply a synonym of "fear," a fact indicated by the theological context from which it emerged.[36] The notion seems to have first appeared in the twelfth century, here (in the *Oxford English Dictionary*'s oldest recorded example) in the verbal form:

> Þe eorðliche lauerd ne mei don na mare bote pinen Þe wrecche licome to deaðe. Ah godalmihitn Þe mei fordon eiðer ȝe Þine wrecche licome and Þine saule. Swilcne lauerd we aȝen to dreden. Þ*et* is godalmihtin.
>
> [The earthly lord may do no more than put the wretched body to death, but God Almighty may destroy both thy wretched body and thy soul. Such a lord we ought to dread, that is God Almighty.][37]

The thematic terms of this construction carry wholesale into early modern usage, as when the "troubled soule" of a late Elizabethan pamphlet describes "dreading [God's] displeasure, whose wrath maketh the deuells to quake."[38] Though occasioned by a fantasy of divine annihilation, the sentiments here are equally predicated on the magnificent power which makes that wrath possible: hence the *Oxford English Dictionary*'s primary definition "to fear greatly, be in mortal fear of; to regard with awe or reverence, venerate."[39] The affective connection between fear and veneration suggests the multiple, and sometimes conflicting, connotations that "dread" variants would begin to accrue in the intervening centuries. In the secular correlate, this basic polarity appears in perhaps the term's most familiar early modern usage: the title of "dread sovereign." The idea of dread was thus multivalenced, a union of anxiety and awe that became implicated in some of the era's primary cultural struggles.

And, as has been well-documented, in the 1590s England's cosmic and social order was dreadfully threatened. Facing an unsettled succession and a moribund queen—and keenly aware of the civil wars that had long ravaged France—Elizabethans were gripped by fear of their immediate political future; "seeing God hath ordayned you our nursing mother," cried one pamphleteer to his sovereign, "wee your children cry vpon you, & most earnestlie beseech you, that by neglecting this motion, you vnnaturallie leaue vs not vnto the evident spoile of the mercilesse bloodie sword."[40] Indeed, that sword continued to threaten: while England was miraculously delivered from the would-be Spanish invaders of 1588, King Philip reassmbled his fleets in the subsequent years, and throughout the 1590s English anxieties were persistently spurred by rumors of a new Spanish assault.[41] Though Philip's naval attempts of 1596 and 1597 came to naught, those on England's coast could again do little but "wayte the cominge of the kinges armada."[42] The natural order proved equally inhospitable: from 1593 to 1597 an "unprecedented series of harvest failures" led to the nation's most devastating famine of the sixteenth century.[43] Missives from the period heartbreakingly chronicle this "harde time of dearth," which led some to speculate that "the course of nature is very much inuerted; our yeares are turned vp-side downe; our sommers are no sommers, our haruests are no haruests; our seed-times are no seed-times."[44] And famine wasn't the only such natural upheaval: English subjects had to contend, in the early years of the decade, with the fact that their nation was "most greviously afflicted with the Pestilence."[45] Frantic letters of the period warned that "the plage is of late in london greatly increased," while the queen released a series of proclamations "for the preseruation of her good Subiectes from the plague."[46] Collectively, these dreadful events of the 1590s were thought by many to foretell the pending annihilation of the world: a collection of texts from the period reflects the growing conviction that "the afflictions and miseries of the world by earthquakes, warres, pestilence, famine and such like" were an index of Christ's imminent arrival.[47]

For such Elizabethans, "our Sauiours coming" promised a glorious resolution to the worldly suffering of the 1590s—and indeed, as we shall see, in the final phase of his life the ruined Essex came to understand deeply that a reverent dread of his creator offered ultimate solace from the whips and scorns of a career at court.[48] But though they were understood as finite, such dreadful times still had to be endured, and the stakes were amplified for those, like Essex, who played an immediate role in directing England's political, social, and religious future. And in the courtly sphere, the era's cosmic and cultural turmoil found a ready correlate: the rampant factionalism that came to plague politics in the declining years of Elizabeth's life. For those in the trenches, the late Elizabethan court indeed seemed a war zone of social violence, and commentators routinely reveal how the envy, emulation, and backbiting that undid Artegall would often emerge along party lines. Sir Francis Bacon, nothing if not a veteran of these wars, observed how common it was to think that "the Principall Part of Policy" is "for a Great Person to governe his Proceedings, according to the Respect of *Factions*"—but when "*Factions* are carried too high, and too violently," he warns, it is a "Signe of Weaknesse in Princes; And much to the Preiudice, both of their Authoritie and Businesse."[49] In the essay "Of Friendship and Factions," the literary polymath (and

Essex associate) Sir William Cornwallis reminds the would-be courtier that "loue wil not, or cannot be vniversall," and that the wise man "must not entertaine the humor of neutrallitie" in the conflicts of high politics.[50] And Sir Robert Naunton, reflecting upon the career of Queen Elizabeth not long after her death, famously declared that "the principall note of her raign, will be, that she ruled much by faction and parties, which herself, both made, upheld, and weakened, as her own great judgement advised."[51] Though the last three decades have seen fierce debate about the nature of factions in Renaissance England—and though Janet Dickinson has importantly challenged overly simplistic views of late Elizabethan factionalism—most historians of the period echo the assessment of Simon Adams: in the 1590s "the Court was nearly torn apart by a factional struggle of major proportions." [52]

In this struggle, the Essex circle was a quintessential faction, and its affective experience in the late Elizabethan courtly sphere was largely occupied with both suffering and inflicting dread. Despite Essex's de facto status as primary favorite, he enjoyed little true dominance over the social domain, and in the 1590s he and his allies found themselves dodging as many attacks as they themselves administered. As such, the struggle for the late Elizabethan court was implicitly an affective struggle over the terms of dread: who is the object of terror, and who is the terrified object? Who demands social reverence, and who inspires social fear? Which party can master the emotional experience of the other?

The ambiguity of this social dread finds an analogy in the term itself: with a single word encompassing verbal, adjectival, and substantive forms (itself a relative anomaly in the English affective lexicon), "dread" also displays, in early modern usage, a notable ability to convey both subjective and objective meaning. That is to say, in each grammatical category, "dread" can equally attach to both the *fearful subject* and the *feared object* that evokes it. Though obscured in conventional phrases like "Dread God" or "Dread Sovereign," there is nonetheless a latent way that dread can announce its capacity to be undone, by entailing its own opposition: in early modern usage, "dread" (like the verbs "let" or "seed") has the capacity to evoke its own antonym, making it what is sometimes called an "autantonym" or "Janus word."[53] Encompassing its own binary, "dread" might lock both subject and object in a zero-sum game of affective negotiation, in which each term, equally *dreadful*, struggles to tip the scales from subjugation to mastery.

Before God and queen, such linguistic games were hardly helpful—but in a different context, one of lateral social contestation, the reciprocity of fear was an important affective circuit. In the 1590s, both the Essex circle and its courtly enemies were infused with dread, though what that statement meant at any particular time is exceedingly difficult to sort out.[54] In this social arena, factional politics ensured that oppositional parties found themselves both inspiring and succumbing to anxiety and terror. This affective warfare, waged under the dreadful skies of the 1590s more generally, ensured that the collective atmosphere of suspicion and treachery was mutually reinforcing, as combatants were locked in a persistent struggle to control the terms of who was dreading, and who was being dreaded. The Janus-faced linguistic potential of "dread," I suggest, is analogous to the Janus-faced affective negotiations that were being contested in the social arena. I turn now to the specific courtly milieu in which dread reigned, by considering both what the Earl of Essex and his men dreaded, and what dread they inspired in their political adversaries.

To begin, then: why did Essex dread his enemies?

The Earl of Essex: Dreadful Subject

In 1593 the Essex partisan Anthony Standen, writing to Anthony Bacon, thought debilitating illness a worthy trade-off from life at court:

> I do begin truly to bless and commend your infirmity, which if you might receive without pain or torment, I would think you in the superlative degree beholding to it, as a cause to retain you from a place, from whence all charity is exiled, and all envy and treachery doth prevail, and where a prince of the most rare virtues and divine parts is assieged with persons so infected with malice.[55]

Court could be a miserable, corrupting, soul-sucking place, and it was especially so in the 1590s. But it was also a critical home for Essex, even though it would ultimately destroy him.

As factionalism soaked into the bedrock of the Elizabethan political scene, and relationships were polarized accordingly, the court became an increasingly oppositional, increasingly dangerous place for men like Essex, who found themselves ever more alienated from their enemies and enmeshed with their friends. It is no wonder, then, that in late 1597 a concerned partisan warned Essex of the forces working against him:

> Pardon mee, that am and euer will be redie prest in all offices to thy seruice, thow art full of wisdom, bountie, and valor, and dost performe all thinges with much honor, and yet mee thinks thow art

> least perfect in securely woorkinge thy owne good, which in this age, and tyme of vncertentie, is most needfull to bee cared for, but by the way let mee tell thee, thy owne patience, I say thy patience hath continually from the beeginninge giuen way to thy crosses, practised by a dubble faction verie stronge against thee.[56]

We have seen in the previous chapter how shared feelings of persecution and alienation generate courtly solidarity, but the advent of factionalism altered this dynamic greatly. Sidney and Leicester faced a noncompliant monarch, and accordingly manifested a symbolic opposition to manage and reclaim feelings of frustration and impotence. But what was largely a symbolic conflict for the previous generation became unsettlingly real for Essex, who, in the final phase of his life, really did face a group of adversaries actively working to undo him.

Indeed, there was a steady stream of rumor and intelligence that enemies had "layd secret plotts, and damnable deuices" to ruin Essex and his allies.[57] Some were probably true, some embellished, and some invented, but each contributed to the collective mood of suspicion, grievance, and moral righteousness that would increasingly settle over Essex House. In 1598, for example, Essex was informed that a network of Jesuit agents was secretly suggesting that "it were a verie merritorious acte to Stabb or kill the Earle of Essex if you can come att him"; a year later, he was told that his enemies plotted "to work some treson . . . agans your person," and was warned to be vigilant against "any suche assasanes."[58] In the final months before the rising, Essex desperately reached out to James VI in Scotland in a last-ditch effort to secure support; enemies at court, Essex bewailed, orchestrated the "corrupting of my servants, stealing of my papers, suborning of false witnesses, procuring of many forged letters in my name, and other such like practises against me."[59] When Essex and his men finally took to the streets in 1601, they did so announcing that the "Earle of Essex should haue beene murdered the night before in his owne house by Sir Walter Rawleigh, the Lord Cobham, and others."[60]

What's more, the fear and suspicion of external adversaries also worked to undo the faction from within, via the possibility that a Judas or Sinon might be lurking in its ranks. We get something of this in an exchange between Gilly Merrick and Henry Cuffe, two of the earl's prominent associates:

> Then soe I here some of our owne famely are very malitious againste vs both, butt esspetaly againste me. The coursses practysed are soe bayse thatt I would hatt my self yf ytt were true, butt I shale better

> satisfie ytt whene I come then to trobele you with a tedyus letter. I am very sorry thatt some of them proffessinge Relygion can be soe malitious. Wee haue envy and malyce inoughe, besydes to haue ytt plottyde and practysed by thos thatt my lord vseth soe nere him.[61]

Consistent with the general atmosphere of paranoia in which he was engulfed, Essex was aware that ostensible supporters might have an ulterior motive. "I haue bene many tymes and deeply wounded by practising libellers," he complained during the time of his disgrace in 1600, "who since my committment have shadowed ther intended mischeefe to me under pretended greefe or passion for me"; in such an environment, the earl had to fear "the corrupcyon of some of hys servantes that had accesse to hys chamber, who myght take & wrytt owt hys loose papers."[62] Even close friends, Essex was warned, needed to be watched carefully: "take heede, and remember, that christ had but twelfe, and on proued a diuell."[63]

In the 1590s, then, life at court entailed very little security: enemies abounded, and even friends could not be trusted. But attendance on the queen was a necessary evil, and because of the importance of this physical presence, the correspondence of the period bubbles with distant courtiers anxiously trying to keep up on the happenings at the power-center. For those unlucky enough to get them, lengthy assignments on the political periphery were often attributed (though not always rightly) to either royal displeasure or the malice of some other courtly notable. But a military man like Essex found himself in a particular bind: he constantly agitated for a foreign deployment that would remove him from the very site of political power. When at sea or in the field, he was not at court, and could not control the machinations of his enemies. Even in his earliest years, Essex was aware that the management of such absence was a primary courtly strategy. In 1587, when Leicester's conduct in the Netherlands was under suspicion, Essex sent word to the Continent that he would guard his stepfather's interests:

> [Queen Elizabeth] hath bene since longe with her counsaile, what is agreed on I know not, [but] I desired her, she wold know yowr enemies and not belieue any thinge they shuld say, yf they layd any matter to yowr chardge, that she wold suspend her iudgemant till she did heare yourself speake. I will watch with the best diligence I can that yowr enemies may not take advauntage of yowr absence.[64]

Only a few years later, when Essex himself had aims on Continental exploits, it was noted that "his frendes here hathe advised him to the contrary, wishing him rather to seke a domesticall greatnesse."[65] In retrospect, Essex apparently found this advice to be spot on, at least according to an account sent to Robert Cecil: upon his disappointing return from France in 1591, the earl was said to be "infinitly discontented," because "he suspecteth my Lord your father [Lord Treasurer Burghley] hath not so much favored him in his absence as he expected."[66]

Throughout his political career, Essex's enemies would regularly capitalize on these periodic absences, and thus the thrill of martial deployment could not be detached from the anxiety that accompanied foreign action. Most notably, Essex was fighting at Cadiz when his primary rival Cecil was promoted to secretary of state, despite the fact that the "queene had given him a faithfull promise not to doe it, and had confirmed her promise by her letter sent to him to Plymmouth before his setting saile."[67] In fact, Essex was advised to be wary of "plausible offers, which may be made unto you to prolong your absence," and was warned of a "plot laid to recoil his lordship, and to keep him aloof by some new employment, which it was presumed would be pleasing to him."[68] Though the earl enjoyed both general popularity and the queen's favor, this alone was not enough to ensure political safety; as Hammer explains, Essex (unlike Leicester) lacked allies "in key posts who could support his initiatives or defend his interests in his absence."[69] But when the tables were turned, Essex found himself paralyzed by his sense of honor: after Robert Cecil left on a special diplomatic envoy in early 1598, the earl refused to take advantage of his rival's departure, despite Francis Bacon's suggestion that "Mr. Secretary's absence" was a fine time to strike.[70] It was thus a dreadful game that a military man like Essex had to play: were the potential rewards of martial glory worth the risk of leaving court?

In the daily struggles of the late Elizabethan courtier, there was much to be anxious about. As Essex was well aware (and was endlessly told), his enemies strove to usurp his social power, and some even strove to take his life; he burned with the desire to engage the enemies of England and the enemies of Christendom, but was plagued with worry about how he would be undone in absence. But dread was not only an affective state that characterized social interaction in this manner: importantly for literary studies, the anxiety and suspicion that marked the Essex circle's experience in the courtly sphere also manifests in the texts that Essex and his allies produced and circulated in its name.

As Hammer has elucidated, Essex's popular reputation as a dashing soldier-playboy obscures the depth of his intellectual curiosity, a dispositional feature that was further cultivated as a matter of prudent policy.[71]

Like that of Sidney, Essex's approach to politics was thus integrated into a larger philosophical and intellectual outlook, which itself helped contribute to the affective mode of his circle.[72] For Essex and his followers, this outlook was famously shaped by the sixteenth century's emerging fondness for Tacitus, the Roman historian with a particular knack for treating political corruption and treachery—and for revealing how virtuous men might resist them.[73] Initially explored on the Continent by thinkers like Machiavelli and Jean Bodin, and cultivated at Cambridge (where Essex and many members of his circle studied), the methods of Tacitus provided a novel way of viewing history for a group of men increasingly interested in mastering the brutal skills required for life at court.[74] This "politic" history, inspired by Tacitus, looked to the past for practical wisdom on the arts of statesmanship, which might be put to mercenary use.[75] In an attempt to examine the often inscrutable phenomena of contemporary politics, a new breed of historical thinkers "concentrated on political causation, searching into the psychology of ruler and ruled; and they analyzed the role of fortune in history, and the extent to which men could plan for the unpredictable."[76] As such, they increasingly tended to the "secondary causes" of history: those historical actors, like Essex, who shaped the world through the force of individual will, and from whose example political wisdom could be extracted.

Though this development, it now seems, was not quite the sharp transition in humanist sensibility described by a previous generation of scholars, there is little doubt that the increasing interest in Tacitus had important implications for early modern thinkers.[77] With this Tacitean approach to history, the Essex circle would eventually find a political playbook well suited to their evolving temperament: as a historian of the tyrant, Tacitus provided ample ammunition for a vigorous critique of courtly corruption. In his 1601 essay "Of Histories," Robert Johnson offers a penetrating description of the Tacitean historical subject:

> Another kind [of history] there is like labyrinths, relating cunning and deceitfull friendshippes, how rage is suppressed with silence, treason disguised in innocence, how the wealthy haue beene proscribed for their riches, and the worthy vndermined for their vertue. These prouoke vs to eschew their viletie and lacke of vertue, and to be rather viceles then greatly vertuous: and although they bee distasted by those who measure Historie by delight, yet they are of most vse in instructing the minde to the like accidents.[78]

"In this ranke," Johnson continues,

> I preferre *Tacitus* as the best that any man can dwel vpon: Hee sheweth the miseries of a torne and declining state, where it was a capitall crime to bee vertuous, and nothing so vnsafe as to be securely innocent, where great mens gestures were particularly interpreted, their actions aggrauated, and construed to proceed from an aspiring intent: and the prince too suspitiously iealous touching points of concurrancie, suppressed men of great deserte, as competitors with them in that chiefest grounde, the loue of the people.

A historian so sensitive to issues of aspiration, jealousy, and popularity proved notable in a social landscape increasingly torn by factionalism. But in addition to its ideological implications, there is another way that the turn to Tacitus appealed to the cutting-edge thinkers of the 1590s: Tacitus's famed style of tough, restrained, and sententious prose was adopted by the politic historians in conscious opposition to the Ciceronian excesses of contemporary academic discourse, echoing Montaigne's call to "fortifie and harden our hearing, against the tendernesse of the cerimonious sound of wordes."[79] By replicating Tacitus's stylistic virility, the scholars of the Essex circle asserted a localized, intellectual identity that mirrored the larger strategies by which Essex announced himself as England's foremost martial presence. Not surprisingly, such verbal considerations fold back into larger issues of historiography: Tacitus offered the politic historians "a style admirably suited to men who aimed at psychological realism and the 'poyse' of political experience in their own work and who admired strong and self-reliant heroes like William I, and Henry IV, and Henry VII."[80]

This linkage between style and ideology would become valuable cover to an intellectual coterie increasingly interested in subversive political philosophy, and increasingly suspicious of prying eyes. For though the Tacitean aphorism lent itself to easy memorization, Tacitus also veiled his insights in famously difficult Latin. Such murkiness was co-opted as a political asset: with it, the politic historians could "conceal their true thoughts in riddling and ambiguous words, both to preserve themselves from immediate persecution and to enable them to await an outcome before committing themselves to a course of action."[81] In his comments on Tacitean style, Johnson underscores this captivating union of masculine bluntness and crafted obliqueness: Tacitus constructs his history, he observes, "with such an art, hiding art, as if hee were *aliud agens*, by enterlacing the *serios* of the tale, with some iudiciall, but strangelie briefe sentences."[82]

The Essex circle's fondness for Tacitus and Tacitean historiography seems to have contributed to an intellectual, political, and stylistic ethos for those in the know—and it was one underwritten by the affective mood of the 1590s. As such, Tacitus was a powerful courtly symbol, insofar as devotion to his works indicated a series of intellectual assumptions about the value of history, a series of political assumptions about the correspondence between imperial Rome and England's own cankered age, and a series of stylistic assumptions about the formal strategies best suited for exploring such matters. In a letter of advice to Fulke Greville from the mid-1590s, Essex himself proclaimed "Tacitus simply the best" of all historians, and this attitude seems to have informed much of the earl's outlook.[83]

We know that Essex read Tacitus actively; less than a year after the earl's death, a letter makes reference to a "paper boke of my lord of Essex notations of Cornelius Tacitus."[84] But it seems that his engagement with the Roman historian was more elaborate still: according to Ben Jonson, in 1591 Essex penned the elaborate, anonymous preface to Sir Henry Savile's partial translation of Tacitus's *Historiae*.[85] In this "seminal document of the Tacitean revival in England," Essex offers lavish praise of the historian who "hath written the most matter with best conceyt in fewest wordes of anie Historiographer ancient or moderne;" Tacitus, he argues, veils his meaning in such obscurity that "the second reading ouer will please thee more than the first, and the third then the second."[86] The preface is capped with a transhistorical conclusion, in which Essex, perhaps slyly, contrasts "our owne happie gouernement" of Elizabeth with the Rome that "did suffer miseries vnder the greatest Tyrant."[87]

Essex's remarks introduce the first extended translation of Tacitus to be published in England, Savile's *The Ende of Nero and Beginning of Galba, Fower Bookes of the Histories of Cornelius Tacitus*. This edition sparked English interest in both Tacitus and the methods of politic history; in addition to its partial translation of the *Historiae*, the volume contained Savile's original essay *The Ende of Nero and Beginning of Galba*, a piece of new-style history designed to bridge the temporal gulf between Tacitus's *Annales* and *Historiae*. Jonson deemed this act of intellectual ventriloquism the edition's greatest virtue:

> But when I read that speciall piece, restor'd
> Where NERO falls, and GALBA is ador'd,
> To thine owne proper I ascribe then more;
> And gratulate the breach, I grieu'd before:
> Which Fate (it seemes) caus'd in the historie,
> Onely to boast thy merit in supply.[88]

By borrowing the robes of Tacitus, Savile acquires license to craft a piece of history in the new politic style: in Savile's creation, for example, the rebel leader Julius Vindex is praised for his attempts "to redeeme his cuntrey from tyranny and bondage" by taking arms against the emperor Nero.[89] As David Womersley argues, the novelty of this reconstruction enables Savile and his readers to explore heterodox categories of political thought, such as the appropriate grounds for tyrannicide and the necessity of military heroes (not unlike Essex) "making successful, principled interventions in the political life of a nation which, in at least some educated and contemporary minds, shared the same underlying form of absolute monarchy as Elizabethan England."[90] To be sure, in a recent article Paulina Kewes has importantly reminded us that the concerns of 1591 were not the concerns of 1601, and that scholars must guard against reading Savile's edition anachronistically: at the moment of publication, she argues, "Savile's volume was neither a jaundiced anatomy of royal envy and courtly corruption nor an antimonarchical manifesto," and thus we should not see it as reflecting viewpoints that Essex and his circle would not come to adopt for several years.[91] But the larger point is that the inherent content of Tacitean history offered fertile soil for the increasingly discontented Essex circle to eventually till—and indeed, as Kewes notes, even in 1591 "Savile was keen to warn his patron Essex about the pitfalls of court intrigue and royal jealousy."[92] In his anonymous preface, Essex himself describes the Tacitean subject as "the miseries of a torne and declining state: The Empire vsurped; the Prince murthered; the people wavering; the souldiers tumultuous; nothing vnlawfull to him that hath power, and nothing so vnsafe as to bee securely innocent"—a catalog of horror that cannot help but inflect Savile's prayer, on the facing page, that Elizabeth find "a Tacitus to describe your most glorious raigne."[93] As the decade continued, and as factionalism ravaged the court, this connection would be ever more appealing for Essex and his ilk, who found themselves ruminating upon one Tacitean lesson in particular: "that a good Prince gouerned by euill ministers is as dangerous as if hee were euill himselfe."[94]

To varying degrees, Tacitus featured in the political thought of numerous men associated with Essex, including (besides Savile) Henry Cuffe, Henry Wotton, Francis and Anthony Bacon, and Antonio Perez. A variety of texts indebted to Tacitus emerged from their collective pen. Of particular note is *The State of Christendom, or, A Most Exact and Curious Discovery of Many Secret Passages, and Hidden Mysteries of the Times*, a political tract first printed in 1657, but written in the 1590s. Though the text has been traditionally attributed to Wotton (who is credited on the title page of the first edition), Alexandra Gajda's recent study suggests that Anthony Bacon is more likely the primary author—but either way, there is no doubt that it emerged from a follower of Essex, and became "a text that shaped the mental world of the Essex circle."[95] Robert Johnson, we have seen, referred to Tacitean history as labyrinthine, and it is thus not surprising that this text's exposure of "secret passages" owes to the Roman historian; the author reveals how the "Competencies, Pretensions, Titles, Quarrels, and Debates" of Europe's princes have "greatly weakned" the Christian fellowship, exemplified most spectacularly by the tyrannical reign of Philip II.[96] While *The State of Christendom* draws some specific material from Tacitus—for example, a description of "the Treasons of Sejan, his policies, and his purposes"—its primary debt to Tacitus is the more general thematic exploration of "the bleak realities of political corruption," and of the steps that subjects might take to counteract it.[97] Like Savile, *The State*'s author borrows the Tacitean mode to advance daring views on the limits of sovereign authority, making it "the most unequivocal statement of the legitimacy of resistance by a non-Catholic English author from the accession of Elizabeth until the civil war."[98] As an affective resource, such resistance would come to prove a valuable refuge for Essex and his followers.

The Earl of Essex: Dreadful Object

In the 1590s, the Earl of Essex and his associates found much to dread in the political sphere; this atmosphere of fear, anxiety, and suspicion was embedded in the texts that their circle produced. Turning now to their courtly opponents, we find that Essex was equally a source of dread for his adversaries: as a popular, martial hero, Essex was an ideal symbol for the disaffected Elizabethans of the 1590s, who sought a champion to deliver them from the social and political unrest cataloged earlier in the chapter. To those who opposed him, Essex cut a terrifying figure, and his capacity for political violence was a grave concern for enemies like Cecil, Raleigh, and eventually Elizabeth herself. And in a further Janus-twist, dread of Essex equally manifested in the textual sphere, though with an inverse trajectory to that which we have just witnessed: for Elizabeth and her agents, textuality was not a refuge from dread, but rather a source of it, as works relating to the earl risked cloaking all manner of seditious content. That Essex might prove dangerous was an increasing concern for both his courtly rivals and Elizabeth. As events proved, this fear was well-founded.

Why, then, did Essex's enemies dread him?

The Earl of Essex, writes his biographer, "lived his life as self-consciously as if it were a work of art, and sought to make himself indisputably the leader of his generation by excelling all of his contemporaries in accomplishments and zeal."[99] As friend to Sidney and stepson to Leicester, Essex was exceptionally well positioned to inherit a wealth of symbolic stock; in the 1580s, the model of Sidney became the blueprint for the courtly persona of the developing Essex, who tapped an array of private and public connections to position himself as his mythological heir. It was the harrowing experience of war that forever cemented the two young men; Essex was knighted for his bravery in the same battle that dealt Sidney his mortal wound, and as he lay dying the shepherd knight bestowed his best sword on his young friend. The mythic potency of this exchange only galvanized the existing connections between them, and when Leicester died in 1588 it was apparent that the young earl would inherit the mantle of the Sidney/Leicester circle. With this pedigree, Essex was poised to seize command of Elizabeth's court and the minds of her subjects: a feature that made him potentially dangerous to an aging, weakening queen.

Even in his earlier years, Essex understood the deep importance of public self-promotion—and though this awareness would build him a circle of devotees, it also put him in perennial conflict with Elizabeth, who did not appreciate being upstaged. After the defeat of the Armada, for example, the earl sponsored the highlight of London's subsequent festivities, at least according to one observer:

> I was, however, present at the last review, which was held by the earl of Essex on the 26th, and which I am assured was the best of them all. There was a company of 60 musketeers, 60 harquebussiers on horseback, and 200 light horse. The uniforms were of orange-coloured cloth, with facings of white silk, and several of the light-horsemen had surcoats of velvet of the same colour, trimmed with silver. . . . A joust was then held in the open field (i.e., without lists), and the earl of Essex ran two tilts against the earl of Cumberland. As they are two of the best horsemen in the country the spectators were much pleased at this.[100]

It is not hard to imagine why this visual display would have pleased the onlookers, and done much for Essex's popularity. Yet at the same time, beneath the celebratory frame, Essex here essentially leads a private army through the streets of London—a convention, to be sure, appropriate to his aristocratic station, but one that ominously prefigures the events of a decade later. One very important spectator, in fact, was not amused with the proceedings:

> Several other gentlemen then joined, and they tilted first two against two, and then four against four; the earl of Essex always running against the earl of Cumberland. When they had finished with the lance they drew their swords, but when her Majesty saw this she made a sign with her hand that they were to cease, but they set to and she shut the window, in order not to see them.

This anecdote exposes a central fault line of Elizabethan aristocratic identity: nobles like Essex struggled with the competing pulls of obedience to the monarch and fidelity to the autonomous individual will. For a man in the business of self-promotion, it was very tempting to side with the latter.[101] As master of the horse, Essex enjoyed "a supervisory role over tournaments, which he exploited to its fullest potential"; this control was most famously exemplified in the Accession Day tilts of 1595, a fulsome celebration of Essex himself.[102] The queen, again, was not happy at his antics: "if she had thought their had bene so moch said of her," Elizabeth was alleged to have remarked, "she wold not haue bene their that Night."[103]

Essex's less ceremonial exploits made for even better publicity—and though his martial triumphs, in the larger sense, were relatively minor, the victories he did command reminded England of his might. The sack of Cadiz, "one of the very few decisive military successes" in England's war with Spain, was an especially potent site for self-presentation; the queen eventually was forced to ban the publication of documents relating to the affair, lest a piece of more partisan propaganda undermine the official account she had constructed.[104] Nonetheless, Essex was popularly commemorated in ballads like "the welcome home of the Earle of Essex the Lord Admirall from the victorious voyage of Cales"—allegedly written spontaneously by Thomas Churchyard "vpon the sodaine sight of the Earle of Essex comming to the Court"—or "Long had the proud *Spainards* advauted to conquer us," which celebrates the "most valyant and hardy" Essex as a paragon of chivalry:

> "Now," quoth the noble Earl, "Courage, my Soldiers all!
> Fight and be valiant, then spoyl you shall have;
> And well rewarded all, from the great to the small:
> But looke that the Women and Children you save!"[105]

In fact, the mythos of the heroic Essex was enough to spark a fashion trend. During the voyage, Essex famously grew a square beard, and as visual images of the victorious earl circulated, so too did his style of grooming.[106] Within two years, this trend among England's young gallants was widespread enough for Everard Guilpin to mock it in *Skialetheia*, his caustic collection of epigrams:

> I know some . . .
> Which scorne to speake to one which hath not bin
> In one of these last voyages: or to one
> Which hauing bin there yet (though he haue none)
> Hath not a Cades-beard.[107]

The Cadiz beard would feature prominently in subsequent visual representations of the earl, and remains today one of his trademark features.

But it is not just the beard of Essex that figures in *Skialetheia*. Much more seriously, Guilpin mocks Essex under the guise of that "great Foelix," who "passing through the street, / Vayleth his cap to each one he doth meet":

> Who would not thinke him perfect curtesie?
> Or the honny-suckle of humilitie?
> The deuill he is as soone: he is the deuill,
> Brightly accoustred to bemist his euill:
> Like a Swartrutters hose his puffe thoughts swell,
> With yeastie ambition: Signior Machiauell
> Taught him this mumming trick, with curtesie
> T'entrench himselfe in popularitie.[108]

As has been long recognized, these lines recall *Richard II*'s famous depiction of Bolingbroke, the man with whom Essex was, and would forever become, linked in popular imagination. For an ambitious peer like Essex, popularity came with the cost of being thought to court it.[109] In a famous letter of advice, Francis Bacon directly addresses the crux of popular support, suggesting a shrewd tactic that recalls the dissembling manner of Guilpin's portrayal, but inverts its trajectory:

> [Popularity] is a thing good in itself, being obtained as your Lordship obtaineth it, that is *bonis artibus*; and besides, well governed, is one of the best flowers of your greatness both present and to come;

> it would be handled tenderly. The only way to quench it *verbis* and not *rebus*. And therefore to take all occations, to the Queen, to speak against popularity and popular courses vehemently; and to tax it in all others: but nevertheless to go on in your honourable commonwealth courses as you do.[110]

Five years later, the rising itself would reveal that Essex had greatly overestimated his own standing with the people—or rather, it would reveal that popularity alone, in this context, was not enough to rouse Londoners to take up arms against the queen's counselors. Unfortunately for Essex, his crowd-pleasing disposition was still said to be damning evidence of ill intentions: immediately after the rebellion, Cecil railed that Essex's "affabilite and Curtosie manifested his desire to be populer," while at his trial it was alleged that Essex "affected popularity and to be the Mynion of the people," thus proving his action "was premeditated and had the deeper roote."[111]

But for his fearful enemies, it was not simply that Essex courted popularity—more dangerous still was with whom, specifically, he was popular. Though he variously occupied roles as both courtier and politician, Essex saw himself primarily as a man of war: it was in war that Essex cemented himself as the heir to Leicester and Sidney, just as it was in war that he secured the loyalty of countless men who would serve him in the coming years. Though his enemies in the 1590s increasingly painted Essex as an unstable warhawk, the earl still openly acknowledged his "friendshippe to the chiefe men of action, and fauour generall to the men of warre":

> For most of them which are accounted the chiefe men of action, I doe intirely loue them: they haue beene my companions both abroad and at home: Some of them began the wars with me, most of them haue had place vnder me, and many of them had me a witnesse of their rising, from Captaynes, Lieuetenants, and priuate men, to these charges which since by their vertues they haue obtayned. Now I knowe their vertue I would chuse them for friends, if I had them not, but before I had tryed them, God in his prouidence chose them for me: I loue them for my owne sake, for I finde sweetenesse in their conuersation, strong assistance in their imployment with mee, and happinesse in their friendshippe.[112]

As his reference to "rising" suggests, Essex was notorious for bestowing knighthoods to his men, often to Elizabeth's fury, and often in contempt of her explicit order to the contrary. Manuscripts from the period are flush with lists of "the knights made at Caliz" or "those that have bene knighted by the Lord Lyvtenent in Ireland."[113]

In fact, during the proceedings against him at York House in 1600, Essex's fondness for knighting was one of the explicit charges levied against him. Before his appointment to Ireland, the panel recalled, "it was a question disputable & in great Consultacion before his goinge over, whithr by reason of his making so many knightes in former employmentes he should haue that authorytye in his Comission or no"; he was ultimately granted authority, but was by the "Queene hir self required to be very sparing in that respect, and to make very few & those of very good desent & quality."[114] But Elizabeth routinely struggled with curbing the will of a warring peer, and the earl's flouting of her proviso was both flagrant and habitual:

> Notwithstandinge which warninge after his Coming ouer into Ireland, he made a great number of knightes which, being by the Queene very much misliked, he was afterwardes by lettres in the Queens name required to hold his hande, and yet after the receipt of those lettres, he made many.

The crown's fears were well-founded. As suggested by one account of his return to London in 1599, Essex commanded a magnetism that drew such soldiers to his physical presence: "His Lordships soddain Retorn out of Ireland, bringes all Sortes of Knights, Captens, Officers, and Soldiers away from thence. . . . This Town is full of them, to the great Discontentment of her Majestie."[115] But at the same time, his charisma was such as to assure loyalty even in absence: only weeks later, he would receive word from Ireland that "the full crie of our poore remnant of freinds is Essex or none, Essex out of hand or all is loste."[116] The ability to command such a following was an asset of enormous power, and it was a source of enormous distress for those to whom it might be directed.

But for that very reason, the sword of popularity cut both ways. Francis Bacon, noting that "her Majesty loveth peace," would famously advise Essex to subdue his "affinity with a martial greatness": such a "militar dependence," he warned, "maketh a suspected greatness."[117] Subsequent events proved this to be sound reasoning. The earl's reputation as a man of arms made it effortless for the crown to construe the rising as an act of open, violent, civil war. Essex and his followers, says one account of the indictment, conspired

> not only to depriue the Queens Maiesty from her Royall seate and dignity but also to procure the death, and destruccion of the Queene, and to procure a Cruell slaughter of her Maiesteies Subjects, to make Cruell warrs within this Realme of England and alter the Relligion established by her Maiesty and so Change the gouernement therof, and for the effecting therof did intend to goe to her Maiesties house at White-Hall her Maiestie beeing then within the sayd house, and by force and power to seaze vpon the Queenes person and to take her into his Custody.[118]

But nonetheless, Essex continued to assert himself fundamentally as a man of the sword, and insisted upon his natural affinity with other such soldiers. "That generally I am affected to the men of warre," he explained, "should not seeme strange to any reasonable man: the graue iudge fauours the student of the lawe, the reuerend Bishoppes the labourers of the ministerie, And I, since her Maiestie hath yeerely vsed my seruice in her late actions, must reckon my selfe to the number of her men of warre."[119]

Essex's ability to court widespread public favor and amass a hard core of military followers made him a formidable opponent for his courtly adversaries; it is not surprising, then, to hear his foe Cecil complain of "how hard termes the erle of Essex standeth to me, and how apt diuers of his followers are to throwe Imputations vppon me."[120] Essex was a dangerous man to have as an enemy, as his rivals were well aware: "I am not wize enough to give yow advise," Raleigh warned Cecil in 1600, "butt if yow take it for a good councall to relent towards this tirant, yow will repent it when it shalbe to late."[121]

For the Essex circle, we have seen, the dread elicited by adversarial courtly interactions had a textual correlate in literary production. There is an analogous dynamic in the crown's response to Essex, though directed to a different end. Whereas the Essex circle adopted the Tacitean ethos to brace themselves against the storm of political corruption, and the Tacitean style to alleviate their fears of exposure within it, the earl's enemies engaged the literary field inversely: for them, textual production threatened to be a site of sedition and subversion, obscuring all manner of treasonous secrets. They found in textuality a source of endless dread—and their efforts centered on shedding light into its depths.

Examples of the Essex circle's engagement with dangerous texts have been well-documented by scholars of the period. Most notable is one of the single most analyzed theatrical moments of the sixteenth century: the specially commissioned performance of *Richard II* by the Lord

Chamberlain's Men on Saturday, February 7, 1601. On this evening, only hours before the earl's rising, a cadre of key Essexian partisans (including, as Gilly Merrick recalls it, "Lord Monteegle, Sir Christephr Blont, Sir Charles Percye, Ellys Iones, and Edward Busshell") famously decided to take some entertainment:

> At the mocyon of Sir Charles Percye and the rest, they went all together to the Globe, over the water wher the Lord Chamberlens men vse to playe, and were ther somwhat before the playe began . . . the play was of Kyng Harry the iiijth, and of the kyllyng of Kyng Richard the second played by the Lord Chamberlens players.[122]

With good reason, literary scholars have long explored how this dramatic performance (almost certainly Shakespeare's *Richard II*) might serve as a particularly meaningful example of how literature participated in the working (and unworking) of early modern political structures; the anecdote is prominently foregrounded in Stephen Greenblatt's introduction to the 1982 collection *The Power of Forms in the English Renaissance*, a de facto manifesto for the budding New Historicist movement.[123] The smoking gun, as the crown investigation would subsequently uncover, is that members of the Essex circle (most notably Percy) actively commissioned this performance from the players:

> Sir Charles Percye, Sir Iosclyne Percye, and the Lord Montegle, with some thre more spoke to some of the players, in the presans of this examinante to haue the playe of the deposyng and kyllyng of Kyng Rychard the second to be played the Saterday next . . . Wher thys examinante and hys fellowes were determyned to haue played some other playe, holdyng that play of Kyng Richard to be so old & so long out of vse as that they shold haue small or no Company at yt. But at their request this examinante and his fellowes were Content to play yt the Saterday and hadd their xls [forty shillings] more then their ordynary for yt and so played yt accordyngly.[124]

That Essex's men actively requested *Richard II*, a play about the deposition of a feeble monarch by a virile, popular nobleman—a nobleman, no less, with whom Essex had been associated in contemporary discourse—proved particularly enticing for those scholars interested in how early modern literary forces circulated within larger fields of power.

Hammer has recently deflated some of the "more extravagant" theories about the relationship of Shakespeare's play to the subsequent rising.[125]

The action on Sunday morning, for example, was a sudden response to a newly discovered plot against the earl (thus Essex's men did not purposely commission the play to prime themselves or London for the next day), while the crown's subsequent investigation into the Lord Chamberlain's players was casual and nonpunitive (and thus sought evidence that might be brought against the conspirators at trial, not to indict the public stage). Yet nonetheless, the royal response to the Essex rising still made a direct correlation between the events on the stage and the events of the next day—thus Francis Bacon says of Merrick, in the crown's official account of the uprising, that "so earnest hee was to satisfie his eyes with the sight of that Tragedie, which hee thought soone after his Lord should bring from the Stage to the State."[126]

Also pressing for the crown was the well-known textual anxiety inspired by the young historian John Hayward—who, in dedicating his *The First Part of the Life and Raigne of King Henrie the IIII* to Essex, would inadvertently bring misfortune upon both himself and his would-be master. [127] In January 1599, Hayward published his prose account (in the Tacitean mode) of the rise of King Henry IV and the deposition of Richard II, in an apparent bid for patronage from the earl.[128] Hayward overshot his mark, producing a volume that was not provocative, but inflammatory: according to the crown's later account,

> 1 he selecteth a storie 200 yere olde, and publisheth it this last yere, intendinge the application of it to this tyme
> 2 [he] maketh choice of that story only, a kinge is taxed for misgovernment, his councell for corrupt[ion] and covetous for there priuate [benefits], the king censured for conferring benefits of hatefull parisites and fauorities, the nobles discontented, the commons groning vnder countinuall taxation. There vppon the king is deposed, and by an erle, and in the ende murdre[d].[129]

The book, which Essex openly denounced, was soon suppressed by authorities for its seditious content. But the text reemerged on the crown's radar during the York House proceedings of June 1600, when the earl was explicitly accused of sponsoring it: "a certaine dangerous seditious Pamphlet, was of late put forth into print, concerning the first yeeres of the raigne of Henry the fourth, but indeed the end of Richard the second, and who thought fit to be Patron of that booke, but my Lord of Essex."[130] Hayward, now imprisoned in the Tower, was construed as the agent of some grander scheme; the book's content was such, reports Bacon, that the queen "would not be persuaded that it was his writing whose name was to it, but that it had some more mischievous author, and said with great indignation that she would have him racked to produce his author."[131] Though Hayward offered a spirited defense of his historiographical autonomy, the events of the earl's rising was all it took for the crown to authenticate its claims about the seditious content of *The Life and Raigne*. Elizabeth's agents immediately seized the opportunity to insert Hayward into its official narrative of the insurrection, and his book was denounced as a blueprint for regicide: Essex's treasonous intentions, it was declared by Cecil in the Star Chamber, "appeared by the booke written of Henry 4th wherein many thinges weare inserted to make this tyme seeme like the tyme of King Richard 2 & that they weare to be reformed by him like as did Henry 4th."[132] For his unsolicited profession of solidarity, Hayward would remain in the Tower until Elizabeth's death.

At other times, the earl and his agents raised the crown's ire by producing propaganda directly. This was the case after the Cadiz raid, when Essex found himself jockeying with Sir Walter Raleigh over credit for the successful action, and actively worked to secure the lion's share of martial glory.[133] Shortly after the assault, Essex's followers in London received a "discourse of our great Action at Calez penned very truly according to his Lordships large instructions," to be "deliuered to some good printer in good characters and with diligence to publish it."[134] Essex's aim, it was reported, was "that it should with the soonest be sett in print, both to stopp all vagrant Rumurs and to inform those that are well affected of the truth of the whole"—but, to insulate the earl from political blowback, it was warned that "nether his Lordships name nor myine not any other [should] be ether openly named, vsed, or soe insinuated."[135] (The letter's writer is Henry Cuffe, one of Essex's several secretaries.)[136] The council, however, sniffed out Essex's plan, and before long Cuffe "was charged by her Maiestie . . . vppon paine of death not to sett forth any discourse of this service without her priuity."[137] As Hammer reveals, such bans "did not deter Essex," but "merely made his propagandising more difficult": despite the queen's warning, the finished document was nonetheless circulated in England, Scotland, France, Italy, and the Low Countries.[138]

Finally, the crown was also deeply fearful of the poetic libels that circulated both before and after the Essex rising. The earl himself was no stranger to this genre; in the early 1590s, he and Raleigh engaged in a poetic flyting over the queen's favor—Essex, punning on his rival's given name, memorably declared that "it is to much to thinke, / So pure a mouth should puddle water drinke"—and Raleigh's anti-court poem

"The Lie" inspired a cluster of satirical responses with apparent ties to Essex and his party.[139] But as the decade progressed, the libel emerged as a valuable weapon in factional warfare, and seems to have been employed vigorously on behalf of Essex. In the immediate aftermath of the rising, several members of the council include remarks on libelers in their general denunciation of Essex and his men. Lord Treasurer Thomas Sackville was particularly incensed:

> First, to the matter of the libellers. In my opinion they deserve death better then open enemies; they are dangerous, & who can be fre from their stroake; they barke in secret, and ought to be subiect to the Censure of death: there ys remedy against the sworde, against gunnshott etc., but none against backebyters & libellers.[140]

This concern was for good reason: a number of anonymous poems survive that actively denounce the enemies of Essex, in a variety of manners. For example, the minor beast fable "A dreame alludinge to my L of Essex, and his adversaries" embeds specific reference to Essex's enemies in its portrayal of "A stately HART" (the earl himself) undone by treacherous machinations: as the fable unfolds, the poet takes shots at Cecil ("a CAMMELS uglie broode"), Raleigh ("His meate blood RAWE"), Cobham ("A muddye BROOKE"), and crown prosecutor Edward Coke ("A leafe wee'le have from Co-oake").[141] This technique is amplified further in "Admir-all weaknes wronges the right," which has been said to offer "a virtual roll-call of Essex's enemies."[142]

Unsurprisingly, it is the "Cankred Cecill" who receives the most venom from the anonymous backbiters on Essex's side.[143] The opening lines of a "Libell against Sir Robert Cecill" offers a representative sample:

> Proude and ambitious wretch that feedest on naught but faction
> Prevaile and fill thy selfe, and burst with vile detraction
> Detraction is thy game, and hathe bene since thie youthe
> And wilbe to thie dyinge daie, He lies that speakes the truthe
> But well I knowe thy bosome is fraught, with naught but scorne.[144]

The attacks against Cecil here recall the terms of anti-Wolsey satires: "First did thy Sire," the poem continues, "and now thy selfe by Machivillian skill / Prevaile, and curbe the Peeres as well befittes your will."[145] In "Chamberlaine Chamberlaine, one of her graces kinn," a poem composed after the earl's execution, Cecil's pretensions are equally mocked in the manner of Skelton:

> Little Cecill tripps up and downe, he Rules bothe Court & Croun
> with his great Burghley Clowne, in his Longe fox-furd gowne
> with his Longe proclamacion, hee saith hee saved the Towne.[146]

Both before and after Essex's death, Cecil is vilified in the anonymous poems that circulated throughout London. It is no wonder, then, that he and his allies were especially incensed that "the Taverns and ordinaries are filled with tales of governement and matters of state . . . which doe falcely and traytorouslye slaunder her sacred Majestie and her whole Counsell."[147]

The crown's concerns were well-founded, at least according to a piece of evidence that suggests an immediate connection between libels and sedition. One week after the failed Essex rising, a cadre of emboldened apprentices had "intended to meete at the Exchange . . . at x of the Clocke in the morninge," to embark upon a dashing caper to liberate the earl from crown captivity.[148] Though the plot was spoiled prematurely, the crown's subsequent investigation revealed their plan of action: "They intended to drawe theire companie together by Libells with hope to have 5000 persons." Without further evidence, it is not clear what form these "libells" took; in the early modern period, the word "libel" had a flexible connotation, with usage signaling both non-moralized texts (the generic "little book") and all manner of written slander and invective. But whatever the precise form, the apprentices apparently thought that such writings could galvanize London to a surprising degree: they anticipated a turnout dwarfing that of the rising itself.

Beneath the dreadful skies of the 1590s, Essex and his enemies were deadlocked in an affective struggle, each fearing, and each feared. After his disgraced return from Ireland, and his subsequent destruction in the proceedings that followed, the terms of the contest changed, as Cecil, Raleigh, and the anti-Essex party powerfully asserted their own mastery over the operation of dread in the courtly sphere. In the final months of his life, as Essex was increasingly choked with terror and paranoia, he was forced to try to reclaim the terms of dread for a final time. This attempt set off a chain of events, both worldly and cosmic, that would drag him to ruin.

The Dreadful End

In the early weeks of 1601, the fears of the Essex circle were boiling over; there seemed little hope of recovery, and the chambers of Essex

House echoed with shadowy reports of plots to destroy the earl. A group of frustrated, alienated followers surrounded the equally disposed Essex, and the mutual mood quickly worsened. Sir John Harington, the queen's godson, records a chilling glimpse of this malaise:

> It resteth wythe me in opynion, that ambition thwarted in its career, dothe speedilie leade on to madnesse; herein I am strengthened by what I learne in my Lord of Essex, who shyftethe from sorrowe and repentaunce to rage and rebellion so suddenlie, as well provethe him devoide of goode reason or righte mynde; in my laste discourse, he uttered strange wordes, borderyninge on suche strange desygns that made me hastene forthe, and leave his presence.[149]

Though likely embellished by hindsight, Harington's report at least partly indicates the affective toll of this dire moment. On the morning of Sunday, February 8, the group's collective dread reached a critical mass: after receiving "ceryetn aduertisementes on the Saterdaye night that his private enymies was vp in armes against him," Essex and his men found themselves pushed to a radical act of resistance.[150] As Essex later told it, the events of that morning were sparked by a spontaneous gathering of his adherents, suddenly united to thwart this attack against their symbolic epicenter:

> [To the charge] that I gathered a Companye togither and that by that means intended forceably. . . . I answere the Company that was gathered togither in my howse assembled themselues vpon intelligence being giuen out vnto them that my life was sought for & that without any priuitye at all vnto me these my seruants and fearefull friends in my howse [were making the reports] knowne amongst them.[151]

As we have seen above, when this group of fearful friends took to the streets, statements of terror and persecution became their rallying cry. Such proclamations served to justify their bold action and incite an atmosphere of collective panic: by assuring onlookers that "they came into the Citty only for safty of their liues," the rebels imagined that London's citizens, equally moved by fear, would be roused to join the cause.[152]

In this desperate action, Essex thus makes a last-ditch attempt to assert his will over his courtly enemies, by orchestrating a final conflict that ensured absolute destruction for the loser. To galvanize his followers,

Essex continued to denounce men like Cecil and Raleigh, the "Athiests and Catterpillers" that perverted the queen's will and sought his own life; with this common enemy, he hoped to assure the group's adherence to both "the lawe of nature" and "good seruice," by casting their action as a political purgative.[153] In the rising's aftermath, however, this maneuver would be deemed a despicable fraud:

> The Earle of Essex [employed] false Suggesting to the Cittizens & others of violence and murder to be intended and attempted against him in his house, thereby to breed a commeseracion in the people of his estate and danger and to drawe them to hatred of such as he Called his priuate enimies.[154]

Essex is charged with inciting panic—a common affective state that might subsequently be retooled into an instrument of violence. During his trial, the earl's alleged strategy is elaborated more specifically:

> Why then did you and the whole Company goe vp and downe the citty through gracious street, Cheapeside and other the Cheefe streets, vpon a purpose to get ayd, and a multitude of Runnigates and Vagabounds which might winde with you villanously to effect that which you had trayterously determined.[155]

The crown's lawyers suggest that Essex is ensnaring those whom he engages, creating an enmeshment in which his fears become their own ("winde with you"). The affective symbiosis serves to collapse the social hierarchy, as both peer and pauper are imagined sympathetic in their mutual dread—a fantasy that doubly triggers the crown's own fear of sedition, linking paranoia over high-level courtly intrigues (coups, assassination attempts, etc.) with fears of popular unrest (religious rising, food riots, etc.).

But Essex's popularity, we have seen, was grossly misjudged. The action fizzled, as London failed to rise (or even open its gates); the party retreated by barge to Essex House, where they staged a perfunctory standoff, before surrendering peacefully to the crown's agents. A week later, Essex and Southampton were tried together for treason; Essex protested his innocence in a rousing defense, but there was little doubt of the outcome. As the prisoners were escorted back to the Tower, "the Axe was carried before them with the edge towardes them."[156] Here they awaited their sentence:

> Nowe you must goe to the place from whence you came, there to be laied on a hurdell, drawen to the place of execution, hanged and cutt down or you bee dead, then your members to be cutt of, and burnt before your faces, your heddes to be cutt of and your bodies to be quartered and dispersed at the Queenes pleasure, And the Lord have mercie on your soules.[157]

Such horrors did not come to pass: Essex would be granted a more honorable beheading, while Southampton escaped the axe entirely. But with the promise of these tortures, as prelude to the eternal uncertainty of oblivion, Essex now faced a different kind of dread.

The dread explored in this chapter has been largely collective in nature: Essex and his allies feared the machinations of his courtly enemies, while his enemies (and Elizabeth) feared that the earl's power and popularity might upend the social order. In the aftermath of his failed rising, however, the Earl of Essex came to know what it was like to be alone. Despite all attempts to rouse her, London did not respond as he had hoped, leaving his action without desperately needed support—and on a day, the most important of Essex's life, where "everything that could go wrong did go wrong."[158] There were, as we have seen, some immediate professions of loyalty to the earl, such as the plot of the apprentices. But Essex himself, awaiting imminent execution, would turn inward and upward. His dread was shifting its object, and the likes of Raleigh and Cecil seemed far less important to him now.

Only days after a defiant performance in the courtroom, the earl suddenly summoned Elizabeth's agents, so that he might "deliuer his knowledge of those Treasons which he had formerly denyed at the Barr."[159] In a marked reversal, Essex began to realize that his priorities had been gravely misaligned. And with a short time to live, he had little interest in the profane bonds that linked him to this world, including those that he had forged with his former allies:

> He did meruailous earnestly desyre that wee would suffer him to speake vnto Cuffe his Secretary, against whom he vehemently complayned vnto vs to haue ben a principall Instigator to theis vyelent courses which he had vndertaken, wherein he protested that he chiefly deysred that he might make yt appeare that he was not the only perswader of theis great offences which they had commytted, but that Blont, Cuffe, Temple, and those other persons who were at the priuate conspiracy at Drury house.

With his eternal soul on the line, Essex was naming names, and he had plans to make sure his conscience was cleared fully. Not content with merely exposing the chief conspirators, the earl revealed that the extent of their intended action was yet unknown to the crown:

> [They] had more dangerous and malycious endes for the disturbance of the Estate then he doth nowe fynde coulde haue ben preuented yf his proiect had gon forwarde, as well appereth by the confusion they drewe him to even in his owne house that morning that he went into the citty.

To be sure, Essex's reimagination of the events was self-interested: here, it is he who was drawn unknowingly into the schemes of these traitors, a bystander swept up in the collective action. To make his peace, Essex affirms that he was not a type of Bolingbroke, but rather a counterpart of King Richard, and thus of Elizabeth herself: noble souls, tragically led to ruin by others. It is thus with no small self-pity that Essex declares to Cuffe, when his secretary was brought before him a final time, that "none hath ben a greater Instigator of me then yourselfe, to all theis my disloyall courses into which I haue fallen."[160]

In what is almost certainly the last poem he ever wrote, Essex reflects upon the dangers of bad fellowship, a social cancer so apt to bring destruction upon the godly:

> Ill company, the cause of many woes,
> The sugred baite, that hideth poysned hooke;
> The rocke unseene that shipwrackt soules o'rethrowes,
> The weeping crocodile that killes with looke,
> The readiest steppe to ruine and decay,
> Grace's confounder, and helle's nearest way.[161]

How many have been ruined by the company they keep, seduced into an unforeseen fall? Yet in these dreadful days, Essex continues, to be social at all is to expose oneself to the agents of corruptions:

> But he is held no sotiable man
> In this corrupted age, that shall refuse
> To keepe accursed company now and than;
> Nay but a foole, unlesse he seeme to chuse
> Their fellowship, and give them highest place,
> That vildest live, and furthest off from grace.[162]

Essex must indict himself with the same charges of bad company that he had so often levied at the queen. With newfound clarity, he reveals the caterpillars in his own garden; Essex discovers that the greater threat is not what was plotted by his rivals, but that which he invited upon himself. It is a moment of royal atonement, as the earl's empathy with Elizabeth provides means for his reintegration into the unity of her symbolic self—not as a profane sovereign, but as anointed conduit of heavenly grace.

In disavowing his earthly ties, Essex did considerable violence to the social ecosystem that had, with his nourishment, come to flourish around him. Though some of the earl's associates would regroup in the court of James I, the fate of the Essex circle's charter members is recorded bluntly by George Carleton, in a letter written just weeks after the rising:

> You must needes here by common report of the vnadvised & mischevous action of the Erle of Essexe & his adeerentes; dangerous to the person of our Quene, fearfull to the state, & mischevous to him & all his partakers, especiallye to thos that were of hys secrett councell & partyes with him in the plott: wherof diuerse haue allreddye suffredd death, thoughe not with him yet after him. Therle himself was beheaded in the tower first, Sir Guillam Merricke & Cuffe his secertarye were after hanged, drawne & quartred att Tiborn, & lastleye Sir Charles Danvers & Sir Christopher Blunt were beheaded on tower hille openlye.[163]

All that outrage, all that turmoil, all that dread, reduced to a few passing lines. Yet, as Carleton continues, there is a larger story here about the frailty of union in this fallen age:

> Ytt was strange to see the beginninge of this action (wherof I was a behollder) & somewhatt strange to consider the circumstances now toward the end. For thes noble & resolute men assured of one an other by their vndoubted valour & combined together by firme oathes, beinge all taken, severed, examined, & the principalls arraygned & condempned, sett in the end before their deathes to such playne confessions & accusations one of an other.

Once embattled in a zero-sum game with their courtly rivals, the Essex men similarly set upon each other—each man determined "to strive who could drawe one an other in deepest."

Denouncing his coconspirators entailed a commitment to atonement, however revisionist the narrative that enabled it; the humbled Essex rejected the facilitators of his earthly ambition, turning toward the unifying promise of faith. In a short poem that seems to date from this period, Essex struggles with such reorientation, seeking an account of how his shattering self is refracted in the hearts and minds of the world at large:

> I am not as I seeme, I seeme and am the same;
> I am as divers deeme, but not as others name;
> I am not as I shoulde; I shoulde be as I saye;
> In wantinge what I woulde, I must be as I maye.
> finis qd Rob: Essex Comes[164]

The poem is obscure to me; I assume that the second line is animated by an implicit opposition of sinner/traitor, while the final line's "wantinge" suggests the ambivalence inherent in his action, insofar as it might entail both desire for the worldly (a successful outcome in the rising; the queen's grace and pardon; etc.) or the sacred (the salvation he turned away from). But whatever its precise meaning, the affective tenor is dizzying for both the poet and his reader, as Essex struggles to disentangle himself from the countless sites of external investment in which his identity had become ensnared.

In "The Passion of a Discontented Minde," Essex's final poem, the earl comes to address his sin and salvation far more directly than in the cryptic epigram above—and in this poetic finale, he devotes no small space to establishing the proper object of creation's dread, and the proper way to be dreadful.[165] For though sinfulness demands that we "live in feare, distrust, and terror"—and though "heav'nly contemplation," in turn, yields a "minde set free from care, disrust, or feare"—Essex still praises the "terror unremovable" of the creator, at "whose sterne lookes all creatures are afraide," and at whom dread is rightly directed as an instrument of salvation (165, 144, 142, 302, 78). Essex was once among those "fond worldings" who "without feare worke Virtue's fowle abuse"—but as he learned to fear, and learned to fear correctly, he seems to have learned that "banishment from everlasting blisse" is our own doing, "Because we fled from him we should have served" (286, 39, 81, 156). Essex acknowledges the informed volition that marked his descent into sin, and his descent away from God:

> Thrise happy sinner was that blessed Saint,
> Who though he fell with puffe of woman's blast,
> Went forth and wept with many a bitter plaint
> And by his teares obtained grace at last;

> But wretched I have falne of mine accord,
> Tenne thousand times against the living Lord. (91–96)

Is it possible that Essex, on some profane level, considered himself equally undone by a "puffe of woman's blast"—but the poem's professed aim is pitched quite differently. "I see my sinnes arraign'd before my face," Essex exclaims, realizing that, through the workings of faith and grace, they might be pressed to a nobler service:

> Thou deepest Searcher of each secret thought,
> Infuse in me thy all-affecting grace;
> So shall my workes to good effects be brought,
> While I peruse my ugly sinnes a space,
> Whose staining filth so spotted hath my soule,
> As nought with wash but teares of inward dole. (73, 19–24).

To complete his confession, the earl thus affirms his rejection of the world and its trappings, committing himself to the infinite unity of dreadful atonement; "so wil I come," Essex promises his maker, "with feare and blushing cheeke, / For giving others what to thee belonge" (338–39).

With this promise, finally, Essex acknowledges the significance of his own guilt, and the significance of the judge by whom it was pronounced. After a struggle to control the meaning of "dread" in the courtly battlefields of the 1590s, Essex is left finally with only awe and reverence for his God and queen. On the morning of February 25, 1601, as he addressed the English nation for a final time, Essex "gave thanks to Almighty God from the bottom of his heart, that his designs, which were so dangerous to the state, succeeded not"—he had, he assured the gathered crowd, "now looked thoroughly and seriously into his sin, and was heartily sorry he had so obstinately defended an unjust cause at the bar."[166] Having shed himself of his company, Essex promised that "he had now learned how vain a thing the blast of popular favour and applause was."[167] Courtly friends and courtly foes mattered little now; it was only God who might "strengthen his mind against the terrors of death."[168] And in facing the dread of oblivion, whatever strength Essex might muster is attributed alone to grace:

> He bewaylded his sinnes with the greatest shewe of true repentaunce. he begged at godes handes strength . . . , acknowledginge his owne weaknes & infirmitie, adding further that there was no man fearfullr in nature than himself, whereof he had a trewe feeling for

> that he had passed some danger & thereby knewe his owne imbecillitie. But gave vs for a note that were beholders that if he shewed any strength or Constancye in that passage it was to be attribututed to godes grace & favour, for he himself was weaker than anye.[169]

After a final prayer, "beesching god that he wold not permitte Sathan to distract him at that instant when the body & soule should be seperated," Essex placed himself on the block, where he "patientlie receaved the stroake of thexecucioner."[170] It took three strikes to remove his head entirely—but, at the very least, "neither bodie, armes nor hedd ever stirred after the First."[171] During the "tyme of his beinge on the scaffold," one witness approvingly observed, "the Erle never uttered worldlie thought." Essex had learned whom to fear, and Essex had learned how to dread.

When, decades later, Sir Henry Wotton reflected on the fate of his patron Essex, he offered his own first hand assessment of political life in the "nasty nineties": at that time, he writes, "there were in Court two names of *Power,* and almost of *Affection,* the *Essexian* and the *Cecilian* with their Adherents." [172] For scholars of the early modern period, his emphasis on power is probably not surprising. But it is the complementary invocation of *affection*—a word that, in contemporary usage, could tellingly signal an emotive passion, a general stirring, a personal affinity, or even an adopted style—that encapsulates my larger argument in this chapter.[173] Factional participation in Renaissance England was no doubt motivated by social self-interest, as an adaptive strategy to achieve one's political and material aims. But, then as now, there is also an affective force to collective identification and in-group membership, and it is this crucial emotional component of social conflict that has been seldom considered by scholars of the period. As we have seen, it did not always feel good to be a member of the Essex faction in the late 1590s—but it always felt like *something,* and it is this something that demands more consideration by future researchers.

NOTES

Introduction

1. Unsurprisingly, there is no consensus in the sciences or humanities on how to delineate the conceptual boundaries of terms like emotion, affect, mood, feeling, sentiment, etc. Because I am interested in how all such phenomena manifest in the Tudor court, this book (like many others on emotion in the early modern period) does not depend on any such taxonomic distinctions. This is in contrast to the particular strand of literary and cultural scholarship that insists upon the categorical difference between affect and emotion; see note 10 below. On the semantic slipperiness of emotion words in the sixteenth century, see Kirk Essary, "Passions, Affections, or Emotions? On the Ambiguity of 16th-Century Terminology," *Emotion Review* (2017): 1–8 [Advance Access: DOI: 10.1177/1754073916679007].

2. For a splendid introduction to this growing field, see Susan Broomhall, ed., *Early Modern Emotions: An Introduction* (London: Routledge, 2017); more generally, see Rob Boddice, "The Affective Turn: Historicizing the Emotions" in *Psychology and History: Interdisciplinary Explorations,* ed. Cristian Tileagă and Jovan Byford (Cambridge: Cambridge University Press, 2014), 147–65; Jan Plamper, *The History of Emotions: An Introduction* (Oxford: Oxford University Press, 2015); and Rob Boddice, *The History of Emotions* (Manchester: Manchester University Press, 2018) [forthcoming].

3. On grief, see G. W. Pigman III, *Grief and English Renaissance Elegy* (Cambridge: Cambridge University Press, 1985); Heather Dubrow, *Shakespeare and Domestic Loss: Forms of Deprivation, Mourning, and Recuperation* (Cambridge: Cambridge University Press, 1999); Margo Swiss and David A. Kent, eds., *Speaking Grief in English Literary Culture: Shakespeare to Milton* (Pittsburgh, Pa.: Duquesne University Press, 2002); and Elizabeth Hodgson, *Grief and Women Writers in the English Renaissance* (Cambridge: Cambridge University Press, 2015). Of more immediate interest is the vast work on melancholy, summarized in David Houston Wood, *Time, Narrative, and Emotion in Early Modern England* (Burlington, Vt.: Ashgate, 2009), 2 n.4. More recent works include Douglas Trevor, *The Poetics of Melancholy in Early Modern England* (Cambridge: Cambridge University Press, 2004); Angus Gowland, *The World of Renaissance Melancholy: Robert Burton in Context* (Cambridge: Cambridge University Press, 2006); Angus Gowland, "Medicine, Psychology, and the Melancholic Subject in the Renaissance," in *Emotions and Health, 1200–1700,* ed. Elena Carrera (Leiden: Brill, 2013), 185–219; Angus Gowland, "Melancholy, Passions and Identity in the Renaissance," in *Passions and Subjectivity in Early Modern Culture*, ed. Brian Cummings and Freya Sierhuis (Burlington, Vt.: Ashgate, 2013), 75–93; Mary Ann Lund, *Melancholy, Medicine and Religion in Early Modern England: Reading "The Anatomy of Melancholy"* (Cambridge: Cambridge University Press, 2010); Drew Daniel, *The Melancholy Assemblage: Affect and Epistemology in*

the English Renaissance (New York: Fordham University Press, 2013); Erin Sullivan, *Beyond Melancholy: Sadness and Selfhood in Renaissance England* (Oxford: Oxford University Press, 2016); and Stephanie Shirilan, *Robert Burton and the Transformative Powers of Melancholy* (New York: Routledge, 2016).

4. Gail Kern Paster, *Humoring the Body: Emotions and the Shakespearean Stage* (Chicago: University of Chicago Press, 2004); and Gail Kern Paster, Katherine Rowe, and Mary Floyd-Wilson, eds., *Reading the Early Modern Passions: Essays in the Cultural History of Emotion* (Philadelphia: University of Pennsylvania Press, 2004). Important forerunners include Gail Kern Paster, *The Body Embarrassed: Drama and the Disciplines of Shame in Early Modern England* (Ithaca, N.Y.: Cornell University Press, 1993); and Michael C. Schoenfeldt, *Bodies and Selves in Early Modern England: Physiology and Inwardness in Spenser, Shakespeare, Herbert, and Milton* (Cambridge: Cambridge University Press, 1999). See also L. E. Semler, "The Renaissance Gets Emotional," *Metascience* 16, no. 1 (2007): 137–41; and Erin Sullivan, "The History of the Emotions: Past, Present, Future," *Cultural History* 2, no. 1 (2013): 93–102.

5. Paster, *Humoring the Body*, 20; Paster, Rowe, and Floyd-Wilson, *Reading the Early Modern Passions*, 18. It is important to note, however, that this "new humoralism," as Richard Strier skeptically calls it (*The Unrepentant Renaissance: From Petrarch to Shakespeare to Milton* [Chicago: University of Chicago Press, 2011], 7), has been criticized for promoting an overly prescriptive, simplified understanding of Renaissance psychophysiology. Angus Gowland, for example, argues that the "humoral subjectivity" of scholars like Paster rests upon "an inaccurate [account] in which the physical qualities of the body are more or less determinative of the functions of the soul" ("Melancholy, Passions and Identity," 75). See also Strier's remarks in Strier and Carla Mazzio, "Two Responses to 'Shakespeare and Embodiment: An E-Conversation,'" *Literature Compass* 3, no. 1 (2005): 15–31; and Richard Meek, "Introduction: Shakespeare and the Culture of Emotion," *Shakespeare* 8, no. 3 (2012): 279–85.

6. Mary Floyd-Wilson and Garrett A. Sullivan Jr., eds., *Environment and Embodiment in Early Modern England* (New York: Palgrave Macmillan, 2007); Garrett A. Sullivan, *Sleep, Romance and Human Embodiment: Vitality from Spenser to Milton* (Cambridge: Cambridge University Press, 2012); Sandra Clark, "*Macbeth* and the Language of the Passions," *Shakespeare* 8, no. 3 (2012): 300–311; Katharine A. Craik and Tanya Pollard, eds., *Shakespearean Sensations: Experiencing Literature in Early Modern England* (Cambridge: Cambridge University Press, 2013); Bridget Escolme, *Emotional Excess on the Shakespearean Stage: Passion's Slaves* (London: Bloomsbury, 2014); and Allison P. Hobgood, *Passionate Playgoing in Early Modern England* (Cambridge: Cambridge University Press, 2014). For a meta-commentary, see Mary Floyd-Wilson et al., "Shakespeare and Embodiment: An E-Conversation," *Literature Compass* 2, no. 1 (2005): 1–15; and Strier and Mazzio, "Two Responses."

7. Robert Cockcroft, *Rhetorical Affect in Early Modern Writing: Renaissance Passions Reconsidered* (New York: Palgrave Macmillan, 2003); Wendy Olmsted, *The Imperfect Friend: Emotion and Rhetoric in Sidney, Milton, and Their Contexts* (Toronto: University of Toronto Press, 2008); Lynn Enterline, *Shakespeare's Schoolroom: Rhetoric, Discipline, Emotion* (Philadelphia: University of Pennsylvania Press, 2012); R. S. White, "'False Friends': Affective Semantics in

Shakespeare," *Shakespeare* 8, no. 3 (2012): 286–99; Susan C. Karant-Nunn, *The Reformation of Feeling: Shaping the Religious Emotions in Early Modern Germany* (Oxford: Oxford University Press, 2010); Joseph Campana, *The Pain of Reformation: Spenser, Vulnerability, and the Ethics of Masculinity* (New York: Fordham University Press, 2012); Steven Mullaney, *The Reformation of Emotions in the Age of Shakespeare* (Chicago: University of Chicago Press, 2015); Daniel Juan Gil, *Before Intimacy: Asocial Sexuality in Early Modern England* (Minneapolis: University of Minnesota Press, 2006); Jennifer C. Vaught, *Masculinity and Emotion in Early Modern English Literature* (Burlington, Vt.: Ashgate, 2008); and Cora Fox, *Ovid and the Politics of Emotion in Elizabethan England* (New York: Palgrave, 2009).

8. R. S. White, Mark Houlahan, and Katrina O'Loughlin, eds., *Shakespeare and Emotions: Inheritances, Enactments, Legacies* (New York: Palgrave, 2015); Fabrizio Ricciardelli and Andrea Zorzi, eds., *Emotions, Passions, and Power in Renaissance Italy* (Amsterdam: Amsterdam University Press, 2015); Michael Champion and Andrew Lynch, eds., *Understanding Emotions in Early Europe* (Turnhout: Brepols, 2015); Susan Broomhall and Sarah Finn, eds., *Violence and Emotions in Early Modern Europe* (New York: Routledge, 2015); Susan Broomhall, ed., *Authority, Gender and Emotions in Late Medieval and Early Modern England* (New York: Palgrave Macmillan, 2015); Susan Broomhall, ed., *Gender and Emotions in Medieval and Early Modern Europe: Destroying Order, Structuring Disorder* (Burlington, Vt.: Ashgate, 2015); Susan Broomhall, ed., *Ordering Emotions in Europe, 1100–1800* (Leiden: Brill, 2015); Richard Meek and Erin Sullivan, eds., *The Renaissance of Emotion: Understanding Affect in Shakespeare and His Contemporaries* (Manchester: Manchester University Press, 2015); and Ronda Arab, Michelle M. Dowd, and Adam Zucker, eds., *Historical Affects and the Early Modern Theater* (New York: Routledge, 2015).

9. In this sense, my approach recalls Barbara H. Rosenwein's influential work on "emotional communities"—that is, social coalitions in which "people adhere to the same norms of emotional expression and value—or devalue—the same or related emotions." See her *Emotional Communities in the Early Middle Ages* (Ithaca, N.Y.: Cornell University Press, 2006), 2. For an overview, see Andrew Lynch, "Emotional Community," in Broomhall, *Early Modern Emotions,* 3–6; see also Barbara H. Rosenwein, *Generations of Feeling: A History of Emotions, 600–1700* (Cambridge: Cambridge University Press, 2016).

10. This method, which has its ultimate philosophical origins in Gilles Deleuze's reading of Baruch Spinoza, draws a sharp contrast between *affect*—a kind of latent energy potential owing to a body's capacity to affect or be affected—and *emotion*—the specific linguistic identification of that energy in action. See Stephanie Trigg, "Affect Theory," in Broomhall, *Early Modern Emotions,* 10–13; and Amanda Bailey and Mario DiGangi, eds., *Affect Theory and Early Modern Texts: Politics, Ecologies, and Form* (New York: Palgrave, 2017). For two general introductions to this approach, see Patricia Ticineto Clough and Jean Halley, eds., *The Affective Turn: Theorizing the Social* (Durham, N.C.: Duke University Press, 2007); and Melissa Gregg and Gregory J. Seigworth, eds., *The Affect Theory Reader* (Durham, N.C.: Duke University Press, 2010). See also Brian Massumi, *Parables for the Virtual: Movement, Affect, Sensation* (Durham, N.C.: Duke University Press, 2002).

11. Natalie Mears, "Courts, Courtiers, and Culture in Tudor England," *The Historical Journal* 46, no. 3 (2003): 704.

12. Patrick Collinson, *Elizabethan Essays* (London: Hambledon, 1994), 11. Mears's "Courts, Courtiers, and Culture" splendidly outlines this historiography.

13. Mears, "Courts, Courtiers, and Culture," 704; see Mears's essay also for a review of relevant scholarship in this vein, where she cites work (besides that of Starkey) by the prominent historians Simon Adams, George Bernard, C. S. L. Davies, Steve Gunn, Eric Ives, Wallace MacCaffrey, and Penry Williams. David Starkey's classic essay is "Representation Through Intimacy: A Study in the Symbolism of Monarchy and Court Office in Early-Modern England," in *Symbols and Sentiments: Cross-Cultural Studies in Symbolism*, ed. Ioan Lewis (New York: Academic, 1977), 187–224, but see also Starkey's "Court and Government," in *Revolution Reassessed: Revisions in the History of Tudor Government and Administration*, ed. Christopher Coleman and David Starkey (Oxford: Clarendon, 1986): 29–58; and "Privy Secrets: Henry VIII and the Lords of the Council," *History Today* 37, no. 8 (1987): 23–31. This work, on balance, challenges the mid-century account of Sir Geoffrey Elton; in its emphasis on interpersonal dynamics, it reanimates "questions first raised by Conyers Read and Sir John Neale in the early twentieth century about the role of ideology and social connections in politics" (Mears, "Courts, Courtiers, and Culture").

14. Ann Cvetkovich, *An Archive of Feelings: Trauma, Sexuality, and Lesbian Public Cultures* (Durham, N.C.: Duke University Press, 2003), 7.

15. See George E. Marcus, W. Russell Neuman, and Michael Mackuen, eds., *Affective Intelligence and Political Judgment* (Chicago: University of Chicago Press, 2000); Cheryl Hall, *The Trouble with Passion: Political Theory beyond the Reign of Reason* (New York: Routledge, 2005); W. Russell Neuman et al., eds., *The Affect Effect: Dynamics of Emotion in Political Thinking and Behavior* (Chicago: University of Chicago Press, 2007); Rebecca Kingston and Leonard Ferry, eds., *Bringing the Passions Back In: The Emotions in Political Philosophy* (Vancouver: University of British Columbia Press, 2008); James E. Fleming, ed., *Passions and Emotions* (New York: New York University Press, 2013); and Martha C. Nussbaum, *Political Emotions: Why Love Matters for Justice* (Cambridge, Mass.: Harvard University Press, 2013). As several scholars remind us, however, it is important not to cartoon the extent of post-Enlightenment hostility to emotion; see Cheshire Calhoun, "Reliable Democratic Habits and Emotions," in Fleming, *Passions and Emotions*, 212–25.

16. Chantal Mouffe, *On the Political* (New York: Routledge, 2005), 6; Chantal Mouffe, "Deliberative Democracy or Agonistic Pluralism?" *Social Research* 66, no. 3 (1999): 755–56. See also Nussbaum, *Political Emotions*.

17. See Antonio Damasio, *Descartes' Error: Emotion, Reason, and the Human Brain* (New York: G.P. Putnam's Sons, 1994); Hanna Damasio et al., "The Return of Phineas Gage: Clues about the Brain from the Skull of a Famous Patient," *Science* 264, no. 5162 (1994): 1102–05; Jonathan Haidt, "The Emotional Dog and Its Rational Tail: A Social Intuitionist Approach to Moral Judgment," *Psychological Review* 108, no. 4 (2001): 814–34; Jonathan Haidt, *The Righteous Mind: Why Good People Are Divided by Politics and Religion* (New York: Pantheon, 2012); Jonathan Haidt and Matthew A. Hersh, "Sexual Morality: The Cultures and Emotions of Conservatives and Liberals," *Journal of Applied Social*

Psychology 31, no. 1 (2001): 191–221; and Jonathan Haidt and Craig Joseph, "Intuitive Ethics: How Innately Prepared Intuitions Generate Culturally Variable Virtues," *Daedalus* 133, no. 4 (2004): 55–66.

18. Damasio, *Descartes' Error*; Antonio Damasio, *The Feeling of What Happens: Body and Emotion in the Making of Consciousness* (New York: Harcourt, 1999); Antonio Damasio, *Looking for Spinoza: Joy, Sorrow, and the Feeling Brain* (New York: Harcourt, 2003); Haidt, *Righteous Mind*; Drew Westen, *The Political Brain: The Role of Emotion in Deciding the Fate of the Nation* (New York: Public Affairs, 2007); William E. Connolly, *Neuropolitics: Thinking, Culture, Speed* (Minneapolis: University of Minnesota Press, 2002), 9. For a response, see Andrew Lee Gluck, *Damasio's Error and Descartes' Truth: An Inquiry into Consciousness, Metaphysics, and Epistemology* (Scranton, Pa.: University of Scranton Press, 2007). See also Jeff Goodwin, James M. Jasper, and Francesca Polletta, eds., *Passionate Politics: Emotions and Social Movements* (Chicago: University of Chicago Press, 2001); Dominique Moïsi, *The Geopolitics of Emotion: How Cultures of Fear, Humiliation, and Hope Are Reshaping the World* (New York: Anchor Books, 2009); Paul Hoggett, *Politics, Identity, and Emotion* (Boulder, Colo.: Paradigm, 2009); and Simon Thompson and Paul Hoggett, eds., *Politics and the Emotions: The Affective Turn in Contemporary Political Studies* (New York: Continuum International, 2012).

19. John Protevi, *Political Affect: Connecting the Social and the Somatic* (Minneapolis: University of Minnesota Press, 2009), xi. See also, for example, Connolly, *Neuropolitics*; and Sara Ahmed, *The Cultural Politics of Emotion* (New York: Routledge, 2004).

20. Janet Staiger, Ann Cvetkovich, and Ann Reynolds, eds., *Political Emotions* (New York: Routledge, 2010), 2. See also Ann Cvetkovich, "Public Feelings," *South Atlantic Quarterly* 106, no. 3 (2007): 459–68; and Ann Cvetkovich and Ann Pellegrini, "Introduction: Public Sentiments," *S&F Online* 2, no. 1 (2003), n.p., http://sfonline.barnard.edu/ps/intro.htm.

21. Donovan Schaefer, "The Promise of Affect: The Politics of the Event in Ahmed's *The Promise of Happiness* and Berlant's *Cruel Optimism*," *Theory & Event* 16, no. 2 (2013), n.p.

22. Dacher Keltner and Jonathan Haidt, "Social Functions of Emotions at Four Levels of Analysis," *Cognition & Emotion* 13, no. 5 (1999): 505; Paul Griffiths and Andrea Scarantino, "Emotions in the Wild: The Situated Perspective on Emotion," in *The Cambridge Handbook of Situated Cognition*, ed. Philip Robbins and Murat Aydede (Cambridge: Cambridge University Press, 2009), 437.

23. Strier, *Unrepentant Renaissance*, 31.

24. Massumi, *Parables*, 37. For Massumi, it is important to note, *affect* is a related, but distinct phenomenon from *emotion*.

25. For some valuable cautions on scientific approaches to literature, see Patrick Colm Hogan, "Science, Literature, and Cultural Colonialism." *Scientific Study of Literature* 1, no. 1 (2011): 165–72.

26. Lalita Pandit Hogan, "Prophesying with Accents Terrible: Emotion and Appraisal in *Macbeth*," in *Toward A Cognitive Theory of Narrative Acts*, ed. Frederick Luis Aldama (Austin: University of Texas Press, 2010), 255.

27. See Lalita Pandit, "Emotion, Perception and Anagnorisis in the Comedy of Errors: A Cognitive Perspective," *College Literature* 33, no. 1 (2006): 94–126; and

[Pandit] Hogan, "Prophesying with Accents Terrible." For Patrick Colm Hogan, see "The Mourning Brain: Attachment, Anticipation, and Hamlet's Unmanly Grief," in *Cognitive Literary Studies: Current Themes and New Directions,* ed. Isabel Jaén and Julien J. Simon (Austin: University of Texas Press, 2012), 89–104, and see also the citations for Hogan throughout the remainder of the notes for this chapter. See also Donald R. Wehrs, "Moral Physiology, Ethical Prototypes, and the Denaturing of Sense in Shakespearean Tragedy," *College Literature* 33, no. 1 (2006): 67–92.

28. Constantina Papoulias and Felicity Callard, "Biology's Gift: Interrogating the Turn to Affect," *Body & Society* 16, no. 1 (2010): 29–56.

29. Ruth Leys, "The Turn to Affect: A Critique," *Critical Inquiry* 37, no. 3 (2011): 434–72.

30. Patrick Colm Hogan, "Literary Brains: Neuroscience, Criticism, and Theory," *Literature Compass* 11, no. 4 (2014): 293. "In correlational criticism," Hogan writes, "the critic takes some theory—whether deconstruction or neuroscience—and finds parallels for its elements and principles in literature" (ibid.).

31. Paster, Rowe, and Floyd-Wilson, *Reading the Early Modern Passions*, 9.

32. Patrick Colm Hogan, *What Literature Teaches Us about Emotion* (Cambridge: Cambridge University Press, 2011), 2. See also his "What Literature Teaches Us about Emotion: Synthesizing Affective Science and Literary Study," in *The Oxford Handbook of Cognitive Literary Studies,* ed. Lisa Zunshine (Oxford: Oxford University Press, 2015), 273–90.

33. Floyd-Wilson et al., "Shakespeare and Embodiment," 4.

34. Stephen Greenblatt, *Learning to Curse: Essays in Early Modern Culture* (New York: Routledge, 1990), 169; Katharine Eisaman Maus, *Inwardness and Theater in the English Renaissance* (Chicago: University of Chicago Press, 1995), 26. Maus, however, influentially argued against this position.

35. Semler, "Renaissance Gets Emotional," 137.

36. White, Houlahan, and O'Loughlin, *Shakespeare and the Emotions*, 8; Strier, *Unrepentant Renaissance,* 17.

37. Paster; *Humoring the Body*, 11; Paster, Rowe, and Floyd-Wilson, *Reading the Early Modern Passions*, 2–3.

38. Gail Kern Paster, "The Pith and Marrow of Our Attribute: Dialogue of Skin and Skull in *Hamlet* and Holbein's *The Ambassadors*," *Textual Practice* 23, no. 2 (2009): 247. On a heuristics of sameness in a different Renaissance context, see Marjorie Rubright, *Doppelgänger Dilemmas: Anglo-Dutch Relations in Early Modern English Literature and Culture* (Philadelphia: University of Pennsylvania Press, 2014).

39. Jean E. Howard, "The New Historicism in Renaissance Studies," *English Literary Renaissance* 16, no. 1 (1986): 20.

40. Paster, "Pith and Marrow," 247.

41. Plamper, it should be noted, is skeptical of adopting this sort of attitude toward scientific claims (History of Emotion, 240–41).

42. Greenblatt, *Learning to Curse*, 222; Judith Newton, "History as Usual? Feminism and the 'New Historicism,'" *Cultural Critique* 9 (1988): 88. For a recent counterargument, however, see Kiernan Ryan, *Shakespeare's Universality: Here's Fine Revolution* (London: Bloomsbury, 2015).

43. Connolly, *Neuropolitics*, 3.

44. Catherine Belsey, "Biology and Imagination: The Role of Culture," in *Human Nature: Fact and Fiction*, ed. Robin Headlam Wells and Johnjoe McFadden (London: Continuum International, 2006), 125.

45. John Dupré, *Human Nature and the Limits of Science* (Oxford: Clarendon, 2001), 4.

46. F. Elizabeth Hart, "Epistemology of Cognitive Literary Studies," *Philosophy and Literature* 25, no. 2 (2001): 320–21. Or, as she puts it elsewhere, a "recognition that all the knowledge humans can experience is, by definition, *mediated*, first by individual bodies and brains, then by brains and minds, and finally by the aggregates of minds we call 'society' or 'culture' and without which (in feedback-loop dependency) individual brains and minds would fail to develop" (Hart, "A Paltry 'Hoop of Gold': Semantics and Systematicity in Early Modern Studies," in *The Return of Theory in Early Modern English Studies: Tarrying with the Subjunctive*, ed. Paul Cefalu and Bryan Reynolds [New York: Palgrave, 2011], 23).

47. Andy Mousley, "Introduction: Shakespeare and the Meaning of Life," *Shakespeare* 5, no. 2 (2009): 135.

48. Luc Faucher, "Constructionisms?" *Emotion Review* 5, no. 4 (2013): 374, 376.

49. N. Katherine Hayles, "Constrained Constructivism: Locating Scientific Inquiry in the Theater of Representation," in *Realism and Representation: Essays on the Problem of Realism in Relation to Science, Literature, and Culture*, ed. George Levine (Madison: University of Wisconsin Press, 1993), 27.

50. Jessie J. Prinz, *Gut Reactions: A Perceptual Theory of Emotion* (Oxford: Oxford University Press, 2004), 134.

51. Ellen Spolsky, "Darwin and Derrida: Cognitive Literary Theory as a Species of Post-Structuralism," *Poetics Today* 23, no. 1 (2002): 47

52. Simon Clarke, "Psychoanalytic Sociology and the Interpretation of Emotion," *Journal for the Theory of Social Behaviour* 33, no. 2 (2003): 147; Paul Cefalu and Bryan Reynolds, "Tarrying with the Subjunctive, an Introduction," in Cefalu and Reynolds, *Return of Theory,* 4. Patrick Colm Hogan has worked extensively on literary universals; see his "Literary Universals," *Poetics Today* 18, no. 2 (1997): 223–49; Patrick Colm Hogan, *The Mind and Its Stories* (Cambridge: Cambridge University Press, 2003); and Lalita Pandit and Patrick Colm Hogan, "Introduction: Morsels and Modules: On Embodying Cognition in Shakespeare's Plays," *College Literature* 33, no. 1 (2006): 1–13.

53. Amy Cook, "Interplay: The Method and Potential of a Cognitive Scientific Approach to Theatre," *Theatre Journal* 59, no. 4 (2007): 579–94; Amy Cook, *Shakespearean Neuroplay: Reinvigorating the Study of Dramatic Texts and Performance through Cognitive Science* (New York: Palgrave Macmillan, 2010); Mary Thomas Crane, *Shakespeare's Brain: Reading with Cognitive Theory* (Princeton, N.J.: Princeton University Press, 2001); Mary Thomas Crane, "Analogy, Metaphor, and the New Science: Cognitive Science and Early Modern Epistemology," in *Introduction to Cognitive Cultural Studies,* ed. Lisa Zunshine (Baltimore, Md.: Johns Hopkins University Press, 2010), 103–14; Arthur F. Kinney, *Shakespeare's Webs: Networks of Meaning in Renaissance Drama* (New York: Routledge, 2004); Arthur F. Kinney, *Shakespeare and Cognition: Aristotle's Legacy and Shakespearean Drama* (New York: Routledge,

2006); Evelyn B. Tribble, *Cognition in the Globe: Attention and Memory in Shakespeare's Theatre* (New York: Palgrave, 2011); and Laurie Johnson, John Sutton, and Evelyn Tribble, eds., *Embodied Cognition and Shakespeare's Theatre: The Early Modern Body-Mind* (New York: Routledge, 2014). See also Martin Pickavé and Lisa Shapiro, eds., *Emotion and Cognitive Life in Medieval and Early Modern Philosophy* (Oxford: Oxford University Press, 2012); Hogan, "Literary Brains"; and Zunshine, *Oxford Handbook of Cognitive Literary Studies*.

54. Susan J. Matt, "Current Emotion Research in History: or, Doing History from the Inside Out," *Emotion Review* 3, no. 1 (2011): 118. See also Faucher, "Constructionisms?"

55. William A. Mason and John P. Capitanio, "Basic Emotions: A Reconstruction," *Emotion Review* 4, no. 3 (2012): 239.

56. Ira J. Roseman, "Emotional Behaviors, Emotivational Goals, Emotion Strategies: Multiple Levels of Organization Integrate Variable and Consistent Responses," *Emotion Review* 3, no. 4 (2011): 434.

57. Protevi, *Political Affect*, 25, 24–25.

58. Jonathan H. Turner and Jan E. Stets, *The Sociology of Emotions* (Cambridge: Cambridge University Press, 2005), 10.

59. Clarke, "Psychoanalytic Sociology," 152.

60. Strier, *Unrepentant Renaissance*, 17.

61. It should be noted, however, that some researchers stress the positive implications of ostensibly negative emotions; see W. Gerrod Parrott, ed., *The Positive Side of Negative Emotions* (New York: Guilford, 2014).

62. Bradley J. Irish, "Gender and Politics in the Henrician Court: The Douglas-Howard Lyrics in the Devonshire Manuscript (BL Add 17492)," *Renaissance Quarterly* 61, no. 1 (2011): 79–114. Though women at court had unequal access to power, it is important to recognize that they did not lack political agency; see Joanne Lee Hocking, "Aristocratic Women at the Late Elizabethan Court: Politics, Patronage and Power," Ph.D. diss., University of Adelaide, 2015.

Chapter 1

1. Cornelis Metsys, *Henricvs Dei Gra[tie] Rex Anglie* (1548), Folger Shakespeare Library, ART 252711. Though the Folger engraving is dated 1548, it first appeared in 1544; see Greg Walker, *Persuasive Fictions: Faction, Faith, and Political Culture in the Reign of Henry VIII* (Aldershot, Eng.: Scholar, 1996), 79.

2. Arthur L. Schwarz, *Vivat Rex! An Exhibition Commemorating the 500th Anniversary of the Accession of Henry VIII* (New York: Grolier Club, 2009), 205.

3. Sebastian Giustinian, *Four Years at the Court of Henry VIII*, trans. Rawdon Brown, 2 vols. (London, 1854), 2:312.

4. See David Starkey, *Henry: Virtuous Prince* (London: Harper, 2008). For recent studies of Henry's afterlife, see Mark Rankin, Christopher Highley, and John N. King, eds., *Henry VIII and His Afterlives: Literature, Politics, and Art* (Cambridge: Cambridge University Press, 2009); and Thomas Betteridge and Thomas S. Freeman, eds., *Henry VIII and History* (Burlington, Vt.: Ashgate, 2012).

5. Sidney Young, ed., *The Annals of the Barber-Surgeons of London* (London, 1890), 522; *L&P* XIII(i), 995; XVI, 590.

6. David Starkey, ed., *The Inventory of King Henry VIII: The Transcript* (London: Harvey Miller, 1998), 263.

7. *L&P* II(i), 411; quoted in Susan Brigden, "Henry Howard, Earl of Surrey, and the 'Conjured League,'" *The Historical Journal* 37, no. 3 (1994): 510.

8. Garrett Mattingly, *Catherine of Aragon* (New York: Vintage Books, 1941), 224–25.

9. Wolsey was deemed *alter rex* by Venetian ambassador Antonio Surian in 1519; see *Calendar of State Papers and Manuscripts Relating to English Affairs, Existing in the Archives and Collections of Venice and in Other Libraries of Northern Italy*, ed. Rawdon Brown et al., 38 vols. (London, 1864–1947), II, 1296.

10. William Shakespeare, *King Henry VIII*, ed. Gordon McMullan (London: Arden Shakespeare, 2000), 1.1.52–53.

11. For this revisionist account, see Peter Gwyn, *The King's Cardinal: The Rise and Fall of Thomas Wolsey* (London: Barrie and Jenkins, 1990) [hereafter *KC*]. This, the most thorough scholarly biography of Wolsey, has greatly informed this chapter. On Wolsey's life, see also Sybil M. Jack's *ODNB* entry, as well as A. F. Pollard, *Wolsey: Church and State in Sixteenth-Century England* (New York: Harper and Row, 1966); S. J. Gunn and and P. G. Lindley, eds., *Cardinal Wolsey: Church, State and Art* (Cambridge: Cambridge University Press, 1991); Stella Fletcher, *Cardinal Wolsey: A Life in Renaissance Europe* (London: Continuum, 2009); and Gavin Schwartz-Leeper, *From Princes to Pages: The Literary Lives of Cardinal Wolsey, Tudor England's "Other King"* (Leiden: Brill, 2016).

12. BL, Egerton MS 2402, fol. 5 (4). Subsequent references to *The Life and Death of Cardinal Wolsey* [hereafter *LD*] refer to this manuscript; numbers in parentheses are keyed to the modern edition of George Cavendish, *The Life and Death of Cardinal Wolsey*, ed. Richard S. Sylvester (London: Oxford University Press, 1959). For scholarly commentary, see Jonathan V. Crewe, "The Wolsey Paradigm?" *Criticism* 30, no. 2 (1988): 153–69; and Mike Pincombe, "A Place in the Shade: George Cavendish and *De Casibus* Tragedy," in *The Oxford Handbook of Tudor Literature, 1485–1603*, ed. Mike Pincombe and Cathy Shrank (Oxford: Oxford University Press, 2009), 372–88.

13. According to Cavendish, Wolsey made a most favorable impression with the speed of his journey to the court of Emperor Maximilian—a round trip that lasted less than four days, and that left King Henry VII "in a great confuse & wonder of his hasty spede" (*LD*, fol. 7^{v} [9]).

14. Cavendish, *LD*, fol. 9^{v} (12).

15. On the early reign of Henry VIII, and Wolsey's place in it, see Gwyn, *KC*; Starkey, *Henry: Virtuous Prince*; and J. J. Scarisbrick, *Henry VIII* (Berkeley: University of California Press, 1968).

16. To become legate *a latere*—that is, legate "from the side" of the pope—was to reach the highest echelon of the church hierarchy besides the pope himself; the word of the legate *a latere*, in theory, was to be regarded as if it had come from the pope's mouth. With this appointment, Wolsey was confirmed the highest-ranking cleric in England, even though his archbishopric of York was, by itself, subordinate to William Warham's archbishopric of Canterbury. For a copy of the announcement, see BL, Cotton MS Vitellius B/III, fol. 267.

17. Desiderius Erasmus, *The Correspondence of Erasmus*, ed. R. A. B. Mynors et al., 15 vols. (Toronto: University of Toronto Press, 1974–2015), 6:366.

18. For a classic account of the divorce, see Henry Ansgar Kelly, *The Matrimonial Trials of Henry VIII* (Stanford, Calif.: Stanford University Press, 1976).

19. *L&P* IV(ii), 4112; Cavendish, *LD,* fol. 39v (74–75).

20. On Campeggio, see Edward Victor Cardinal, *Cardinal Lorenzo Campeggio, Legate to the Courts of Henry VIII and Charles* (Boston: Chapman and Grimes, 1935); and William E. Wilkie, *The Cardinal Protectors of England: Rome and the Tudors before the Reformation* (Cambridge: Cambridge University Press, 1974).

21. Henry's chances of receiving a favorable verdict in the 1529 legatine trial were not helped by the pacification of the Continental scene. One month before the trial's July adjournment, the Treaty of Barcelona confirmed peace between the papacy and the empire; one month after, the Treaty of Cambrai brought Francis and Charles to friendly terms. Such tidings did little for Henry's cause.

22. For an extensive discussion of the varied strategies through which Henrician writers brought forward complaints at court, see Greg Walker, *Writing under Tyranny: English Literature and the Henrician Reformation* (Oxford: Oxford University Press, 2005).

23. On Skelton's complex relationship to the Henrician court, see Greg Walker, "John Skelton and the Royal Court," in *John Skelton and Early Modern Culture: Papers Honoring Robert S. Kinsman*, ed. David R. Carlson (Tempe, Ariz.: Arizona Center for Medieval and Renaissance Studies, 2008), 3–18.

24. For the first half of the twentieth century, Wolsey was assumed to be the aggregate referent for the play's multiple vice figures; more recently, however, critics have equally associated the play with the "expulsion of the minions" of 1519, in which a gang of courtly favorites was restricted access within the king's household. See William O. Harris, *Skelton's Magnyfycence and the Cardinal Virtue Tradition* (Chapel Hill: University of North Carolina Press, 1965); Greg Walker, *Plays of Persuasion: Drama and Politics at the Court of Henry VIII* (Cambridge: Cambridge University Press, 1991), chap. 3; and John Scattergood, "Skelton's *Magnyfycence* and the Tudor Royal Household," *Medieval English Theatre* 15 (1993): 21–48.

25. For the poems of Skelton, discussed below, see *John Skelton: The Complete English Poems*, ed. John Scattergood (New York: Penguin Books, 1983), the edition from which I quote in this chapter. For general treatments, see William Nelson, "Skelton's Quarrel with Wolsey," *PMLA* 51, no. 2 (1936): 377–98; Delmas Crisp, "Cardinal Wolsey in Skelton's Poetry," *Innisfree* 2 (1975): 47–61; Greg Walker, *John Skelton and the Politics of the 1520s* (Cambridge: Cambridge University Press, 1988); Jane Griffiths, *John Skelton and Poetic Authority: Defining the Liberty to Speak* (Oxford: Clarendon, 2006); David R. Carlson, "Protestant Skelton: The Satires of 1519–1523 and the *Piers Plowman* Tradition," in Carlson, *John Skelton and Early Modern Culture,* 215–38; and Schwartz-Leeper, *From Princes to Pages*.

26. For discussion of this bizarre poem, see (in addition to Walker, *John Skelton*, and Schwartz-Leeper, *From Princes to Pages*) John M. Berdan, "Speke, Parrot: An Interpretation of Skelton's Satire," *Modern Language Notes* 30, no. 5 (1915): 140–44; John Chalker, "The Literary Seriousness of John Skelton's 'Speke, Parrot,'" *Neophilologus* 44, no. 1 (1960): 39–47; F. W. Brownlow, "*Speke, Parrot*: Skelton's Allegorical Denunciation of Cardinal Wolsey," *Studies in Philology* 65 (1968): 124–39; Nancy Coiner, "Galathea and the Interplay of Voices in Skelton's *Speke,*

Parrot," in *Subjects on the World's Stage: Essays on British Literature of the Middle Ages and the Renaissance*, ed. David G. Allen and Robert A. White (Newark, N.J.: University of Delaware Press, 1995), 88–99; and Simon Brittan, "Skelton's 'Speke Parott': Language, Madness and the Role of the Court Poet," *Renaissance Forum* 4, no. 1 (1999), http://www.hull.ac.uk/renforum/v4no1/brittan.htm.

27. See Paul E. McLane, "Prince Lucifer and the Fitful 'Lanternes of Lyght': Wolsey and the Bishops in Skelton's *Colyn Cloute*," *Huntington Library Quarterly* 43, no. 3 (1980): 159–79; and John Burrow, "The Argument of Skelton's *Collyn Clout*," *The Chaucer Review* 51, no. 4 (2016): 469–77.

28. Greg Walker, in his important full-length study *John Skelton and the Politics of the 1520s*, persuasively argues that the satirical performances must not be attributed to the poet's genuine conviction, but rather as a bid for patronage elsewhere. Shortly after producing his anti-Wolsey trilogy, Skelton dedicated "The Garlande or Chapelet of Laurell" to the cardinal, who apparently went on to sponsor two of the poet's final works, "Howe the Douty Duke of Albany" (1523–26) and "A Replycacion" (1528) (see Walker, *John Skelton,* chap. 6).

29. "Le Historye Cardinalis Eboracensis," in George Cavendish, *Metrical Visions*, ed. A. S. G. Edwards (Columbia: University of South Carolina Press, 1980). Cavendish, it must be noted, didn't compose the poem until years after his master's death.

30. Both poems are reprinted in the first volume of Frederick J. Furnivall, ed., *Ballads from Manuscripts*, 2 vols. (London, 1868–73).

31. On this text, see Walker, *Plays of Persuasion*, chap. 4; Greg Walker, *Reading Literature Historically: Drama and Poetry from Chaucer to the Reformation* (Edinburgh: Edinburgh University Press, 2013), chap. 2; and Schwartz-Leeper, *From Princes to Pages,* 24–36.

32. William Roy and Jerome Barlowe, *Rede Me and Be Nott Wrothe*, ed. Douglas H. Parker (Toronto: University of Toronto Press, 1992).

33. For discussion of the poem's structure, see Roy and Barlowe, *Rede Me and Be Nott Wrothe*, ed. Parker, 5–7.

34. See Donald Lateiner and Dimos Spatharas, eds., *The Ancient Emotion of Disgust* (Oxford: Oxford University Press, 2017), 18–21, 25–27. (Though disgust, it should be noted, doesn't figure into Catherine Keane, *Juvenal and the Satiric Emotions* [Oxford: Oxford University Press, 2015]). On scatology and satire generally, see Jae Num Lee, *Swift and Scatological Satire* (Albuquerque: University of New Mexico Press, 1971); Sidney Shrager, *Scatology in Modern Drama* (New York: Irvington, 1982), chap. 6; John R. Clark, *The Modern Satiric Grotesque and Its Traditions* (Lexington: University Press of Kentucky, 1991); Bruce Boehrer, "The Privy and Its Double: Scatology and Satire in Shakespeare's Theatre," in *A Companion to Shakespeare's Works, Volume IV: The Poems, Problem Comedies, Late Plays,* ed. Richard Dutton and Jean E. Howard (Malden, Mass.: Blackwell, 2003), 69–88; and David Musgrave, *Grotesque Anatomies: Menippean Satire since the Renaissance* (Newcastle upon Tyne, Eng.: Cambridge Scholars, 2014).

35. The word's etymology is discussed below. On disgust in the early modern period, see Benedict Robinson, "Disgust c. 1600," *ELH* 81, no. 2 (2014): 553–83; and Natalie K. Eschenbaum and Barbara Correll, eds., *Disgust in Early Modern Literature* (New York: Routledge, 2016). For disgust in the classical world, see Robert A. Kaster, "The Dynamics of 'Fastidium' and the Ideology of Disgust,"

Transactions of the American Philological Association 131 (2001): 143–89; and Lateiner and Spatharas, *Ancient Emotion of Disgust*.

36. Mary Douglas, *Purity and Danger: An Analysis of Concepts of Pollution and Taboo* (London: Routledge and Kegan Paul, 1966), 35. The importance of disgust in the early modern period may reflect Norbert Elias's controversial "civilizing hypothesis"—an argument for the increasing importance of institutionalized shame in the historical transition from the Middle Ages to modernity. Given the chronological sweep of Elias's argument, his more specific handling of data raises skepticism in some readers. For a snapshot of this debate, see Stephen Mennell and Johan Goudsblom, "Civilizing Processes—Myth or Reality? A Comment on Duerr's Critique of Elias," *Comparative Studies in Society and History* 39, no. 4 (1997): 729–33. For the current purposes, it is unnecessary to engage Elias's diachronic argument—but it is notable that he finds "court society" as the engine of the civilizing process, the site where "the moderation of passions, sublimation, is unmistakable and inevitable" (Elias, *The Civilizing Process: Sociogenetic and Psychogenetic Investigations* [Oxford: Blackwell, 1994], 246).

37. That the human response to disgust seems to be cross-culturally consistent is not, of course, to suggest that the *elicitors* of disgust are universal; see Uri Berger and David Anaki, "Demographic Influences on Disgust: Evidence from a Heterogeneous Sample," *Personality and Individual Differences* 64 (2014): 67–71, and see below.

38. First articulated by Darwin (see below), the universal disgust face involves, primarily, the gaping of the mouth and the wrinkling of the nose—a physiological response apt for the expulsion of food and the avoidance of noxious smells. (However, different domains of disgust—such as food-response disgust, animal-reminder disgust, or moral disgust—do seem to modulate our precise facial response; see Paul Rozin, Laura Lowery, and Rhonda Ebert, "Varieties of Disgust Faces and the Structure of Disgust," *Journal of Personality and Social Psychology* 66, no. 5 [1994]: 870–81.) On the disgust face, see Paul Ekman and Wallace V. Friesen, "Constants across Cultures in the Face and Emotion," *Journal of Personality and Social Psychology* 17, no. 2 (1971): 124–29; Sherri C. Widen and James A. Russell, "Children's and Adults' Understanding of the 'Disgust Face,'" *Cognition & Emotion* 22, no. 8 (2008): 1513–41; and Maren Westphal, George A. Bonanno, and Anthony D. Mancini, "Attachment and Attentional Biases for Facial Expressions of Disgust," *Journal of Social & Clinical Psychology* 33, no. 2 (2014): 169–86. Finally, it must be especially noted that Ekman's theories of facial recognition have been highly controversial; see James A. Russell, "Is There Universal Recognition of Emotion from Facial Expressions? A Review of the Cross-Cultural Studies," *Psychological Bulletin* 115, no. 1 (1994): 102–41; and Ruth Leys, *From Guilt to Shame: Auschwitz and After* (Princeton, N.J.: Princeton University Press, 2007), 138–45.

39. The somatic response to disgust includes "lowered blood pressure and galvanic skin response, nausea and actions including stopping, dropping the object of disgust and shuddering"; see Valerie Curtis, Robert Aunger, and Tamer Rabie, "Evidence That Disgust Evolved to Protect from Risk of Disease," *Proceedings of the Royal Society of London B (Biological Sciences)* 271, sup. 1 (2004): S131.

40. On neuro-anatomical activation, see below.

41. For discussion of recent research on disgust, see Bunmi O. Olatunji and Craig N. Sawchuk, "Disgust: Characteristic Features, Social Manifestations, and Clinical Implications," *Journal of Social and Clinical Psychology* 24, no. 7 (2005): 932–62; Valerie Curtis, "Why Disgust Matters," *Philosophical Transactions of the Royal Society B: Biological Sciences* 366, no. 1583 (2011): 3478–90; Joshua M. Tybur et al., "Disgust: Evolved Function and Structure," *Psychological Review* 120, no. 1 (2013): 65–84; Hanah A. Chapman and Adam K. Anderson, "Things Rank and Gross in Nature: A Review and Synthesis of Moral Disgust," *Psychological Bulletin* 139, no. 2 (2013): 300–327; and Ditte Marie Munch-Jurišić, "Perpetrator Abhorrence: Disgust as a Stop Sign," *Metaphilosophy* 45, no. 2 (2014): 270–87.

42. See William Ian Miller, *The Anatomy of Disgust* (Cambridge, Mass.: Harvard University Press, 1998); Robert Rawdon Wilson, *The Hydra's Tail: Imagining Disgust* (Edmonton: University of Alberta Press, 2002); Winfried Menninghaus, *Disgust: Theory and History of a Strong Sensation*, trans. Howard Eiland and Joel Golb (Albany: SUNY Press, 2003); Martha C. Nussbaum, *Hiding from Humanity: Disgust, Shame, and the Law* (Princeton, N.J.: Princeton University Press, 2004); Martha C. Nussbaum, *From Disgust to Humanity: Sexual Orientation and Constitutional Law* (Oxford: Oxford University Press, 2010); William A. Cohen and Ryan Johnson, eds., *Filth: Dirt, Disgust, and Modern Life* (Minneapolis: University of Minnesota Press, 2005); and Carolyn Korsmeyer, *Savoring Disgust: The Foul & the Fair in Aesthetics* (Oxford: Oxford University Press, 2011).

43. See, for example, the following exchange: Judith A. Toronchuk and George F. R. Ellis, "Disgust: Sensory Affect or Primary Emotional System?" *Cognition & Emotion* 21, no. 8 (2007): 1799–1818; Judith A. Toronchuk and George F. R. Ellis, "Criteria for Basic Emotions: Seeking DISGUST?" *Cognition & Emotion* 21, no. 8 (2007): 1829–32; Jaak Panksepp, "Criteria for Basic Emotions: Is DISGUST a Primary 'Emotion'?" *Cognition & Emotion* 21, no. 8 (2007): 1819–28.

44. Charles Darwin, *The Expression of the Emotions in Man and Animals* (New York, 1873), 257–61.

45. A. Angyal, "Disgust and Related Aversions," *Journal of Abnormal and Social Psychology* 36, no. 3 (1941): 394. With his emphasis on social taboos, Freud was a notable dissenter; he associated disgust primarily with sexual aversion. See *Three Essays on the Theory of Sexuality*, ed. James Strachey (New York: Basic Books, 2000), 17–18.

46. Paul Rozin and April E. Fallon, "A Perspective on Disgust," *Psychological Review* 94, no. 1 (1987): 23. The second half of the definition reflects the fact that the contagious properties of disgust follow the two basic laws of "sympathetic magic" first articulated by nineteenth-century anthropologists: the law of *contagion* suggests that once an object has been in contact with an object of disgust, it is forever contaminated, while the law of *similarity* suggests that sterile objects may be deemed offensive if they share properties (appearance, smell, etc.) with objects of disgust. See Paul Rozin, Linda Millman, and Carol Nemeroff, "Operation of the Laws of Sympathetic Magic in Disgust and Other Domains," *Journal of Personality and Social Psychology* 50, no. 4 (1986): 703–12; Paul Rozin and Carol Nemeroff, "The Laws of Sympathetic Magic: A Psychological Analysis of Similarity and Contagion," in *Cultural Psychology: Essays on*

Comparative Human Development, ed. James W. Stigler, Richard A. Shweder, and Gilbert Herdt (Cambridge: Cambridge University Press, 1990), 205–32; and S. Rachman, "Pollution of the Mind," *Behaviour Research and Therapy* 32, no. 3 (1994): 311–14.

47. See Yolanda Martins and Patricia Pliner, "'Ugh! That's Disgusting!': Identification of the Characteristics of Foods Underlying Rejections Based on Disgust," *Appetite* 46, no. 1 (2006): 75–85; and Birgit Mayer et al., "A Disgust Mood State Causes a Negative Interpretation Bias, But Not in the Specific Domain of Body-Related Concerns," *Behaviour Research and Therapy* 47, no. 10 (2009): 876–81.

48. Jonathan Haidt et al., "Body, Psyche, and Culture: The Relationship between Disgust and Morality," *Psychology and Developing Societies* 9, no. 1 (1997): 111. Unsurprisingly, a great deal of literature considers disgust in terms of a disease-avoidance model; see Valerie Curtis and Adam Biran, "Dirt, Disgust, and Disease: Is Hygiene in Our Genes?" *Perspectives in Biology and Medicine* 44, no. 1 (2001): 17–31; Curtis, Aunger, and Tamer, "Evidence That Disgust Evolved"; M. Rubio-Godoy, Robert Aunger, and Valerie Curtis, "Serotonin—a Link between Disgust and Immunity?" *Medical Hypotheses* 68, no. 1 (2007): 61–66; Richard J. Stevenson and Betty M. Repacholi, "Does the Source of an Interpersonal Odour Affect Disgust? A Disease Risk Model and Its Alternatives," *European Journal of Social Psychology* 35, no. 3 (2005): 375–401; and Graham C. L. Davey, "Disgust: The Disease-Avoidance Emotion and Its Dysfunctions," *Philosophical Transactions of the Royal Society B: Biological Sciences* 366, no. 1583 (2011): 3453–65.

49. See Jonathan Haidt, Clark McCauley, and Paul Rozin, "Individual Differences in Sensitivity to Disgust: A Scale Sampling Seven Domains of Disgust Elicitors," *Personality and Individual Differences* 16, no. 5 (1994): 701–13.

50. Ibid., 712, for the following quotations.

51. The saliency of the "animal reminder" category of disgust can be demonstrated by a piece of experiential evidence: of all the fluids produced by the human body, tears are almost universally acknowledged to be the least revolting. This seems to correlate with the fact that, with minor exception, tears (in their affective function) are a uniquely human phenomenon. See Sherry B. Ortner, "Sherpa Purity," *American Anthropologist* 75, no. 1 (1973): 57.

52. Bunmi O. Olatunji et al., "The Structure of Disgust: Domain Specificity in Relation to Contamination Ideation and Excessive Washing," *Behaviour Research and Therapy* 43, no. 8 (2005): 1069–86; Bunmi O. Olatunji et al., "The Disgust Scale: Item Analysis, Factor Structure, and Suggestions for Refinement," *Psychological Assessment* 19, no. 3 (2007): 281–97; Bunmi O. Olatunji et al., "Core, Animal Reminder, and Contamination Disgust: Three Kinds of Disgust with Distinct Personality, Behavioral, Physiological, and Clinical Correlates," *Journal of Research in Personality* 42, no. 5 (2008): 1243–59; and Bunmi O. Olatunji et al., "The Three Domains of Disgust Scale: Factor Structure, Psychometric Properties, and Conceptual Limitations," *Assessment* 19, no. 2 (2012): 205–25; as well as Joshua M. Tybur, Debra Lieberman, and Vladas Griskevicius, "Microbes, Mating, and Morality: Individual Differences in Three Functional Domains of Disgust," *Journal of Personality and Social Psychology* 97, no. 1 (2009): 103–22; and Tybur et al., "Disgust." Many discrete studies have investigated disgust in terms of (literal and symbolic) contamination fears; see Rachman, "Pollution

of the Mind"; S. Rachman, "Fear of Contamination," *Behaviour Research and Therapy* 42 (2004): 1227–55; Carol Nemeroff and Paul Rozin, "The Contagion Concept in Adult Thinking in the United States: Transmission of Germs and of Interpersonal Influence," *Ethos* 22, no. 2 (1994): 158–86; Paul Rozin et al., "The Borders of the Self: Contamination Sensitivity and Potency of the Body Apertures and Other Body Parts," *Journal of Research in Personality* 29, no. 3 (1995): 318–40; Nichole Fairbrother, Sarah J. Newth, and S. Rachman, "Mental Pollution: Feelings of Dirtiness without Physical Contact," *Behaviour Research and Therapy* 43, no. 1 (2005): 121–30; and Daniel M. T. Fessler and Kevin J. Haley, "Guarding the Perimeter: The Outside-Inside Dichotomy in Disgust and Bodily Experience," *Cognition & Emotion* 20, no. 1 (2006): 3–19.

53. Unsurprisingly, this general avoidance function of disgust seems to be particularly active in those with phobias and anxiety disorders. See, for example, Graham C. L. Davey, Sarah Bickerstaffe, and Benie A. MacDonald, "Experienced Disgust Causes a Negative Interpretation Bias: A Causal Role for Disgust in Anxious Psychopathology," *Behaviour Research and Therapy* 44, no. 10 (2006): 1375–84.

54. Jorge Moll et al., "The Moral Affiliations of Disgust: A Functional MRI Study," *Cognitive and Behavioral Neurology* 18, no. 1 (2005): 68.

55. See Edward B. Royzman and John Sabini, "Something It Takes to Be an Emotion: The Interesting Case of Disgust," *Journal for the Theory of Social Behaviour* 31, no. 1 (2001): 29–59; Robin L. Nabi, "The Theoretical versus the Lay Meaning of Disgust: Implications for Emotion Research," *Cognition and Emotion* 16, no. 5 (2002): 695–703; and Roberto Gutierrez, Roger Giner-Sorolla, and Milica Vasiljevic, "Just an Anger Synonym? Moral Context Influences Predictors of Disgust Word Use," *Cognition and Emotion* 26, no. 1 (2012): 53–64.

56. See Jonathan Haidt, Silvia Helena Koller, and Maria G. Dias, "Affect, Culture, and Morality, or Is It Wrong to Eat Your Dog?" *Journal of Personality and Social Psychology* 65, no. 4 (1993): 613–28.

57. Bodily and sociomoral domains overlap semantically, for example, in *degout* (French), *ekel* (German), *otvrashchenie* (Russian), *asco* (Spanish), *go-at* (Hebrew), *ken'o* (Japanese), *aw-shin* (Chinese), and *ghenna* (Bengali). See Haidt et al., "Body, Psyche, and Culture," 117.

58. On moral disgust, see, for example, Roger Giner-Sorolla et al., "Emotions in Sexual Morality: Testing the Separate Elicitors of Anger and Disgust," *Cognition and Emotion* 26, no. 7 (2012): 1208–22; Chapman and Anderson, "Things Rank and Gross in Nature"; and Westphal, Bonanno, and Mancini, "Attachment and Attentional Biases."

59. Douglas, *Purity and Danger*, 138.

60. See Edward B. Royzman, Robert F. Leeman, and John Sabini, "'You Make Me Sick': Moral Dyspepsia as a Reaction to Third-Party Sibling Incest," *Motivation and Emotion* 32, no. 2 (2008): 100–108.

61. See Gary D. Sherman, Jonathan Haidt, and James A. Coan, "The Psychophysiology of Moral Disgust: Throat Tightness and Heart Rate Deceleration," unpublished manuscript. I am thankful to Dr. Sherman for sharing his study with me.

62. Royzman, Leeman, and Sabini, "'You Make Me Sick,'" 100. See also H. A. Chapman et al., "In Bad Taste: Evidence for the Oral Origins of Moral Disgust," *Science* 323, no. 1222 (2009): 1222–26; Kendall J. Eskine, Natalie A. Kacinik,

and Jesse J. Prinz, "A Bad Taste in the Mouth: Gustatory Disgust Influences Moral Judgment," *Psychological Science* 22, no. 3 (2011): 295–99; and Rachel S. Herz, "Verbal Priming and Taste Sensitivity Make Moral Transgressions Gross," *Behavioral Neuroscience* 128, no. 1 (2014): 20–28.

63. Moll et al., "Moral Affiliations of Disgust," 75. On the neuroanatomy of disgust, see Bruno Wicker et al., "Both of Us Disgusted in *My* Insula: The Common Neural Basis of Seeing and Feeling Disgust," *Neuron* 40, no. 3 (2003): 655–64; P. Wright et al., "Disgust and the Insula: fMRI Responses to Pictures of Mutilation and Contamination," *NeuroReport* 15, no. 15 (2004): 2347–51; Elisa Ciaramelli et al., "Damage to the Ventromedial Prefrontal Cortex Reduces Interpersonal Disgust," *Social Cognitive and Affective Neuroscience* 8, no. 2 (2013): 171–80; and Charmaine Borg et al., "Disgust Trait Modulates Frontal-Posterior Coupling as a Function of Disgust Domain," *Social Cognitive and Affective Neuroscience* 8, no. 3 (2013): 351–58. For a critique, see Ruth Leys, "'Both of Us Disgusted in My Insula': Mirror Neuron Theory and Emotional Empathy," *Nonsite.org 5* (2012), http://nonsite.org/article/%E2%80%9Cboth-of-us-disgusted-in-my-insula%E2%80%9D-mirror-neuron-theory-and-emotional-empathy.

64. See Sarah L. Marzillier and Graham C. L. Davey, "The Emotional Profiling of Disgust-Eliciting Stimuli: Evidence for Primary and Complex Disgusts," *Cognition & Emotion* 18, no. 3 (2004): 313–36.

65. Moll et al., "Moral Affiliations of Disgust," 69.

66. Paul Rozin et al., "The CAD Triad Hypothesis: A Mapping between Three Moral Emotions (Contempt, Anger, Disgust) and Three Moral Codes (Community, Autonomy, Divinity)," *Journal of Personality and Social Psychology* 76, no. 4 (1999): 576; Richard A. Shweder et al., "The 'Big Three' of Morality (Autonomy, Community, Divinity) and the 'Big Three' Explanations of Suffering," in *Morality and Health,* ed. Allan M. Brandt and Paul Rozin (New York: Routledge, 1997), 138.

67. See Stephen Jay Gould, "Exaptation: A Crucial Tool for Evolutionary Psychology," *Journal of Social Issues* 47 (1991): 43–65; and Stephen Jay Gould and Elisabeth S. Vrba, "Exaptation—A Missing Term in the Science of Form," *Paleobiology* 8, no. 1 (1982): 4–15. On disgust as exaptation, see Royzman, Leeman, and Sabini, "'You Make Me Sick,'" 100.

68. Haidt et al., "Body, Psyche, and Culture," 108.

69. Simone Schnall et al., "Disgust as Embodied Moral Judgment," *Personality and Social Psychology Bulletin* 34, no. 8 (2008): 1105.

70. See Thalia Wheatley and Jonathan Haidt, "Hypnotic Disgust Makes Moral Judgments More Severe," *Psychological Science* 16, no. 10 (2005): 780–84.

71. Bioethicist Leon Kass, former chairman (2001–2005) of the President's Council on Bioethics, has famously argued for the "wisdom of repugnance"—that is, the ability of visceral disgust responses to communicate a fundamental moral truth, above and beyond the dictates of pure rationality. (Kass employs this concept to oppose issues such as human cloning.) The philosopher Martha Nussbaum, on the other hand, has forcefully argued against a disgust-based morality. See Leon R. Kass, "The Wisdom of Repugnance," *The New Republic* 216, no. 22 (1997): 17–26; Nussbaum, *Hiding from Humanity*; Nussbaum, *From Disgust to Humanity*; Roger Kimball, "Does Shame Have a Future?" *New Criterion* 23, no. 1 (2004): 4–9; and Munch-Jurišić, "Perpetrator Abhorrence."

72. Paul Rozin et al., "Disgust: Preadaptation and the Cultural Evolution of a Food-Based Emotion," in *Food Preference and Taste: Continuity and Change*, ed. Helen Macbeth (Providence, R.I.: Berghahn Books, 1997), 73, 72. See also Erin E. Buckels and Paul D. Trapnell, "Disgust Facilitates Outgroup Dehumanization," *Group Processes & Intergroup Relations* 16, no. 6 (2013): 771–80.

73. Lasana T. Harris and Susan T. Fiske, "Perceiving Humanity or Not: A Social Neuroscience Approach to Dehumanized Perception," in *Social Neuroscience: Toward Understanding the Underpinnings of the Social Mind*, ed. Alexander Todorov, Susan T. Fiske, and Deborah A. Prentice (Oxford: Oxford University Press, 2011), 125, 126.

74. John Florio, *A Worlde of Wordes, or Most Copious, and Exact Dictionarie in Italian and English* (London, 1598), 370. Florio confirms the generalized form in the definition of Disparére, which he renders "a disopinion, a diuersitie in conceit. . . . Also a disgust or vnkindnes" (108). Incidentally, the word "distaste" seems to have entered the language near-concurrently with "disgust"; its first recorded appearance (in the verbal form) occurs in 1586 (Oxford English Dictionary, "distaste, v.").

75. Randle Cotgrave, *A Dictionarie of the French and English Tongues* (London, 1611), Bb; Aavi^{v}.

76. Anthony Copley, *Another Letter of Mr. A.C. to His Dis-Iesuited Kinseman* (London, 1602), 25.

77. See, for example, Christopher Bagshaw, *A Sparing Discouerie of Our English Iesuits, and of Fa. Parsons Proceedings Vnder Pretence of Promoting the Catholike Faith in England* (London, 1601), 33; Robert Parsons, *A Manifestation of the Great Folly and Bad Spirit of Certayne in England Calling Themselues Secular Priestes* (Antwerp, 1602), 92; and Robert Parsons, *A Treatise Tending to Mitigation Towardes Catholike-Subiectes in England* (Saint-Omer, 1607), 78.

78. See the discussion of pre-Cartesian physiology in the "Introduction."

79. Mikhail Bakhtin, *Rabelais and His World*, trans. Hélène Iswolsky (Bloomington: Indiana University Press, 1984), 29.

80. Note that this response is directed from both ends of the social hierarchy; a satirical vocabulary is largely shared by populist (in, for example, the folk ballad tradition) and aristocratic (in, for example, letters and official accounts) attacks on Wolsey. An approach to this data set thus benefits from the more general caution of Susan Signe Morrison, who has recently argued that we must "temper Bakhtin's misleading implication that the folk enjoyed excreta while aristocrats and clerics disdained them; [because] negative and positive views of excreta cut across class divisions"; see Morrison, *Excrement in the Late Middle Ages: Sacred Filth and Chaucer's Fecopoetics* (New York: Palgrave 2008), 7.

81. According to Gwyn, there are only two surviving near-contemporary images of Wolsey. The first, by an unknown artist, is the image that immortalized the notion of a fat Wolsey; Gwyn, however, notes that "it was never intended to be an accurate representation." The other portrait, of French origin in 1567, "suggests a much thinner man" (*KC*, xvi).

82. Skelton, *Speke, Parott*, line 492.

83. Cavendish, *LD*, fol. 17^{v} (28).

84. Ibid., 37^{v} (70–71).

85. Giustinian, *Four Years*, 2:315.

86. *L&P* III(i), 634, 647.

87. John Skelton, *Why Come Ye Nat to Courte?* lines 1078–84. Skelton's image of the pig being cloaked as a fish was apparently proverbial: in *Confutation of Tyndale's Answer*, for example, Thomas More speaks of the "llollardes . . . that put a pygge in to the water, on good frydate / and sayd go in pygge and come oute pyke / and so when they had chaunged the name, the toke yt for fyshe and ete yt." This passage is quoted and discussed in Charles Clay Doyle, "Lenten Fare and the Language of Falsehood: Pig and Pike, Fish and Fowl," *Albion* 10 (1978): 29.

88. Polydore Vergil, *The Anglica Historia of Polydore Vergil A.D. 1485–1537*, ed. Denys Hay (London: Royal Historical Society, 1950), 293.

89. Skelton, *Why Come Ye Nat to Courte?* line 71. In *Magnyfycence*, it is worth noting, the vice figures Fansy and Courtly Abusyon are both associated with fatness; see Schwartz-Leeper, *From Princes to Pages*, 35.

90. Skelton, *Why Come Ye Nat to Courte?* lines 217–26.

91. Thomas Churchyard, "Thomas Wolsey," in *The Mirror for Magistrates*, ed. Lily B. Campbell (New York: Barnes and Noble, 1960), lines 22–27.

92. Skelton, *Collyn Clout*, lines 649–59. Skelton's use of "mammock" ("A scrap or shred, a broken or torn piece"), in the *OED*'s first recorded example, is suggestive: though the term entails a general association with shredding and tearing, many of the more notable usages in the *OED* have an oral component, as in the examples of Shakespeare ("Hee did so set his teeth, and teare it. Oh, I warrant how he mammockt it") and Milton ("The obscene, and surfeted Priest scruples not to paw, and mammock the sacramentall bread"). See both "mammock, *v.*" and "mammock, *n.*"

93. See Jack's discussion in the *ODNB* entry.

94. Roy and Barlowe, *Rede Me and Be Nott Wrothe*, lines 1167–74.

95. Skelton, *Why Come Ye Nat to Courte?* lines 1167–70.

96. Garrett Mattingly, *Further Supplement to Letters, Despatches and State Papers, Relating to the Negotiations Between England and Spain* (London: H.M. Stationery Office, 1940), 164.

97. "Surely if he had been promiscuous," Gwyn continues, "international gossip would have soon got hold of it" (*KC*, xvii).

98. Skelton, *Why Come Ye Nat to Courte?* Epilogue, line 36.

99. Skelton, *Why Come Ye Nat to Courte?* lines 1181–85, 1197–1201.

100. ["Neapolitano morbo gravatum
Malagmate cataplasmate stratum,
Pharmacopole ferro foratum,
Nihilo magis alleviatum,
Nihilo melius aut medicatum . . .
A modo ergo ganea
Abhoreat ille ganeus,
Dominus male creticus,
Aptius dictus tetricus,
Phanaticus freneticus."]

Skelton, *Why Come Ye Nat to Courte?* Epilogue, lines 6–10; 14–18 (Scattergood's translation, 494).

101. Skelton, *Speke, Parott*, lines 509–10.

102. "Of the Cardnall Wolse," line 21.
103. "An Impeachment of Wolsey," line 197.
104. Skelton, *Why Come Ye Nat to Courte?* lines 294–98; 304–5.
105. Roy and Barlowe, *Rede Me and Be Nott Wrothe*, line 3414.
106. "Of the Cardnall Wolse," lines 26–27.
107. Frank Whigham, "Reading Social Conflict in the Alimentary Tract: More on the Body in Renaissance Drama," *ELH* 55, no. 2 (1988): 333–50. Similarly, Paster argues that "scatology was a primary discourse in the period for the expression of aggression in unequal power relations" (*Humoring the Body*, 51–52); see also Bruce Thomas Boehrer, *The Fury of Men's Gullets: Ben Jonson & the Digestive Canal* (Philadelphia: University of Pennsylvania Press, 1997). This is hardly a phenomenon restricted to the early modern period; researchers have devoted significant attention to how disgust informs the operation of class prejudice. See Gordon Hodson and Kimberly Costello, "Interpersonal Disgust, Ideological Orientations, and Dehumanization as Predictors of Intergroup Attitudes," *Psychological Science* 18, no. 8 (2007): 691–98.
108. Roy and Barlowe, *Rede Me and Be Nott Wrothe*, line 196.
109. Skelton, *Why Come Ye Nat to Courte?* lines 487–94.
110. Skelton, *Collyn Clout*, lines 643–47.
111. These are the words of Thomas Wyatt, who found himself facing treason charges for (among other things) having ambiguously linked King Henry to the figure of the cart. For discussion of this, and the cart figure generally, see the introduction to George Puttenham, *The Art of English Poesy*, ed. Frank Whigham and Wayne A. Rebhorn (Ithaca, N.Y.: Cornell University Press, 2007), 1–3. Whigham and Rebhorn suggest that the word was imbued with "multivalent and near-sulfuric energy" (2); the Wyatt line is quoted at 3.
112. On the varied textures of the word "defilement," see Frank Whigham, *Seizures of the Will in Early Modern English Drama* (Cambridge: Cambridge University Press, 1996), 196.
113. Giustinian, *Four Years*, 2:314.
114. Skelton, *Collyn Clout*, lines 703–7.
115. "Of the Cardnall Wolse," lines 12–14.
116. "An Impeachment of Wolsey," lines 2–3, 29–30.
117. Skelton, *Collyn Clout*, lines 989; 991–92.
118. TNA, SP 1/14, fol. 179. See the introduction to the next chapter for discussion of Suffolk's role in this passage.
119. William Tyndale, *Expositions and Notes on Sundry Portions of the Holy Scriptures: Together with The Practice of Prelates*, ed. Henry Walter (Cambridge: Cambridge University Press, 1849), 308. Tyndale's expression suggests that the witchcraft involves a misdirection of the king's erotic attention; Wolsey is perhaps implicitly linked to anti-papal notions of clerical sodomy.
120. Skelton, *Why Come Ye Nat to Courte?* lines 658–66.
121. On sympathetic magic, see note 46 above.
122. Giustinian, *Four Years*, 2:314.
123. Edward Hall, *Chronicle Containing the History of England* (London, 1809), 767. The "boke," to my knowledge, does not survive (if it existed at all), but the complaints have been recorded in Hall; see also below.
124. Skelton, *Why Come Ye Nat to Courte?* lines 401–9.

125. Roy and Barlowe, *Rede Me and Be Nott Wrothe*, 50.
126. Ibid., 52.
127. Ibid., lines 9, 10–14.
128. Ibid., lines 19–21.
129. Ibid., lines 22–23, 28.
130. Churchyard, "Thomas Wolsey," lines 365–73.
131. Skelton, *Magnyfycence*, lines 2351–58.
132. TNA, SP 1/44, fol. 43^{v}. For Wolsey's downfall, see Gwyn, *KC*, chaps. 13–14; G. W. Bernard, "The Fall of Wolsey Reconsidered," *Journal of British Studies* 35, no. 3 (1996): 277–310; E. W. Ives, "The Fall of Wolsey," in Gunn and Lindley, *Cardinal Wolsey,* 286–315; and Patrick Hornbeck, "The Conversion of the Cardinal? Pride and Penitence in Some Tudor Histories of Thomas Wolsey," *HTS Teologiese Studies/Theological Studies* 72, no. 1 (2016): 1–10.
133. Hall, *Chronicle Containing the History of England*, 759.
134. *L&P* IV(iii), 5953, 5983.
135. For more detail, see Bradley J. Irish, "'Not Cardinal, but King:' Thomas Wolsey and the Henrician Diplomatic Imagination," in *Authority and Diplomacy from Dante to Shakespeare*, ed. Jason Powell and William T. Rossiter (Burlington, Vt.: Ashgate, 2013), 85–100.
136. Cavendish, *LD*, fol. 50 (98).
137. See, for example, *L&P* IV(iii), 6019: "I have heard that Wolsey has just been put out of his house, and all his goods taken into the King's hands. . . . They accuse him of [so many things] that he is quite undone."
138. After his arrest, Cavendish reports, Wolsey received good news: "[The king] hathe commaundyd me first to sey vnto you that you shold assure your self that he berythe you as myche good wyll & fauour as euer he dyd and wyllyth you to be of good chere" (*LD*, fol. 85^{v}–86 [172]).
139. For foreign bodies and social pathology in a different context, see Jonathan Gil Harris, *Foreign Bodies and the Body Politic: Discourses of Social Pathology in Early Modern England* (Cambridge: Cambridge University Press, 1998).
140. Hall, *Chronicle Containing the History of England*, 764.
141. *OED*, "scab, *n.*" Our most familiar usage—"the crust which forms over a wound or sore during cicatrization"—was also available.
142. Edward Coke, *The Fourth Part of the Institutes of the Laws of England* (London, 1797), 89–90.
143. Hall, *Chronicle Containing the History of England*, 768.
144. Furthermore, the image of whispering, in which Wolsey's speech is being implanted into the king's brain, (inversely) recalls the ventriloquism described above by Giustinian, in which the cardinal co-opted the king's verbal prerogative.
145. *OED*, "impostume, *n.* 2.a." The *OED* first records this metaphoric usage in 1565, though it seems likely that it may have been available earlier.
146. *L&P* IV(iii), 6335.
147. Cavendish, *LD*, fol. 67 (133).
148. Gwyn, *KC*, 618.
149. On Wolsey's fall, see note 132.
150. Cavendish, *LD*, fols. 79^{v}–80 (159–60).
151. Ibid., fol. 81 (162).
152. Ibid., fol. 83^{v} (167).

153. Ibid., fol. 84 (168). "Avoid" here means "belch/expel."

154. Ibid., fol. 84; 85 (168, 171).

155. See *OED*.

156. Cavendish, *LD*, fol. 86 (173).

157. Despite his personal relations with Wolsey, Cavendish's account is no simple hagiography: the cardinal's death, he reflects, reveals "thend and Fall of pryde and arrogauncye of suche men, exalted by Fortune to honour & highe dygnytes" (fol. 90 [182]).

158. Ibid., fol. 86–86^{v} (173–74).

159. Ibid., fol. 88^{v} (178).

160. That is to say, in the satires, Wolsey is the explicit object of both material and moral disgust; in Cavendish's narrative, the second term is essentially absent, but is implied nonetheless through the account of Wolsey's physical degeneration.

161. Francesco Guicciardini, *The Historie of Guicciardin Conteining the Warres of Italie and Other Partes* (London, 1579), 1139.

162. Charles Wriothesley, *A Chronicle of England during the Reigns of the Tudors, from A.D. 1485 to 1559*, ed. William Douglas Hamilton, 2 vols. (Westminster, 1875–77), 1:16. Wriothesley's cousin Thomas spent his early career in Wolsey's service, and would eventually become lord chancellor himself. On early modern purgatives, see Gail Kern Paster, "Purgation as the Allure of Mastery: Early Modern Medicine and the Technology of the Self," in *Material London, Ca. 1600,* ed. Lena Cowen Orlin (Philadelphia: University of Pennsylvania Press, 2000), 193–205.

163. ["tomó alguna ponzoña para morir, por no venir á otra muerte más vergonzosa."] Mariano Roca de Togores Molins, ed., *Crónica del Rey Enrico Otavo de Ingalaterra* (Madrid, 1874), 36.

164. John Foxe, *The Unabridged Acts and Monuments Online or TAMO* (1583 edition), HRI Online Publications: Sheffield, 2011, http://www.johnfoxe.org, 1020, for this and the next quote. For a discussion of Wolsey's portrayal by Foxe, see Schwartz-Leeper, *From Princes to Pages,* chap. 3; see also Thomas Freeman, "Hands Defiled with Blood: Henry VIII in Foxe's *Book of Martyrs*," in Betteridge and Freeman, *Henry VIII and History,* 87–118.

165. Foxe, *Unabridged Acts and Monuments* (1583), 2138, 2137, 1811.

166. Hall, *Chronicle Containing the History of England*, 774, for this and the next quotation. More generally, see Lucas, "From Perfect Prince."

167. Thomas Thomas, *Dictionarium Linguae Latinae et Anglicanae* (London, 1587), Kkk iiij^{v}–v. (In fact, some researchers argue that "indignation" is simply the word we use for moralized disgust; see Moll et al., "Moral Affiliations of Disgust.") "Stomach" might also "designate the inward seat of passion, emotion, secret thoughts, affections, or feelings" (*OED*, *n.* 6.a.).

168. Thomas Cromwell, *The Life and Letters of Thomas Cromwell*, ed. Roger Bigelow Merriman, 2 vols. (Oxford: Clarendon, 1902), 1:36.

169. Cavendish, *LD*, fol. 85^{v} (172).

170. Julia Kristeva, *Powers of Horror: An Essay on Abjection*, trans. Leon S. Roudiez (New York: Columbia University Press, 1982), 2, for this and the following quotation.

171. ["Yo creo que adivinó que yo le queria hacer dar otra muerte."] Molins, *Crónica*, 37.

172. Kristeva, *Powers of Horror*, 4, for this and the following quotation.

Chapter 2

1. Hall, *Chronicle Containing the History of England*, 758.

2. S. J. Gunn, *Charles Brandon, Duke of Suffolk, c. 1484–1545* (Oxford: Basil Blackwell, 1988), 2.

3. *L&P* III(i), 1284.

4. ["ex Dama procerem fecit."] *L&P* I(ii), 2610; see Gunn, *Charles Brandon*, 26.

5. Persius, *The Satires of Persius*, trans. W. S. Merwin (London: Anvil Press Poetry, 1981), 78; see Llewelyn Morgan, "Satire," in *A Companion to Latin Literature,* ed. Stephen Harrison (Malden, Mass.: Blackwell, 2005), 183 for original text and discussion of the passage.

6. François Foppens, ed., *Lettres du Roi Louis XII et du Cardinal George d'Amboise*, 4 vols. (Brussels, 1712), 4:197.

7. TNA, SP 1/14, fol. 179. See chapter 1, page 39.

8. See chapter 1, page 25.

9. See David Konstan and Keith Rutter, eds., *Envy, Spite and Jealousy: The Rivalrous Emotions in Ancient Greece* (Edinburgh: Edinburgh University Press, 2003).

10. On Surrey's elegies to Wyatt, see C. W. Jentoft, "Surrey's Five Elegies: Rhetoric, Structure, and the Poetry of Praise," *PMLA* 91, no. 1 (1976): 23–32; Frederic B. Tromly, "Surrey's Fidelity to Wyatt in 'Wyatt Resteth Here,'" *Studies in Philology* 77, no. 4 (1980): 376–87; William A. Sessions, "Surrey's Wyatt: Autumn 1542 and the New Poet," in *Rethinking the Henrician Era: Essays on Early Tudor Texts and Contexts,* ed. Peter C. Herman (Urbana: University of Illinois Press, 1994), 168–92; José María Pérez Fernández, "'Wyatt Resteth Here': Surrey's Republican Elegy," *Renaissance Studies* 18, no. 2 (2004): 208–38; Walker, *Writing under Tyranny,* chap. 16; and Ryan Hackenbracht, "Mourning the Living: Surrey's 'Wyatt Resteth Here,' Henrician Funerary Debates, and the Passing of National Virtue," *Renaissance & Reformation/Renaissance et Réforme* 35, no. 2 (2012): 61–82. I plan on treating the role of envy in the Wyatt elegies in a separate study.

11. See Jonathan V. Crewe, *Trials of Authorship: Anterior Forms and Poetic Reconstruction from Wyatt to Shakespeare* (Berkeley: University of California Press, 1990), chap. 2; Stephen Guy-Bray, "'We Two Boys Together Clinging': The Earl of Surrey and the Duke of Richmond," *English Studies in Canada* 21, no. 2 (1995): 138–50; and Candice Lines, "The Erotic Politics of Grief in Surrey's 'So Crewell Prison,'" *SEL Studies in English Literature* 46, no. 1 (2006): 1–26.

12. For a modern biography of Fitzroy, see Beverley Anne Murphy, *Bastard Prince: Henry VIII's Lost Son* (Stroud, Eng.: Sutton, 2001), and her entry in the *ODNB*.

13. *CSPS*, IV(i), 228 for this and the next quotation.

14. *L&P* XI, 40; TNA, SP 1/105, fol. 74v.

15. *L&P* XI, 147.

16. Wriothesley, *Chronicle*, 1:53. Some scholars, such as Murphy, place his death on the 23rd (see *ODNB*).

17. *L&P* XI, 221.

18. TNA, SP 1/105, fol. 249; 248v. George Cotton was the gentleman usher and "somtyme gouernor to the late Duke of Richmont" (SP 1/107, fol. 88); his brother Richard was the clerk comptroller of Richmond's household. See Charles John Longcroft, *A Topographical Account of the Hundred of Bosmere, in the County of Southampton, Including the Parishes of Havant, Warblington, and Hayling* (London, 1857), 329. On Richmond's burial, see Nicola Clark, "The Gendering of Dynastic Memory: Burial Choices of the Howards, 1485–1559," *The Journal of Ecclesiastical History* (2017): 1–19 [Advance Access: DOI:10.1017/S0022046916001500].

19. TNA, SP 1/122, fol. 238v.

20. See R. W. Hoyle, *The Pilgrimage of Grace and the Politics of the 1530s* (Oxford: Oxford University Press, 2001).

21. As we will see, Surrey here anticipates a maneuver of the great Elizabethan favorites, such as the earls of Leicester and Essex, who routinely feigned sickness for strategic ends. George Puttenham, for example, noted that a courtier may "feign himself sick to shun the business in court" (*Art of English Poesy*, 379).

22. William A. Sessions, *Henry Howard, the Poet Earl of Surrey: A Life* (Oxford: Oxford University Press, 1999), 129–30. This, the current scholarly biography of Surrey, should be used in conjunction with Edwin Casady, *Henry Howard, Earl of Surrey* (New York: Modern Language Association, 1938); Jessie Childs, *Henry VIII's Last Victim: The Life and Times of Henry Howard, Earl of Surrey* (London: Vintage Books, 2006); and Susan Brigden's excellent *ONDB* entry. Note that it is unclear whether Surrey was born in late 1516 or early 1517; accordingly, when I refer to his age throughout, it is an approximation.

23. See 33 Henry VIII c.12, in *Statutes of the Realm*, 11 vols. (London, 1810–28), 3:845–49. This "Acte for Murther and malicious Bloudshed within the Courte" codified the standing penalties for violence near the king in 1541.

24. On this phenomenon generally, see Mervyn James, *Society, Politics and Culture: Studies in Early Modern England* (Cambridge: Cambridge University Press, 1986), chap. 8; see also William A. Sessions, "'Enough Survives': The Earl of Surrey and European Court Culture," *History Today* 41, no. 6 (1991): 48–54.

25. See Brigden, "Henry Howard"; and Peter R. Moore, "The Heraldic Charge against the Earl of Surrey, 1546–47," *The English Historical Review* 116, no. 467 (2001): 557–83.

26. On envy as a character trait, see Richard H. Smith et al., "Dispositional Envy," *Personality and Social Psychology Bulletin* 25, no. 8 (1999): 1007–20.

27. Ibid., 1007; see also Helmut Schoeck, *Envy: A Theory of Social Behaviour* (New York: Harcourt, Brace and World, 1969).

28. See René Girard, *A Theater of Envy: William Shakespeare* (Oxford: Oxford University Press, 1991).

29. W. Gerrod Parrott and Richard H. Smith, "Distinguishing the Experiences of Envy and Jealousy," *Journal of Personality and Social Psychology* 64, no. 6 (1993): 906

30. Maria Miceli and Cristiano Castelfranchi, "The Envious Mind," *Cognition & Emotion* 21, no. 3 (2007): 450.

31. See Richard H. Smith et al., "Subjective Injustice and Inferiority as Predictors of Hostile and Depressive Feelings in Envy," *Personality and Social Psychology Bulletin* 20, no. 6 (1994): 705–11.

32. Peter Salovey and Judith Rodin, "Provoking Jealousy and Envy: Domain Relevance and Self-Esteem Threat," *Journal of Social and Clinical Psychology* 10, no. 4 (1991): 397.

33. See Niels van de Ven, Marcel Zeelenberg, and Rik Pieters, "Leveling Up and Down: The Experiences of Benign and Malicious Envy," *Emotion* 9, no. 3 (2009): 419–29; and Niels van de Ven, "Envy and Its Consequences: Why It Is Useful to Distinguish between Benign and Malicious Envy," *Social and Personality Psychology Compass* 10, no. 6 (2016): 337–49.

34. For envy in the Renaissance, see R. B. Gill, "The Renaissance Conventions of Envy," *Medievalia et Humanistica* 9 (1979): 215–30; and Lynn S. Meskill, *Ben Jonson and Envy* (Cambridge: Cambridge University Press, 2009); on the Middle Ages, see Jessica Rosenfeld, "Envy and Exemplarity in *The Book of Margery Kempe*," *Exemplaria* 26, no. 1 (2014): 105–21; on the classical period, see Konstan and Rutter, *Envy, Spite, and Jealousy*; and Ed Sanders, *Envy and Jealousy in Classical Athens: A Socio-Psychological Approach* (Oxford: Oxford University Press, 2014).

35. The association of envy and visual appraisal is made explicit, for example, when Bacon describes how frustrated courtiers "become secretly discontent, and look upon men and matters with an evil eye." For this passage and discussion, see Frank Whigham, *Ambition and Privilege: The Social Tropes of Elizabethan Courtesy Theory* (Berkeley: University of California Press, 1984), 173.

36. Thomas Wilson, *A Christian Dictionarie* (London, 1612), 126.

37. Ovid, *Ovid's Metamorphosis*: *The Arthur Golding Translation, 1567*, ed. John Frederick Nims (Philadelphia: Paul Dry Books, 2000), 2.959–60.

38. Geffery Whitney, *A Choice of Emblemes, and Other Deuises, for the Moste Parte Gathered Out of Sundrie Writers, Englished and Moralized* (Leiden, 1586), 94.

39. Edmund Spenser, *The Faerie Queene*, ed. A. C. Hamilton et al., 2nd ed. (Harlow, Eng.: Pearson, 2007), I.iv.30.5–9. See also V.xii.28–37, where Enuie and Detraction aid the Blatant Beast in their assault of Artegall; I treat this passage briefly in chapter 3.

40. Alexander Barclay, trans., *The Ship of Fools* (Edinburgh, 1874), 252–53. As the concluding lines of this passage suggest, envy also had a formal identity in the conventions of Renaissance satire; with this envy topos, early modern satirists denounced their enemies, critics, and slanderers with epithets of railing, barking, and biting. See Gill, "Renaissance Conventions."

41. William Cornwallis, *Essayes* (London, 1600), Lvii–Lvii^{v}.

42. E. A., *The Politicke and Militarie Discourses of the Lord de la Nouue* (London, 1587), 269. For emulation, see Eric S. Mallin, "Emulous Factions and the Collapse of Chivalry: Troilus and Cressida," *Representations* 29 (1990): 145–79; Meskill, *Ben Jonson*, 7, 62–65; Maggie Kilgour, *Milton and the Metamorphosis of Ovid* (Oxford: Oxford University Press, 2012), 231–42; and Vernon Guy Dickson, *Emulation on the Shakespearean Stage* (Burlington, Vt.: Ashgate, 2013).

43. Thomas Elyot, *The Image of Gouernance Compiled of the Actes and Sentences Notable, of the Moste Noble Emperour Alexander Seuerus* (London, 1541), 77^{v}; John Palsgrave, *Ioannis Palsgraui Londoniensis, Ecphrasis Anglica in Comoediam Acolasti, The Comedye of Acolastus Translated into Oure Englysshe Tongue* (London, 1540), bi^{v}.

44. Miceli and Castelfranchi, "Envious Mind," 473.

45. On memory generally in Surrey's works, see Andrew Hiscock, *Reading Memory in Early Modern Literature* (Cambridge: Cambridge University Press, 2011), chap. 1. It should be noted here that "So crewell prison" has a tantalizingly curious relationship to Surrey's "When Windesor walles"—a sonnet in which a melancholic speaker, situated in Windsor Castle, contrasts (abstractly) his prior happy life with his current misery. Some have read it as a pseudo-elegy for Richmond—Stephen Guy-Bray calls "So crewell prison" and "When Windesor walles" two "versions of the same poem"; see Guy-Bray, *Homoerotic Space: The Poetics of Loss in Renaissance Literature* (Toronto: University of Toronto Press, 2002), 110.

46. "So crewell prison," in Henry Howard, Earl of Surrey, *Poems*, ed. Emrys Jones (Oxford: Clarendon, 1964), lines 1–4. Subsequent citations to Surrey's poetry refer to this edition.

47. Lines, "Erotic Politics," 4.

48. *Aeneid*, in Surrey, *Poems,* lines 2:716–20.

49. Ibid., lines 2:688–90.

50. See also Crewe's more general discussion of Surrey's "murderous/suicidal/amatory poetics" in *Trials of Authorship*, 75.

51. Sessions, *Henry Howard*, 266–67, suggests that Surrey probably didn't begin his translation until 1543.

52. Smith et al., "Dispositional Envy," 1009.

53. See Maria Testa and Brenda Major, "The Impact of Social Comparisons after Failure: The Moderating Effects of Perceived Control," *Basic and Applied Social Psychology* 11, no. 2 (1990): 205–18.

54. Surrey, "So crewell prison," lines 18–20.

55. Ibid., 29–32.

56. In chapter 3, I treat such hunting poems in more detail.

57. On the distinction between envy and jealousy, see, for example, Parrott and Smith, "Distinguishing the Experiences."

58. The third party, however, may be entirely abstracted, as in the (somewhat obsolete, but fully comprehensible) construction "the miser is jealous of his money." See Luke Purshouse, "Jealousy in Relation to Envy," *Erkenntnis* 60, no. 2 (2004): 185.

59. Parrott and Smith, "Distinguishing the Experiences," 907; see also Bernd H. Schmitt, "Social Comparison in Romantic Jealousy," *Personality and Social Psychology Bulletin* 14, no. 2 (1988): 374–87.

60. Nicholas Breton, *Pasquils Mistresse* (London, 1600), F4^{v}.

61. Richard Taverner, *The Second Booke of the Garden of Wysedome* (London, 1542), 4–4^{v}; see *OED,* "cuckquean, *n.*"

62. Wilson, *Christian Dictionarie*, 244–45. Wilson also notes the theological context: "God [is] saide to bee Iealous, when the marriage betweene him and his Church, is violated and broken."

63. Quoted and discussed in Richard H. Bell, *Provoked to Jealousy: The Origin and Purpose of the Jealousy Motif in Romans 9–11* (Tübingen: Mohr Siebeck, 1994), 40 n. 185.

64. Acts 5:17, *The Geneva Bible: 1560 Edition* (Peabody, Mass.: Hendrickson, 2007).

65. Surrey, "So crewell prison," line 9. Of course, we are here also squarely in the realm of homosociality, and a reading of the sequence can be informed by Eve Kosofsky Sedgwick's familiar notion that women, when objectified erotically, often serve "the primary purpose of cementing the bonds of men with men" (Sedgwick, *Between Men: English Literature and Male Homosocial Desire* [New York: Columbia University Press, 1985], 26).

66. Surrey, "So crewell prison," lines 25–28.

67. Ibid., lines 13–16.

68. Kenneth Burke, *A Rhetoric of Motives* (Berkeley: University of California Press, 1969), 131. The italics are Burke's. See also Whigham, *Ambition and Privilege*, 78.

69. Lines, "Erotic Politics," 5; Surrey, "So crewell prison," lines 33–40.

70. Surrey, "So crewell prison," lines 43, 45–48. "Lief" is an Old/Middle English word of intimacy: "beloved, a dear one; a friend, sweetheart, mistress; occas. a wife" (*OED*). That the designation conveys both erotic and nonerotic content is suggestive in this context.

71. Surrey, "So crewell prison," lines 49–50.

72. R. Clifton Spargo notes that narcissism "is often the concealed content of manifestly excessive grief," and we may see underneath Surrey's emotional posture how "concern for the other" becomes in actuality "an only too articulate expression of self-concern"; see Spargo, *The Ethics of Mourning: Grief and Responsibility in Elegiac Literature* (Baltimore, Md.: Johns Hopkins University Press, 2004), 22.

73. Surrey, "So crewell prison," lines 51–54.

74. Crewe notes that Surrey's hollow plaints "mourn a defeated rival, whose death has been wished upon him, and whose death is also necessary as a cause of renewed plaint" (*Trials of Authorship*, 74).

75. R. Horacio Etchegoyen and Clara R. Nemas, "Salieri's Dilemma: A Counterpoint between Envy and Appreciation," *International Journal of Psychoanalysis* 84, no. 1 (2003): 45.

76. Richard H. Smith and Sung Hee Kim, "Comprehending Envy," *Psychological Bulletin* 133, no. 1 (2007): 56.

77. Miceli and Castelfranchi, "Envious Mind," 453.

78. Francis Bacon, "Of Envy," in *The Works of Francis Bacon*, ed. James Spedding, Robert Leslie Ellis, and Douglas Denon Heath, 14 vols. (London, 1857–74), 6:394. For discussion of this passage, see Whigham, *Ambition and Privilege*, 174.

79. See Peter M. Sacks, *The English Elegy: Studies in the Genre from Spenser to Yeats* (Baltimore, Md.: Johns Hopkins University Press, 1985), chap. 1.

80. Jahan Ramazani, *Poetry of Mourning: The Modern Elegy from Hardy to Heaney* (Chicago: University of Chicago Press, 1994), 4.

81. Brigden, *ODNB*, n.p.

82. George Frederick Nott, ed., *The Works of Henry Howard Earl of Surrey and of Sir Thomas Wyatt the Elder*, 2 vols. (London, 1815–16), 1.167; see Sessions, *Henry Howard*, 228–30.

83. *Acts of the Privy Council of England*, ed. John Roche Dasent, 32 vols. (London, 1890–1907), 1:104. On this poem, see Andrew W. Taylor, "Glass Houses: Surrey, Petrarch, and the Religious Poetics of the 'London' Invective," *The Review of English Studies* 57, no. 231 (2006): 433–55; and Mike Rodman

Jones, "License and Lutheranism: Diplomatic Gossip, Religious Identity, and the Earl of Surrey," in Powell and Rossiter, *Authority and Diplomacy*, 121–33.

84. David Potter, *Henry VIII and Francis I: The Final Conflict, 1540–47* (Leiden: Brill, 2011), 8. The following section owes much to Potter's analysis.

85. Childs, *Henry VIII's Last Victim*, 203.

86. ["gloriam suorum maiorum non modo aequare, sed etiam ualde exuperare."] Vergil, *Angelica Historia*, 196–97 (Hay's translation).

87. Scarisbrick, *Henry VIII*, 445.

88. Potter, *Henry VIII and Francis I*, 187.

89. ["les pires jambes du monde"; "marcher beaucoup plus lentement pour la gravité et indisposicion dud. Sr. roy."] Quoted ibid., 167 (Potter's translation, 167–68).

90. *L&P* XIX(i), 518. Or it least it was in all likelihood worn then; see http://www.metmuseum.org/Collections/search-the-collections/23936.

91. *CSPS*, VI(ii), 235.

92. *CSPS*, VI(ii), 250. Though Chapuys is indirect, it seems that the earl had taken certain issue with "the officers in Flanders."

93. TNA, SP 1/184, fol. 221.

94. Thomas Rymer, *Foedera, Conventiones, Literae, et Cujuscunque Generis Acta Publica*, 20 vols. (London, 1704–35), 15:56.

95. Sessions, *Henry Howard*, 288. For a description of Henry's entry, see Rymer, *Foedera*, 15:56.

96. ["Locumtenetem & Capitaneum Generalem, Ducemque Primarium & Gubernatorem"] Rymer, *Foedera*, 15:80.

97. Sessions, in a slightly different formulation, argues that "the two Henrys were held in a kind of triangular desire by the dream of honour both held and Surrey could articulate" (*Henry Howard*, 310).

98. M. Bryn Davies, "Surrey at Boulogne," *Huntington Library Quarterly* 23, no. 4 (1960): 339.

99. TNA, SP 1/208, fol. 76. Norfolk was not alone in this assessment: in the same missive Surrey is informed that "[Secretary] Paget desired me to wright to you in no wise to anymate the kyng to kepe Boleyne."

100. TNA, SP 1/209, fol. 116^{v}. For his plans, see, for example, TNA, SP 1/213, fol. 24ff.

101. *CSPS*, VIII, 126.

102. TNA, SP 1/210, fol. 28. This document is faded; I have supplemented my transcription with the calendared summary in *L&P* XX(ii), 738.

103. TNA, SP 1/211, fol. 153^{v}.

104. TNA, SP 1/210, fol. 28.

105. Ibid., fol. 29.

106. Ibid., fol. 28^{v}.

107. TNA, SP 1/213, fol. 24–28; see Potter, *Henry VIII and Francis I*, 287–90.

108. Sessions, *Henry Howard*, 319; quoted in Davies, "Surrey at Boulogne," 345. The anecdote, Davies notes, may be apocryphal (346).

109. TNA, SP 1/213, fol. 49, 49^{v}; *CSPS*, VIII, 184.

110. TNA, SP 1/213, fol. 58; see Childs, *Henry VIII's Last Victim*, 243.

111. Edward Herbert, *The Life and Raigne of King Henry the Eighth* (London, 1649), 538.

112. Sessions, *Henry Howard*, 325.

113. Susan Brigden ("Henry Howard," 520) has shown how the animosity between the two has traditionally been overemphasized, and there were certainly periods of reconciliation—but, as will become apparent, the tension escalated in the final months of the reign.

114. TNA, SP 1/214, fol. 115, 115^{v}.

115. Martin A. Sharp Hume, ed., *Chronicle of King Henry VIII of England: Being a Contemporary Record of Some of the Principal Events of the Reigns of Henry VIII and Edward VI* (London, 1889), 147.

116. TNA, SP 1/215, fol. 87^{v}, 150.

117. *CSPS*, VIII, 226.

118. TNA, SP 1/227, fol. 109^{v}. These words, to be sure, emerge from interrogations designed to prove Surrey's treasonous aims, and must be taken as such.

119. Herbert, *Life and Raigne*, 563.

120. In a way, Surrey and Dudley were rivals in the purest aristocratic sense: in 1540 they ran against each other in the May Day tournaments. More seriously, however, it was Dudley who replaced Surrey as naval commander of the French theater. In July 1546, shortly after Seymour, Dudley, and Paget orchestrated a peace with France—that entailed the eventual return of Boulogne—Surrey wrote to the lord admiral an apparently alarming letter, unfortunately now lost, which (in Dudley's words) "conteyned so many parables that I do not perfectly vnderstand it, [and] I requier you to share vnto the kinges maieste" (TNA, SP 1/221, fol. 181). See Childs, *Henry VIII's Last Victim*, 255.

121. Quoted in Nott, *Works of Henry Howard Earl of Surrey*, 1:lxxxviii; Appendix ci. Childs notes the possibility that the demeanor remark may have referred to Norfolk's other son, Lord Thomas (*Henry VIII's Last Victim*, 354 n. 29).

122. *State Papers*, I, CVII.

123. See Sessions, *Henry Howard*, chap. 13, and the notes within.

124. TNA, SP 1/223, fol. 36.

125. Sessions, *Henry Howard*, 351.

126. Ibid., 338, 333.

127. T. B. Howell and Thomas Jones Howell, eds., *A Complete Collection of State Trials and Proceedings for High Treason and Other Crimes and Misdemeanors*, 34 vols. (London, 1816–28), 1:453; Wriothesley, *Chronicle*, 1:176. See Sessions, *Henry Howard*, 358–59.

128. TNA, SP 1/227, fol. 101.

129. TNA, SP 1/227, fol. 107^{v}, 129. The issue of corruption, as we saw mentioned above in the letter of Surrey's recall, emerged from the (dare I say, envious) accusations of Lord Grey of Wilton, a man displaced by Surrey's Boulogne command in 1545. See Childs, *Henry VIII's Last Victim*, 256–57; and Sessions, *Henry Howard*, 328–29.

130. TNA, SP 1/227, fol. 103–103^{v}.

131. TNA, SP 1/227, fol. 107.

132. TNA, SP 1/227, fol. 105^{v}, 112, 112^{v}.

133. Herbert, *Life and Raigne*, 563.

134. TNA, SP 1/227, fol. 105, for this and the following quotations.

135. Ibid., fol. 107; 104^{v}.

136. Ibid., fol. 112^{v}; 123; 115.

137. Ibid., fol. 112[v].

138. *CSPS*, IX, 3–4.

139. Childs, *Henry VIII's Last Victim*, 262, 261, 262.

140. ["era argumento euidente que se queria alçar por rey."] *CSPS*, IX, 3; Antonio De Guaras, *The Accession of Queen Mary*, ed. Richard Garnett (London, 1892), 34.

141. Moore, "Heraldic Charge," 580.

142. Herbert, *Life and Raigne*, 567.

143. See Childs, *Henry VIII's Last Victim*, 286.

144. Herbert, *Life and Raigne*, 565.

145. TNA, SP 1/227, fol 111[v].

146. Ibid., fol. 123.

147. ["fieri et depingi causavit juxta et conjunctim cum propriis armis insigniis ipsius Henrici HOWARD dicta arma et insignia dicti Dom. Regis nunc"; "falsè malitiosè et proditoriè optans volens et desiderans. . . . illustrissimum et serenissimum Dominum nostrum Regem de juribus dignitate titulis nominibusque status sui regalis deprivare"; "ad dishaereditandum et interrumpendum dictum excellentissimum Dominum Edwardum Principem de vero et indubitato titulo suo in et ad dictam Coronam."] Quoted in Nott, *Works of Henry Howard Earl of Surrey*, 1:Appendix lxxix–lxxx.

148. Herbert, *Life and Raigne*, 565; Wriothesley, *Chronicle*, 1:177.

149. Herbert, *Life and Raigne*, 569.

150. TNA, SP 1/227, fol. 182[v]; *CSPS*, VIII, 370.

151. TNA, SP 1/227, fol. 183[v]. See also David M. Head, *The Ebbs and Flows of Fortune: The Life of Thomas Howard, Third Duke of Norfolk* (Athens: University of Georgia Press, 1995), 226–28.

152. TNA, SP 1/227, fol. 105; Herbert, *Life and Raigne*, 564.

153. Sessions, *Henry Howard*, xi.

154. Childs, *Henry VIII's Last Victim*, 249.

155. ["Gratulamur et toti Regno, quod Henrici invictissimi maximique Regis humeris suffultum, et armis defensum; tuâ alterius Henrici, operâ clarissimum apud exteras nationes nomen consecutum videatur; dum Gallis, praeter invidiam, ploratum, tuique horrorem, reliquum feceris nihil."] Quoted in Nott, *Works of Henry Howard Earl of Surrey*, 1:172 (Childs's translation, from *Henry VIII's Last Victim*, 250).

156. See Clarence H. Miller's entry in the *ODNB*; see also the brief discussion in Childs, *Henry VIII's Last Victim*, 309; and Sessions, *Henry Howard*, 291–92.

157. ["Norfolchi genus antiquum"; "Magna libris, maiora armia, & maxima fido / Consilio"; "Vnus at heu demptus fatis crudelibus Heros / Praepositus cunctis poterat Surreyus esse / Ni fera surgentes Lachesis truncâsset honores, / Obliquoque nocens incautis fascine liuor."] Thomas Chaloner, *De Rep. Anglorum Instauranda Libri Decem* (London, 1579), 45–46.

158. ["Inuidiosa duo manus"; "poenas liuentum à sanguine dudum / Exegit Nemesis."] Ibid., 46, for this and the following quote.

159. ["fatale Britannae / Iam toties aulae"; "speratos patriae praecerpere fructus / Tune impunè potes"].

160. ["Dignum erit vt studio gens aemula prodeat aquo"; "Indigitesque suos imitandos ducat in actus."] Chaloner, *De Rep. Anglorum*, 45.

161. ["Super omnia, illi *Invidiam* in se concitant maximè, qui Fortunarum suarum Amplitudinem, insolenter & tumidè ostentant."] Translated in Bacon, "Of Envy," *Works*, 6:395. It is worth noting that Sir Francis actively oversaw the translation of his essays—conceiving that "the Latin volume of them (being in the universal language) may last as long as books last" (ibid., 6:373)—so my lie is a white one. Latin text from *Francisci Baconi . . . Operum Moralium et Civilium Tomus* (London, 1638), 167.

162. Thomas Amyot, "Transcript of an Original Manuscript, Containing a Memorial from George Constantyne to Thomas Lord Cromwell," *Archaeologia* 23 (1831): 62.

Chapter 3

1. Spenser, *Faerie Queene*, V.xii.26.4; 27.7.

2. Ibid., V.xii.41.2–3; 42.2.

3. Ibid., VI.i.4.4.

4. On Leicester's life, see, for example, Simon Adams, *Leicester and the Court: Essays on Elizabethan Politics* (Manchester: Manchester University Press, 2002); Adams's *ODNB* entry; and Susan Doran, *Elizabeth I & Her Circle* (Oxford: Oxford University Press, 2015), chap. 5. On Sidney, see Malcolm William Wallace, *The Life of Sir Philip Sidney* (Cambridge: Cambridge University Press, 1915); Katherine Duncan-Jones, *Sir Philip Sidney, Courtier Poet* (New Haven, Conn.: Yale University Press, 1991); and Alan Stewart, *Philip Sidney: A Double Life* (London: Chatto and Windus, 2000).

5. The high stakes of courtly interaction were especially primed to generate frustrated and disappointed courtiers. In fact, Frank Whigham notes that a "central employment of the tropes of courtesy was to relieve these strains, by postponing, accounting for, or mystifying the various levels of personal failure" (*Ambition and Privilege*, 21).

6. Naomi I. Eisenberger, "Why Rejection Hurts: The Neuroscience of Social Pain," in *The Oxford Handbook of Social Exclusion*, ed. C. Nathan DeWall (Oxford: Oxford University Press, 2013), 152–62; and Terry K. Borsook and Geoff MacDonald, "Social Pain," in DeWall, *Oxford Handbook of Social Exclusion*, 163–76.

7. For an analysis of Elizabeth's marriage suits, see Susan Doran, *Monarchy and Matrimony: The Courtships of Elizabeth I* (London: Routledge, 1996), which greatly informs what follows.

8. Ibid., 41.

9. Simon Adams, Ian W. Archer, and G. W. Bernard, eds., "'A Journall' of Matters of State Happened from Time to Time . . . ," in *Religion, Politics, and Society in Sixteenth-Century England*, ed. Ian W. Archer et al. (Cambridge: Cambridge University Press, 2003), 66.

10. Adams, *Leicester and the Court*, 47.

11. Samuel Haynes, ed., *A Collection of State Papers: Relating to Affairs in the Reigns of King Henry VIII, King Edward VI, Queen Mary and Queen Elizabeth: From the Year 1542 to 1570* (London, 1740), 364.

12. For the petition and Elizabeth's response, see William Camden, *The History of the Most Renowned and Victorious Princess Elizabeth* (London, 1688), 25–27.

13. Doran, *Monarchy and Matrimony*, 64.

14. ["nunca la Reina se determinará en casarse conmigo, porque tiene determinacion de casarse con algun gran Príncipe."] *Colección de Documentos Inéditos para la Historia de España*, 112 vols. (Madrid, 1842–95), 89:116.

15. Doran, *Monarchy and Matrimony*, 65.

16. On the Dutch revolt, see Charles Wilson, *Queen Elizabeth and the Revolt of The Netherlands* (Berkeley: University of California Press, 1970); Geoffrey Parker, *The Dutch Revolt* (London: Penguin Books, 1985); Alastair Duke, *Reformation and Revolt in the Low Countries* (London: Hambledon, 1990); Martin van Gelderen, *The Political Thought of the Dutch Revolt, 1555–1590* (Cambridge: Cambridge University Press, 1992); Jonathan I. Israel, *The Dutch Republic: Its Rise, Greatness, and Fall, 1477–1806* (Oxford: Clarendon, 1998); Susan Doran, *Elizabeth I and Foreign Policy, 1558–1603* (New York: Routledge, 2000); Graham Darby, ed., *The Origins and Development of the Dutch Revolt* (London: Routledge, 2001); Hugh Dunthorne, *Britain and the Dutch Revolt, 1560–1700* (Cambridge: Cambridge University Press, 2013); and, more generally, Anne Somerset, *Elizabeth I* (London: Phoenix Giant, 1991). See also Bradley J. Irish, "The Sidneys and Foreign Affairs, 1575–1578: An Unpublished Letter of Sir Henry Sidney," *ELR* 45, no. 1 (2015): 90–119.

17. See Israel, *Dutch Republic*, 138–39. The Dutch Council of State was an advisory body that reported to Margaret of Parma, then-Spanish governor (and half-sister to King Philip).

18. Duke, *Reformation and Revolt*, 130–38. It is important to note, however, that at this time countless Dutch (comprising the majority of the southern provinces) favored both Catholicism and reconciliation with Spain.

19. On Orange, see K. W. Swart, *William of Orange and the Revolt of the Netherlands, 1572–84*, ed. R. P. Fagel et al., trans. J. C. Grayson (Burlington, Vt.: Ashgate, 2003).

20. See Israel, *Dutch Republic*, 156–60. Installed in September 1567, this Conseil des Troubles would prove "highly effective" in its charge: "some 8950 persons, from all levels of society, were investigated and sentenced for treason or heresy, or both, more than one thousand being executed" (ibid., 156–57).

21. Dudley Digges, ed., *The Compleat Ambassador: or Two Treaties of the Intended Marriage of Queen Elizabeth* (London, 1655), 129. The "augmentation" (as I take it) refers to the economic value of asserting control of the region.

22. In 1569, a handful of Catholic noblemen from the northern counties unsuccessfully rose against Elizabeth, with hopes of installing Mary, Queen of Scots on the English throne.

23. Somerset, *Elizabeth I*, 287.

24. TNA, SP 70/140, fol. 189.

25. See Swart, *William of Orange*, 164.

26. TNA, SP 15/25, fol. 53.

27. TNA, SP 83/3, #39. (For sections of the state papers that are inconsistently foliated, I cite by document number.)

28. TNA, SP 15/25, fol. 53.

29. TNA, SP 83/3, #5.

30. Ibid.

31. Ibid.

32. TNA, SP 83/5, #69, for this and the following quotations in this paragraph.

33. On courtly ontology, see Whigham, *Ambition and Privilege*, chap. 2.

34. Mark R. Leary, "Varieties of Interpersonal Rejection," in *The Social Outcast: Ostracism, Social Exclusion, Rejection, and Bullying*, ed. Kipling D. Williams, Joseph P. Forgas, and William von Hippel (New York: Psychology, 2005), 36; see also Kipling D. Williams, Joseph P. Forgas, and William von Hippel, "Emotional Responses to Interpersonal Rejection," *Dialogues in Clinical Neuroscience* 17, no. 4 (2015): 435–41.

35. Joseph Berger, Susan J. Rosenholtz, and Morris Zelditch Jr., "Status Organizing Processes," *Annual Review of Sociology* 6 (1980): 479, 482.

36. Bernardo A. Huberman, Christoph H. Loch, and Ayse Önçüler, "Status as a Valued Resource," *Social Psychology Quarterly* 67 (2004): 103. Though research on stigma has primarily (and quite understandably) focused on traditionally ostracized social categories, scholars have equally noted that groups can be stigmatized for their positively exceptional qualities. See also Deborrah E. S. Frable, Tamela Blackstone, and Carol Scherbaum, "Marginal and Mindful: Deviants in Social Interactions," *Journal of Personality and Social Psychology* 59, no. 1 (1990): 140–49; Elizabeth C. Pinel, "Stigma Consciousness: The Psychological Legacy of Social Stereotypes," *Journal of Personality and Social Psychology* 76, no. 1 (1999): 114–28; and Leary, "Varieties of Interpersonal Rejection."

37. Cameron Anderson et al., "The Local-Ladder Effect: Social Status and Subjective Well-Being," *Psychological Science* 23, no. 7 (2012): 764; Leary, "Varieties of Interpersonal Rejection," 37.

38. Katherine B. Curhan et al., "Subjective and Objective Hierarchies and Their Relations to Psychological Well-Being: A U.S./Japan Comparison," *Social Psychological and Personality Science* 5, no. 8 (2014): 855; Nancy E. Adler et al., "Relationship of Subjective and Objective Social Status with Psychological and Physiological Functioning: Preliminary Data in Healthy, White Women," *Health Psychology* 19, no. 6 (2000): 586. See also Michael W. Kraus, Nancy Adler, and Teh-Way David Chen, "Is the Association of Subjective SES and Self-Rated Health Confounded by Negative Mood? An Experimental Approach," *Health Psychology* 32, no. 2 (2013): 138–45.

39. Anderson et al., "Local-Ladder Effect," 765.

40. Naomi I. Eisenberger, "The Neural Sociometer: Brain Mechanisms Underlying State Self-Esteem," *Journal of Cognitive Neuroscience* 23, no. 11 (2011): 3448; Mark R. Leary et al., "Self-Esteem as an Interpersonal Monitor: The Sociometer Hypothesis," *Journal of Personality and Social Psychology* 68, no. 3 (1995): 520.

41. Mark R. Leary, "Making Sense of Self-Esteem," *Current Directions in Psychological Science* 8, no. 1 (1999): 32; Mark R. Leary et al., "Calibrating the Sociometer: The Relationship between Interpersonal Appraisals and State Self-Esteem," *Journal of Personality and Social Psychology* 74, no. 5 (1998): 1290. See also Mark R. Leary and Roy F. Baumeister, "The Nature and Function of Self-Esteem: Sociometer Theory," *Advances in Experimental Social Psychology* 32 (2000): 1–62; and Sandra L. Murray et al., "Calibrating the Sociometer: The Relational Contingencies of Self-Esteem," *Journal of Personality and Social Psychology* 85, no. 1 (2003): 63–84.

42. Leary et al., "Self-Esteem as an Interpersonal Monitor," 520.

43. For background on schism, see Fabio Sani and John Todman, "Should We Stay or Should We Go? A Social Psychological Model of Schisms in Groups," *Personality and Social Psychology Bulletin* 28, no. 12 (2002): 1647–55; Claire M. Hart and Mark Van Vugt, "From Fault Line to Group Fission: Understanding Membership Changes in Small Groups," *Personality and Social Psychology Bulletin* 32, no. 3 (2006): 392–404; and Dominic J. Packer, "On Being Both With Us and Against Us: A Normative Conflict Model of Dissent in Social Groups," *Personality and Social Psychology Review* 12, no. 1 (2008): 50–72.

44. Fabio Sani, "Schism in Groups: A Social Psychological Account," *Social and Personality Psychology Compass* 2, no. 2 (2008): 718; Fabio Sani, "When Subgroups Secede: Extending and Refining the Social Psychological Model of Schism in Groups," *Personality and Social Psychology Bulletin* 31, no. 8 (2005): 1077.

45. Sani, "When Subgroups Secede," 1074.

46. Ibid., 1076; Sani, "Schism in Groups," 723.

47. Colin Wayne Leach et al., "Group Devaluation and Group Identification," *Journal of Social Issues* 66, no. 3 (2010): 536, 535.

48. Chris Jenks, *Subculture: The Fragmentation of the Social* (London: Sage, 2005), 7. On the background of subculture, see Shane Blackman, "Subculture Theory: An Historical and Contemporary Assessment of the Concept for Understanding Deviance," *Deviant Behavior* 35, no. 6 (2014): 496–512.

49. Nicholas Emler and Stephen Reicher, "Delinquency: Cause or Consequence of Social Exclusion?" in *The Social Psychology of Inclusion and Exclusion*, ed. Dominic Abrams, Michael A. Hogg, and José M. Marques (New York: Psychology, 2005), 232, 231.

50. Dominic Abrams, Michael A. Hogg, and José M. Marques, "A Social Psychological Framework for Understanding Social Inclusion and Exclusion," in Abrams, Hogg, and Marques, *Social Psychology of Inclusion and Exclusion*, 10.

51. See Mark R. Leary, Jean M. Twenge, and Erin Quinlivan, "Interpersonal Rejection as a Determinant of Anger and Aggression," *Personality and Social Psychology Review* 10, no. 2 (2006): 111–32.

52. Ibid., 112; Jiyoung Park et al., "Social Status and Anger Expression: The Cultural Moderation Hypothesis," *Emotion* 13, no. 6 (2013): 1128.

53. See Larissa Z. Tiedens, Phoebe C. Ellsworth, and Batja Mesquita, "Sentimental Stereotypes: Emotional Expectations for High- and Low-Status Group Members," *Personality and Social Psychology Bulletin* 26, no. 5 (2000): 560–75; Larissa Z. Tiedens, "Anger and Advancement versus Sadness and Subjugation: The Effect of Negative Emotion Expressions on Social Status Conferral," *Journal of Personality and Social Psychology* 80, no. 1 (2001): 86–94; Shlomo Hareli, Noga Shomrat, and Ursula Hess, "Emotional versus Neutral Expressions and Perceptions of Social Dominance and Submissiveness," *Emotion* 9, no. 3 (2009): 378–84; Park et al., "Social Status"; and Ursula Hess, "Anger Is a Positive Emotion," in Parrott, *Positive Side of Negative Emotions*, 55–75. We may recall the subtitle of Gordon Braden's seminal study *Renaissance Tragedy and the Senecan Tradition: Anger's Privilege* (New Haven, Conn.: Yale University Press, 1985).

54. Brad J. Bushman and Roy F. Baumeister, "Threatened Egotism, Narcissism, Self-Esteem, and Direct and Displaced Aggression: Does Self-Love or Self-Hate Lead to Violence?" *Journal of Personality and Social Psychology* 75, no. 1 (1998): 227; Jean M. Twenge and W. Keith Campbell, "'Isn't It Fun to Get the Respect

That We're Going to Deserve?' Narcissism, Social Rejection, and Aggression," *Personality and Social Psychology Bulletin* 29, no. 2 (2003): 263.

55. David K. Sherman and Geoffrey L. Cohen, "Accepting Threatening Information: Self-Affirmation and the Reduction of Defensive Biases," *Current Directions in Psychological Science* 11, no. 4 (2002): 119; Hart Blanton et al., "When Bad Things Happen to Good Feedback: Exacerbating the Need for Self-Justification with Self-Affirmations," *Personality and Social Psychology Bulletin* 23, no. 7 (1997): 690.

56. Jean M. Twenge and Roy F. Baumeister, "Social Exclusion Increases Aggression and Self-Defeating Behavior While Reducing Intelligent Thought and Prosocial Behavior," in Abrams, Hogg, and Marques, *Social Psychology*, 27–46.

57. Carolyn C. Morf and Frederick Rhodewalt, "Unraveling the Paradoxes of Narcissism: A Dynamic Self-Regulatory Processing Model," *Psychological Inquiry* 12, no. 4 (2001): 177–96; Kipling D. Williams and Cassandra L. Govan, "Reacting to Ostracism: Retaliation or Reconciliation?" in Abrams, Hogg, and Marques, *Social Psychology,* 47–62; Leary, Twenge, and Quinlivan, "Interpersonal Rejection"; and C. Nathan DeWall and Jean M. Twenge, "Rejection and Aggression: Explaining the Paradox," in DeWall, *Oxford Handbook,* 113–20.

58. Williams and Govan, "Reacting to Ostracism," 58.

59. Albert Camus, *The Myth of Sisyphus, and Other Essays* (New York: Vintage Books, 1983), 121.

60. For discussion of such New Historicist treatments of courtly protest, see below.

61. One strand of queer theory similarly explores the productive possibilities of failure; see, for example, Judith Halberstam, *The Queer Art of Failure* (Durham, N.C.: Duke University Press, 2011).

62. On "emotional work," see Arlie Russell Hochschild, *The Managed Heart: Commercialization of Human Feeling* (Berkeley: University of California Press, 2003).

63. *The Lady of May*, in Philip Sidney, *Miscellaneous Prose of Sir Philip Sidney,* ed. Katherine Duncan-Jones and Jan van Dorsten (Oxford: Clarendon, 1973), 21.15.

64. This critical tradition is discussed below.

65. Sidney, *Lady of May*, 25.4–6.

66. Duncan-Jones, *Courtier Poet*, 149.

67. Indeed, rationality is the criterion through which Duncan-Jones more broadly suggests that *The Lady of May* is most probably misread as a reflection of Elizabethan policy; "in broad terms," she suggests, "it seems unlikely that Sidney would be so rash as to use his uncle's public entertainment of the Queen to force a statement from her on such grave matters" (*Courtier Poet*, 149). Yet this approach has difficulty honoring what we know to be a bedrock fact of Sidney's personal and political life: his short career was full of decisions that, in retrospect, seem rash. I am thus in full agreement with the position of Derek B. Alwes, who suggests that the fullest readings of the shepherd knight are those open to "retrieving (or at least conceiving of) a Sidney both capable of and motivated to pursue a tactless and indeed dangerous challenge to his monarch's authority" (Alwes, *Sons and Authors in Elizabethan England* [Newark, N.J.: University of Delaware Press, 2004], 72).

68. For the historical state of the early modern forest, see Dan Beaver, "Ancient Liberties, Royal Honour, and the Politics of Commonweal in English Forests, 1558–1625," in *The Oxford Handbook of the Age of Shakespeare*, ed. R. Malcolm Smuts (Oxford: Oxford University Press, 2016), 139–55.

69. TNA, SP 1/128, fol. 93.

70. Jeffrey S. Theis, in fact, argues that "sylvan pastoral" should be recognized as a distinct mode in the period; see *Writing the Forest in Early Modern England: A Sylvan Pastoral Nation* (Pittsburgh: Duquesne University Press, 2009). On early modern pastoral, see, for example, Sukanta Chaudhuri, *Renaissance Pastoral and Its English Developments* (Oxford: Clarendon, 1989); Todd A. Borlik, *Ecocriticism and Early Modern English Literature: Green Pastures* (New York: Routledge, 2011); Andrew Hadfield, "Foresters, Ploughman, and Shepherds: Versions of Tudor Pastoral," in Pincombe and Shrank, *Oxford Handbook of Tudor Literature, 537–54;* Ken Hiltner, *What Else Is Pastoral: Renaissance Literature and the Environment* (Ithaca, N.Y.: Cornell University Press, 2011); and Katherine C. Little, *Transforming Work: Early Modern Pastoral and Late Medieval Poetry* (Notre Dame, Ind.: University of Notre Dame Press, 2013).

71. Louis Adrian Montrose, "Of Gentlemen and Shepherds: The Politics of Elizabethan Pastoral Form," *ELH: English Literary History* 50, no. 3 (1983): 418.

72. Renato Poggioli, *The Oaten Flute: Essays on Pastoral Poetry and the Pastoral Ideal* (Cambridge, Mass.: Harvard University Press, 1975), 1; Judith Deborah Haber, *Pastoral and the Poetics of Self-Contradiction: Theocritus to Marvell* (Cambridge: Cambridge University Press, 1994), 1; Puttenham, *Art of English Poesy*, 127–28.

73. Montrose, "Of Gentlemen and Shepherds," 438.

74. I touch upon the 1580s in the conclusion of this chapter. It is important to note that Sidney's immortal identity as the Shepherd Knight risks contaminating our assessment of his early career.

75. The most complete is that of Philippa Berry, who (among other things) views it alongside Neoplatonic and Petrarchan discourses of mastery; see *Of Chastity and Power: Elizabethan Literature and the Unmarried Queen* (New York: Routledge, 1989), 90ff.

76. Robert Withington, *English Pageantry: An Historical Outline*, 2 vols. (Cambridge, Mass.: Harvard University Press, 1918–20), 1:74.

77. Catherine Bates, *Masculinity and the Hunt: Wyatt to Spenser* (Oxford: Oxford University Press, 2013), 1, 11.

78. *L&P* III, 2305.

79. Hall, *Chronicle Containing the History of England*, 512.

80. BL, Additional MS 31922. See Raymond G. Siemens, "English Lyrics of the *Henry VIII* Manuscript," Ph.D. dissertation, University of British Columbia, 1997.

81. BL, Additional MS 31922, fol. 39^{v}.

82. Richard Grafton, *Grafton's Chronicle*, 2 vols. (London, 1809), 1:221.

83. Francis James Child, ed., *English and Scottish Ballads*, 8 vols. (Boston, 1857–60), 5:427. On outlaws in the wild, see Sarah Harlan-Haughey, *The Ecology of the English Outlaw in Medieval Literature* (New York: Routledge, 2016).

84. See Edward Berry, "Sidney's May Game for the Queen," *Modern Philology* 86, no. 3 (1989): 256. I return to his insights below. For the Sidney performance

of 1574, see *Report on the Manuscripts of Lord de L'isle & Dudley Preserved at Penshurst Place,* 6 vols. (London, 1925–66), 1:268.

85. Jeffrey L. Singman, "Munday's Unruly Earl," in *Playing Robin Hood: The Legend as Performance in Five Centuries*, ed. Lois Potter (Newark, N.J.: University of Delaware Press, 1998), 64.

86. *A Collection of Old Ballads: Corrected from the Best and Most Ancient Copies Extant* (London, 1723), 67; R. B. Dobson and J. Taylor, *Rymes of Robyn Hood: An Introduction to the English Outlaw* (Pittsburgh, Pa.: University of Pittsburgh Press, 1976), 79. See also Berry, "Sidney's May Game."

87. See Meredith Skura, "Anthony Munday's 'Gentrification' of Robin Hood," *ELR: English Literary Renaissance* 33, no. 2 (2003): 155–80. On the development of the Robin Hood legend more generally in the period, see Thomas H. Ohlgren, *Robin Hood: The Early Poems, 1465–1560: Texts, Contexts, and Ideology* (Newark, N.J.: University of Delaware Press, 2007).

88. Hall, *Chronicle Containing the History of England*, 513.

89. Edwin Davenport, "The Representation of Robin Hood in Elizabethan Drama: *George a Greene* and *Edward I*," in Potter, *Playing Robin Hood*, 58.

90. For an overview, see Erzsébet Stróbl, "The Figure of the Wild Man in the Entertainments of Elizabeth I," in *Writing the Other: Humanism versus Barbarism in Tudor England*, ed. Zsolt Almási and Mike Pincombe (Newcastle upon Tyne: Cambridge Scholars, 2008), 59–78; she argues that "the wild man tradition was an integral part of the artistic imagery of early modern England in general, and of the courtly discourse in particular" (61). See also Robert Hillis Goldsmith, "The Wild Man on the English Stage," *The Modern Language Review* 53, no. 4 (1958): 481–91; Roger Bartra, *Wild Men in the Looking Glass: The Mythic Origins of European Otherness*, trans. Carl T. Berrisford (Ann Arbor: University of Michigan Press, 1994); Anne Barton, "The Wild Man in the Forest," *Comparative Criticism* 18 (1996): 21–54; and John Twyning, *Forms of English History in Literature, Landscape, and Architecture* (Basingstoke, Eng.: Palgrave, 2012), chap. 3.

91. Berry, *Chastity and Power*, 90.

92. Berry notes that the figure might display "a connection with the unconscious and all the terrors it concealed" (ibid.).

93. Richard Bernheimer, *Wild Men in the Middle Ages: A Study in Art, Sentiment, and Demonology* (Cambridge, Mass.: Harvard University Press, 1952), 20.

94. Bartra, *Wild Men in the Looking Glass*, 133.

95. See Stróbl, "Figure of the Wild Man," 71.

96. Indeed, I have suggested how notions of wildness seemed to capture a particular brand of fractious and oppositional energy, and it is thus not surprising that the figure developed an implicit association with a group of equally particular subversive political subjects: the "wilde and mysguyded men" of Ireland, Scotland, and the surrounding borders, the perennial thorns in the side of English governance (BL, Cotton MS Caligula B/III, fol. 116).

97. Albert Feuillerat, ed., *Documents Relating to the Office of the Revels in the Time of Queen Elizabeth* (Louvain, 1908), 193, 227; Withington, *English Pageantry*, 1:72.

98. See Hall, *Chronicle Containing the History of England*, 580, 799; *L&P* II(ii), 1494, 1499, 1502; *L&P* III, 2305.

99. Though distinct, both characters were associated in the Renaissance: in 1633, for example, a pageant for Charles I staged "Bacchus crowned with ivie, and naked from the shoulders up . . . , by him stood Silenus [and] Silvanus." See William Drummond, *The Poems of William Drummond of Hawthornden*, ed. William Macdowall (Edinburgh, 1832), 267.

100. See Timothy Husband, *The Wild Man: Medieval Myth and Symbolism* (New York: Metropolitan Museum of Art, 1980), 11. In the context of our current discussion on oppositionality, to speak of satyrs is to naturally glance at the Renaissance association between woodland creatures and those poets who (as Puttenham puts it) "tax the common abuses and vice of the people in rough and bitter speeches"—"their invectives were called satires, and themselves satyrics" (Puttenham, *Art of English Poesy*, 116). As Whigham and Rebhorn explain in their notes to this passage, the famous conjunction of these notions was based on a false etymology of the Latin *satira/satura*—though the misunderstanding may also indicate a further connection between wildness and opposition, deeply embedded within the history of early modern literary culture. (Puttenham, it should be noted, avoids the confusion.)

101. See Paul Thompson, "The English, the Trees, the Wild, and the Green: Two Millennia of Mythological Metamorphoses," in *The Roots of Environmental Consciousness: Popular Tradition and Personal Experience*, ed. Stephen Hussey and Paul Thompson (London: Routledge, 2000), 20–54. Though the Celtic green man, it seems, was sometimes benign, this was certainly not uniform: as with, for example, the terrifying (and antisocial) naturalism of the Green Knight. See also Stróbl, "Figure of the Wild Man," 66.

102. Arthur Beatty, "The St. George, or Mummers' Plays: A Study in the Protology of the Drama," *Transactions of the Wisconsin Academy of Sciences, Arts, and Letters* 15 (1907): 291.

103. Ernst Cassirer, *The Individual and the Cosmos in Renaissance Philosophy*, trans. Mario Domandi (Chicago: University of Chicago Press, 2010), 75. For discussion, see Michael Wintroub, "Civilizing the Savage and Making a King: The Royal Entry Festival of Henri II (Rouen, 1550)," *Sixteenth Century Journal* 29, no. 2 (1998): 478.

104. See Wintroub, "Civilizing the Savage"; and Wayne A. Rebhorn, *The Emperor of Men's Minds: Literature and the Renaissance Discourse of Rhetoric* (Ithaca, N.Y.: Cornell University Press, 1995), 217–18.

105. Bernheimer, *Wild Men*, 101; see also Stróbl, "Figure of the Wild Man," 64.

106. The image is reproduced in Max Herrmann, *Forschungen zur Deutschen Theatergeschichte des Mittelalters und der Renaissance* (Berlin, 1914), 281.

107. Michael Wintroub, *A Savage Mirror: Power, Identity, and Knowledge in Early Modern France* (Stanford, Calif.: Stanford University Press, 2006), 249.

108. Sarah Thornton, *Club Cultures: Music, Media and Subcultural Capital* (Middletown, Conn.: Wesleyan University Press, 1996), 11. Her subsequent elaborations are also telling: "subcultural capitals fuel rebellion against, or rather escape from, the trappings of parental class. The assertion of subcultural distinction relies, in part, on a fantasy of classlessness" (12).

109. See Elizabeth Goldring, "Gascoigne and Kenilworth: The Production, Reception, and Afterlife of *The Princely Pleasures*," *ELR* 44, no. 3 (2014): 363–87.

110. Robert Laneham, *A Letter*, printed in *John Nichols's The Progresses and Public Processions of Queen Elizabeth I,* ed. Elizabeth Goldring et al., 5 vols. (Oxford: Oxford University Press, 2014), 2:233ff.; George Gascoigne, *The Princelye Pleasures*, printed in *John Nichols's The Progresses and Public Processions of Queen Elizabeth I*, 2:287ff. Subsequent citations of the performance will appear parenthetically in text.

111. See, for example, Susan Doran's discussion in "Juno versus Diana: The Treatment of Elizabeth I's Marriage in Plays and Entertainments, 1561–1581," *The Historical Journal* 38, no. 2 (1995): 266ff.; and Goldring, "Gascoigne and Kenilworth," 363. For other readings of the event, see Catherine Bates, *The Rhetoric of Courtship in Elizabethan Language and Literature* (Cambridge: Cambridge University Press, 1992), chap. 3; Susan Frye, *Elizabeth I: The Competition for Representation* (Oxford: Oxford University Press, 1993), chap. 2; Sandra Logan, *Text/Events in Early Modern England: Poetics of History* (Burlington, Vt.: Ashgate, 2007), chap. 2; Elizabeth Goldring, "Portraiture, Patronage, and the Progresses: Robert Dudley, Earl of Leicester, and the Kenilworth Festivities of 1575," in *The Progresses, Pageants, and Entertainments of Queen Elizabeth I,* ed. Jayne Elisabeth Archer, Elizabeth Goldring, and Sarah Knight (Oxford: Oxford University Press, 2007), 163–88; Fox, *Ovid and the Politics of Emotion*, chap. 1; Janette Dillon, "Pageants and Propaganda: Robert Langham's *Letter* and George Gascoigne's *Princely Pleasures at Kenilworth,*" in Pincombe and Shrank, *Oxford Handbook of Tudor Literature,* 623–36; Amy L. Tigner, *Literature and the Renaissance Garden from Elizabeth I to Charles II: England's Paradise* (Burlington, Vt.: Ashgate, 2012), chap. 1; Lesley Mickel, "Royal Self-Assertion and the Revision of Chivalry: *The Entertainment at Kenilworth* (1575), Jonson's *Masque of Owls* (1624), and *The King's Entertainment at Welbeck* (1633)," *Modern Language Review* 109, no. 4 (2014): 953–76; and Elizabeth Zeman Kolkovich, *The Elizabethan Country House Entertainment* (Cambridge: Cambridge University Press, 2016), chap. 1.

112. Richard C. McCoy, *The Rites of Knighthood: The Literature and Politics of Elizabethan Chivalry* (Berkeley: University of California Press, 1989), 18.

113. On Leicester as Arthur, see Frye, *Elizabeth I*, 68–69.

114. Kolkovich, *Elizabethan Country House Entertainment*, 34.

115. Lawrence Stone, *The Crisis of the Aristocracy, 1558–1641* (Oxford: Clarendon, 1965), 221.

116. On the notion of *magnificence* in this context, see Mary E. Hazard, "A Magnificent Lord: Leicester, Kenilworth, and Transformations in the Idea of Magnificence," *Cahiers Élisabéthains* 31 (1987): 11–35.

117. Associated already with the Welsh-born Tudor dynasty, Arthurian myth became crucial political fodder during Henry's struggles with Rome. The historical Arthur, it was claimed by the crown, had ruled as "emperor" of the British realm—a title duty-bound to English kings, surpassing even the authority of popes. See, for example, David Starkey, "King Henry and King Arthur," *Arthurian Literature* 16 (1998): 171–96.

118. In fact, Elizabeth pushed back against this challenge. At one point during the festivities, the queen discovers the Lady of the Lake, presiding over one of the castle's pools, which she had "kept . . . syns king Arthurz dayz." But when the gracious lady offered to yield her domain, Elizabeth responds with a splendid

barb: "we had thought indeed the Lake had been oours, and doo you call it yourz noow? Well we wyll heerin common more with yoo hereafter" (Goldring et al., *John Nichols's The Progresses and Public Processions of Queen Elizabeth I*, 2:245). For discussion, see Frye, *Elizabeth I*, 69.

119. Indeed, it has also been suggested that one event—plans for which are described by Gascoigne, but which was subsequently canceled—advocated for intervention in the Dutch cause. In it, a "captaine with twentie or thyrtie shotte" delivers a captive mistress from the clutches of the wicked Sir Bruse; Leicester, who would have likely played the captain himself, is thus portrayed as a liberating military hero (Goldring et al., *John Nichols's The Progresses and Public Processions of Queen Elizabeth I*, 2:308). See Frye, *Elizabeth I*, 78ff.

120. ["La Majestad de la Reina, que está tan léjos de aquí como digo, en un castillo de Milord de Lecester, nombrado Quilinghuorth, á donde el Conde la ha servido y hecho muchas fiestas, yendo un dia á caza, como se dice, un traidor la tiró con una ballesta, al cual prendieron luégo, aunque otros dicen que lo hizo tirando á los venados sin pensar mal, y la vira pasó por junto á la Reina sin hacerla daño, gracias á Dios.]; *Colección de Documentos Inéditos*, 91:88. On this moment, see also Frye, *Elizabeth I*, 56–57.

121. See Doran, "Juno versus Diana," 267.

122. Frye, *Elizabeth I*, 71.

123. For the complexities of "Deepe desire," see Bates, *Rhetoric of Courtship*, 58–60.

124. John N. King notes that, despite being "her chief favorite and the English subject most likely to win her in marriage, in all likelihood he had already abandoned genuine hope for the success of his suit" ("Queen Elizabeth I: Representations of the Virgin Queen," *Renaissance Quarterly* 43, no. 1 [1990]: 45).

125. R. W. Maslen, *Elizabethan Fictions: Espionage, Counter-Espionage, and the Duplicity of Fiction in Early Elizabethan Prose Narratives* (Oxford: Clarendon, 1997), 114; George Gascoigne, "Gascoignes Wodmanship," in *A Hundreth Sundrie Flowres,* ed. G. W. Pigman III (Oxford: Clarendon, 2000), line 14. Bates notes that "Gascoigne's particular brand of wood- (or wild-) manship marks . . . his pointed exclusion" from the political mainstream of "Elizabeth's acknowledged and favoured subjects"; see Bates, *Masculinity and the Hunt,* 116.

126. On Lee, see E. K. Chambers, *Sir Henry Lee: An Elizabethan Portrait* (Oxford: Clarendon, 1936); and Sue Simpson, *Sir Henry Lee (1536–1611): Elizabethan Courtier* (Burlington, Vt.: Ashgate, 2014). There is much debate about the actual authorship of the Woodstock entertainment, which survives in two major forms: an elaborate manuscript presented to the queen by Gascoigne at New Year 1576, and the anonymous *The Queenes Maiesties Entertainement at Woodstock*, published ten years after the fact. Whoever penned the actual text, the device was certainly orchestrated by those with connection to the Leicester party. See Goldring et al., *John Nichols's The Progresses and Public Processions of Queen Elizabeth I*, 2:410; and the discussion in Gabriel Heaton, *Writing and Reading Royal Entertainments: From George Gascoigne to Ben Jonson* (Oxford: Oxford University Press, 2010), chap. 1.

127. On this event, see J. W. Cunliffe, "The Queenes Majesties Entertainment at Woodstocke," *PMLA* 26, no. 1 (1911): 92–141; Berry, *Of Chastity and Power,* 100–101; Doran, "Juno versus Diana"; Matthew Woodcock, "The Fairy

Queen Figure in Elizabethan Entertainments," in *Elizabeth I: Always Her Own Free Woman,* ed. Carole Levin, Jo Eldridge Carney, and Debra Barrett-Graves (Burlington, Vt.: Ashgate, 2003), 97–115; Gabriel Heaton, "The Queen and the Hermit: The 'Tale of Hemetes' (1575)," in *Elizabeth I and the Culture of Writing,* ed. Peter Beal and Grace Ioppolo (London: British Library, 2007), 87–114; Heaton, *Writing and Reading,* chap. 1; and Erzsébet Stróbl, "Entertaining the Queen at Woodstock, 1575," in *The Oxford Handbook of Tudor Drama,* ed. Thomas Betteridge and Greg Walker (Oxford: Oxford University Press, 2012), 429–45.

128. Woodcock, "Fairy Queen Figure," 106, echoing Cunliffe's view in "Queenes Majesties"; Heaton, *Writing and Reading*, 26, echoing Doran's view in "Juno versus Diana." Stróbl, "Entertaining the Queen," 437, falls into the former camp; Berry, *Of Chastity and Power*, 101, the latter.

129. Goldring et al., *John Nichols's The Progresses and Public Processions of Queen Elizabeth I*, 2:409–10. Subsequent citations to this entertainment will appear parenthetically, in text.

130. As we will see further in *The Lady of May*, the hermit is another permutation of courtly antisociality.

131. See *OED*, "dainty, adj." 5c: "with infin.: Disinclined or reluctant (*to do*)."

132. Doran notes that something of Leicester is also seen in Gaudina, the "active and passionate lover who had refused to accept objections to an unequal match and had embarked on an adventurous quest to rescue her knight" ("Juno versus Diana," 268).

133. Berry, *Of Chastity and Power*, 101.

134. Like that of the foresters, it is also a homosocial community.

135. See Berry, *Of Chastity and Power*, 101; Doran, "Juno versus Diana," 268.

136. Doran, "Juno versus Diana," 268.

137. Linda Shenk, *Learned Queen: The Image of Elizabeth I in Politics and Poetry* (New York: Palgrave, 2009), chap. 2.

138. Sidney, *The Lady of May*, 21.1–5. In this section, citations to the performance will appear parenthetically in text.

139. To be sure, such management strategies did nothing to make conventional tournament forms any safer for *participants*: I refer here to the ways that their symbolic meaning is processed for *spectators*. Mock combat had high stakes, as Henry VIII of England would learn from several near disasters, and as Henri II of France would miss the opportunity to learn from further. But, in terms of formal conventions, the violence at Wanstead entailed an unexpected and jarring burst of verisimilitude, puncturing the usual fiction of ritualized combat.

140. TNA, SP 63/124, fol. 158.

141. Bates, *Rhetoric of Courtship*, 63. See also Bates, *Masculinity and the Hunt*, 213–17.

142. Duncan-Jones, *Courtier Poet*, 149.

143. S. K. Orgel, "Sidney's Experiment in Pastoral: *The Lady of May*," *Journal of the Warburg and Courtauld Institutes* 26, no. 1–2 (1963): 202; Louis Adrian Montrose, "Celebration and Insinuation: Sir Philip Sidney and the Motives of Elizabethan Courtship," *Renaissance Drama* 8 (1977): 16, 18.

144. Orgel, "Sidney's Experiment," 202; Montrose, "Celebration and Insinuation," 20.

145. See Berry, "Sidney's May Game for the Queen," 253ff.

146. Dobson and Taylor, *Rymes of Robyn Hood*, 106 (italics in original).

147. Marie Axton, "The Tudor Mask and Elizabethan Court Drama," in *English Drama: Forms and Development*, ed. Marie Axton and Raymond Williams (Cambridge: Cambridge University Press, 1977), 37ff., for the preceding quotation and further discussion of the conversion.

148. BL, Additional MS 31922, fol. 66.

149. Or, as with Hemetes, a retired knight—a figure equally virile and active.

150. Bates, *Masculinity and the Hunt*, 40. Indeed, as Bates later notes (ibid., 211–13), Sidney seems to have had an ambivalent opinion on aristocratic blood sports; he "was wont to say," records Sir John Harington, "that next hunting, he liked hauking worst," while he haughtily dismisses as "idiotic hunting" ("ridiculas venationes") in a much-cited letter to Languet. See John Harington, *A New Discourse of a Stale Subject, Called The Metamorphosis of Aiax* (London, 1596), 31; and Sir Philip Sidney, *The Correspondence of Sir Philip Sidney,* ed. Roger Kuin, 2 vols. (Oxford: Oxford University Press, 2012), 1:202, 200.

151. Alwes, *Sons and Authors*, 70 (italics in original).

152. Sidney, *The Lady of May*, 30.20ff. for what follows. The precise attribution of this song is baffling. Neither the original printed text (in the 1598 edition of the *Arcadia*) nor the sole independent manuscript witness give any sense that the speech was divided—yet the concluding lines contain an internal division ("Thus joyful I in chosen tunes rejoice. . . . Thus woeful I in woe this salve do find") that seems to suggest that both Therion and Espilus participated. Duncan-Jones and Van Dorsten, going further, attribute the entire second tale to Therion (*Miscellaneous Prose*). See Robert Kimbrough and Philip Murphy, "The Helmingham Hall Manuscript of Sidney's *The Lady of May*: A Commentary and Transcription," *Renaissance Drama* 1 (1968): 103–19.

153. Sidney, *The Covntess of Pembrokes Arcadia* (London, 1593), fol. 214. See Stephen Greenblatt, "Murdering Peasants: Status, Genre, and Representation of Rebellion," *Representations* 1 (1983): 1–29; and Richard M. Berrong, "Changing Depictions of Popular Revolt in Sixteenth-Century England: The Case of Sidney's Two *Arcadias*," *The Journal of Medieval and Renaissance Studies* 19, no. 1 (1989): 15–33.

154. Goldring et al.,*John Nichols's The Progresses and Public Processions of Queen Elizabeth I*, 2:814.

155. Doran, "Juno versus Diana," 272. In *The Lady of May*, Elizabeth's virginity is emphasized (though perhaps not celebrated) by Leicester's mock-worship; for discussion, see Louis Adrian Montrose, "Gifts and Reasons: The Contexts of Peele's *Araygnement of Paris*," *ELH: English Literary History* 47, no. 3 (1980): 443.

156. Louis Adrian Montrose, *The Subject of Elizabeth: Authority, Gender, and Representation* (Chicago: University of Chicago Press, 2006), 70.

157. George Peele, *The Araygnement of Paris* (London, 1584), Aii^{v}.

158. Montrose, "Gifts and Reasons," 444.

159. Montrose, "Of Gentlemen and Shepherds," 427.

160. Spenser, *The Faerie Queene*, IV.iv.39.

161. Ibid., IV.iv.42.

Chapter 4

1. ["Res est solliciti plena timoris amor."] Ovid, *Heroides*, ed. Arthur Palmer (Oxford: Clarendon, 1898), Ep. 1, line 12.

2. It appears, for example, in the familiar letters of both Erasmus and Sidney; see Erasmus, *Correspondence*, 1:135; and Sidney, *Correspondence of Sir Philip Sidney*, 1:44.

3. R. B. Wernham, *The Return of the Armadas: The Last Years of the Elizabethan War against Spain, 1595–1603* (Oxford: Clarendon, 1994), chap. 12.

4. TNA, SP 12/264, fol. 51; CP 33/49.

5. TNA, SP 12/264, fol. 46.

6. TNA, SP 12/264, fol. 56; CP 33/49.

7. TNA, SP 12/264, fol. 57.

8. Geoffrey Parker, "The *Dreadnought* Revolution of Tudor England," *The Mariner's Mirror* 82, no. 3 (1996): 286.

9. Samuel Purchas, *Purchas His Pilgrimes in Fiue Bookes* . . . (London, 1625), 1950.

10. The quote is from James McDermott's *ODNB* entry. See also Stephen Johnston, "Making Mathematical Practice: Gentlemen, Practitioners and Artisans in Elizabethan England," Ph.D. dissertation, University of Cambridge, 1994, chap. 3.

11. Parker, "*Dreadnought* Revolution," 269.

12. TNA, SP 12/264, fol. 58.

13. Ibid., fol. 46.

14. John Donne, "The Storme," lines 43–48, 65, 52 in John Donne, *The Complete English Poems*, ed. C. A. Patrides (London: Everyman, 1985); see Steve Mentz, "Donne at Sea: The Islands Voyage and Poetic Form," *Forum for Modern Language Studies* 49, no. 4 (2013): 355–68. A year before, Donne had also served with Essex in the more successful raid on Cadiz.

15. TNA, SP 12/264, fol. 46[v].

16. Ibid., fol. 56.

17. Sheldon Solomon, Jeff Greenberg, and Tom Pyszczynski, "The Cultural Animal: Twenty Years of Terror Management Theory and Research," in *Handbook of Experimental Existential Psychology*, ed. Jeff Greenberg, Sander L. Koole, and Tom Pyszczynski (New York: Guilford, 2004), 14.

18. Ibid., 16, for this and the next quote.

19. Jeff Greenberg, Tom Pyszczynski, and Sheldon Solomon, "The Causes and Consequences of a Need for Self-Esteem: A Terror Management Theory," in *Public Self and Private Self*, ed. Roy F. Baumeister (New York: Springer-Verlag, 1986), 198; Solomon, Greenberg, and Pyszczynski, "Cultural Animal," 17.

20. Solomon, Greenberg, and Pyszczynski, "Cultural Animal," 20.

21. Jamie Goldenberg et al., "Of Mice and Men, and Objectified Women: A Terror Management: Account of Infra-Humanization," *Group Processes & Intergroup Relations* 12, no. 6 (2009): 765. It is important to recognize that the findings of terror management theory are not bound to a secular context: because "belief in supernatural agents with omniscient and omnipotent powers can assuage existential anxiety," religion is crucial to the theory, insofar as "one of the most important functions of religious belief is reducing the terror surrounding the prospect of one's mortality" (Mike Friedman and W. Steven Rholes, "Successfully

Challenging Fundamentalist Beliefs Results in Increased Death Awareness," *Journal of Experimental Social Psychology* 43, no. 5 [2007]: 794; Mike Friedman, "Religious Fundamentalism and Responses to Mortality Salience: A Quantitative Text Analysis," *The International Journal for the Psychology of Religion* 18, no. 3 [2008]: 231). Indeed, "religious beliefs are particularly well suited to mitigate death anxiety because they are all encompassing, rely on concepts that are not easily disconfirmed, and promise literal immortality" (Kenneth E. Vail III et al., "A Terror Management Analysis of the Psychological Functions of Religion," *Personality and Social Psychology Review* 14, no. 1 [2010]: 84). See also Scott Atran and Ara Norenzayan, "Religion's Evolutionary Landscape: Counterintuition, Commitment, Compassion, Communion," *Behavioral and Brain Sciences* 27, no. 6 (2004): 713–30; Mike Friedman and W. Steven Rholes, "Religious Fundamentalism and Terror Management," *The International Journal for the Psychology of Religion* 18, no. 1 (2008): 36–52; Matthew Vess et al., "Exploring the Existential Function of Religion: The Effect of Religious Fundamentalism and Mortality Salience on Faith-Based Medical Refusals," *Journal of Personality and Social Psychology* 97, no. 2 (2009): 334–50; and Lee Ellis and Eshah A. Wahab, "Religiosity and Fear of Death: A Theory-Oriented Review of the Empirical Literature," *Review of Religious Research* 55, no. 1 (2013): 149–89.

22. Kenneth E. Vail III et al., "When Death Is Good for Life: Considering the Positive Trajectories of Terror Management," *Personality and Social Psychology Review* 16, no. 4 (2012): 312.

23. Solomon, Greenberg, and Pyszczynski, "Cultural Animal," 26; Mario Mikulincer, Victor Florian, and Gilad Hirschberger, "The Existential Function of Close Relationships: Introducing Death into the Science of Love," *Personality and Social Psychology Review* 7, no. 1 (2003): 20.

24. Solomon, Greenberg, and Pyszczynski, "Cultural Animal," 18; Jeroen Vaes, Nathan A. Heflick, and Jamie L. Goldenberg, "'We Are People': Ingroup Humanization as an Existential Defense," *Journal of Personality and Social Psychology* 98, no. 5 (2010): 751; Eddie Harmon-Jones et al., "Terror Management Theory and Self-Esteem: Evidence That Increased Self-Esteem Reduced Mortality Salience Effects," *Journal of Personality and Social Psychology* 72, no. 1 (1997): 24.

25. Jeff Greenberg, Sheldon Solomon, and Jamie Arndt, "A Basic but Uniquely Human Motivation: Terror Management," in *Handbook of Motivation Science,* ed. James Y. Shah and Wendi L. Gardner (New York: Guilford, 2008), 118; Goldenberg et al., "Of Mice and Men," 766.

26. Florette Cohen et al., "Fatal Attraction: The Effects of Mortality Salience on Evaluations of Charismatic, Task-Oriented, and Relationship-Oriented Leaders," *Psychological Science* 15, no. 12 (2004): 847; Florette Cohen and Sheldon Solomon, "The Politics of Mortal Terror," *Current Directions in Psychological Science* 20, no. 5 (2011): 316.

27. Jeff Greenberg and Spee Kosloff, "Terror Management Theory: Implications for Understanding Prejudice, Stereotyping, Intergroup Conflict, and Political Attitudes," *Social and Personality Psychology Compass* 2, no. 5 (2008): 1883.

28. Will Tosh, *Male Friendship and Testimonies of Love in Shakespeare's England* (London: Palgrave, 2016), 160; Alexandra Gajda, *The Earl of Essex and Late Elizabethan Political Culture* (Oxford: Oxford University Press, 2012), 143.

29. For Essex's life, see Paul E. J. Hammer, *The Polarisation of Elizabethan Politics: The Political Career of Robert Devereux, 2nd Earl of Essex, 1585–1597* (Cambridge: Cambridge University Press, 1999); Paul E. J. Hammer, "The Earl of Essex," in Smuts, *Oxford Handbook of the Age of Shakespeare*, 37–50; and Hammer's entry on Essex in the *ODNB*. Like all scholars of Essex, I am deeply indebted to his work. See also James, *Society, Politics and Culture,* chap. 9; Janet Dickinson, *Court Politics and the Earl of Essex, 1589–1601* (London: Pickering and Chatto, 2012); Gajda, *Earl of Essex*; Annaliese Connolly and Lisa Hopkins, eds., *Essex: The Cultural Impact of an Elizabethan Courtier* (Manchester: Manchester University Press, 2013); and Doran, *Elizabeth I & Her Circle*, chap. 7. For Walter Devereux, see J. J. N. McGurk's *ODNB* entry.

30. John Stow, *The Annales of England* (London, 1601), 1233.

31. Camden, *History of the Most Renowned*, 624.

32. Quoted in Paul E. J. Hammer, "Myth-Making: Politics, Propaganda and the Capture of Cadiz in 1596," *The Historical Journal* 40, no. 3 (1997): 627.

33. Arthur Collins, ed., *Letters and Memorials of State*, 2 vols. (London, 1746), 2:127.

34. Folger MS, V.a.164, fol. 24.

35. Patrick Collinson, "Ecclesiastical Vitriol: Religious Satire in the 1590s and the Invention of Puritanism," in *The Reign of Elizabeth I: Court and Culture in the Last Decade*, ed. John Guy (Cambridge: Cambridge University Press, 1995), 170. See this essay collection for the era generally—but, for an important corrective to the notion that this period was uniformly grim, see Dickinson, *Court Politics;* Janet Dickinson, "Leadership in the 1590s," in *Leadership and Elizabethan Culture,* ed. Peter Iver Kaufman (New York: Palgrave, 2013), 89–101; and Janet Dickinson and Neil Younger, "Just How Nasty Were the 1590s?" *History Today* 64, no. 7 (2014): 10–16.

36. In fact, the most thorough philosophical treatment of dread emerges from this theological context; see Søren Kierkegaard, *The Concept of Dread*, trans. Walter Lowrie (Princeton, N.J.: Princeton University Press, 1944). The title is also translated as *The Concept of Anxiety*, as in the edition of Reidar Thomte (Princeton, N.J.: Princeton University Press, 1980). For a general introduction to the text, see Robert L. Perkins, ed., *International Kierkegaard Commentary: The Concept of Anxiety* (Macon, Ga.: Mercer University Press, 1985).

37. Richard Morris, ed., *Old English Homilies and Homiletic Treatises* (London, 1868), 20–21. (Morris's translation.)

38. John Hayward, *The Sanctuarie of a Troubled Soule* (London, 1601), 102.

39. *OED*, "dread, *v*."

40. Peter Wentworth, *A Pithie Exhortation to Her Maiestie for Establishing Her Successor to the Crowne* (Edinburgh, 1598), 8. On the succession controversy generally during Elizabeth's reign, see Mortimer Levine, *The Early Elizabethan Succession Question, 1558–1568* (Stanford, Calif.: Stanford University Press, 1966); Anne McLaren, "The Quest for a King: Gender, Marriage, and Succession in Elizabethan England," *The Journal of British Studies* 41, no. 3 (2002): 259–90; David Scott Wilson-Okamura, "Spenser and the Two Queens," *ELR* 32, no. 1 (2002): 62–84; Lisa Hopkins, *Drama and the Succession to the Crown, 1561–1633* (Burlington, Vt.: Ashgate, 2011); and Susan Doran and Paulina Kewes, eds., *Doubtful and Dangerous: The Question of Succession in Late Elizabethan*

England (Manchester: Manchester University Press, 2014). On Elizabethan awareness of the French civil wars, see Lisa Ferraro Parmelee, *Good Newes from Fraunce: French Anti-League Propaganda in Late Elizabethan England* (Rochester, N.Y.: University of Rochester Press, 1996).

41. See Wernham, *Return of the Armadas*, chap. 9; and De Lamar Jensen, "The Spanish Armada: The Worst-Kept Secret in Europe," *The Sixteenth Century Journal* 19, no. 4 (1988): 621–41.

42. CP 175/117.

43. Steve Rappaport, *Worlds within Worlds: Structures of Life in Sixteenth-Century London* (Cambridge: Cambridge University Press, 1989), 137. For general discussion, see John Bohstedt, *The Politics of Provisions: Food Riots, Moral Economy, and Market Transition in England, c. 1550–1850* (Burlington, Vt.: Ashgate, 2010).

44. TNA, SP 12/263, fol. 191; George Abbot, *An Exposition Vpon the Prophet Ionah* (London, 1600), 366.

45. Camden, *History of the Most Renowned*, 477. See Paul Slack, *The Impact of Plague in Tudor and Stuart England* (London: Routledge and Kegan Paul, 1985), 151.

46. TNA, SP 46/57, fol. 99; *Orders, Thought Meete by Her Maiestie, and Her Priuie Counsell to Be Executed Throughout the Counties of This Realme* (London, 1593), A1.

47. William Perkins, *The Works of That Famovs and Worthie Minister of Christ in the Vniversitie of Cambridge, M.W. Perkins*, 3 vols. (Cambridge, 1608–09), 3:470; see also Anthony Marten, *A Second Sound, or Warning of the Trumpet Vnto Judgement* (London, 1589), 2–4^{v}; and Sheltco à Geveren, *Of the End of This Worlde, and the Seconde Comming of Christ* (London, 1589), 9^{v}–10. On Tudor apocalypticism, see Richard Bauckham, *Tudor Apocalypse: Sixteenth Century Apocalypticism, Millenarianism and the English Reformation* (Oxford: Sutton Courtenay, 1978); and Bernard Capp, "The Political Dimension of Apocalyptic Thought," in *The Apocalypse in English Renaissance Thought and Literature*, ed. C. A. Patrides and Joseph Wittreich (Manchester: Manchester University Press, 1984), 93–124. In 1580 there was much literary response to the Dover Straits earthquake, one of the largest seismic events in British history; see G. Neilson, R. M. W. Musson, and P. W. Burton, "The 'London' Earthquake of 1580, April 6," *Engineering Geology* 20 (1984): 113–41.

48. Perkins, *Works of That Famovs and Worthie Minister*, 3:470.

49. Francis Bacon, "Of Faction," in *Bacon's Essays and Colours of Good and Evil*, ed. W. Aldis Wright (London, 1862), 207, 209.

50. Cornwallis, *Essayes*, E1^{v}; E2. Essex knighted Cornwallis in the Irish campaign of 1599.

51. Robert Naunton, *Fragmenta Regalia, or Observations on the Late Queen Elizabeth* (London, 1641), 6.

52. Adams, *Leicester and the Court*, 47; see Dickinson, *Court Politics*. The debate centers on whether claims of factionalism (like that of Naunton's) have been exaggerated, and whether it was a more restricted social phenomenon than has been usually thought. On faction see, for example, E. W. Ives, *Faction in Tudor England* (London: Historical Association, 1979); David Starkey, "From Feud to Faction: English Politics Circa 1450–1550," *History Today* 32, no. 11

(1982): 16–22; Paul E. J. Hammer, "'Absolute and Sovereign Mistress of Her Grace'? Queen Elizabeth I and Her Favourites, 1581–1592," in *The World of the Favourite*, ed. J. H. Elliott and L. W. B. Brockliss (New Haven, Conn.: Yale University Press, 1999), 38–53; Paul E. J. Hammer, "Patronage at Court, Faction, and the Earl of Essex," in Guy, *Reign of Elizabeth I*, 65–86; Adams, *Leicester and the Court;* Mears, "Courts, Courtiers, and Culture"; Natalie Mears, *Queenship and Political Discourse in the Elizabethan Realms* (Cambridge: Cambridge University Press, 2005); and Mary Partridge, "Images of the Courtier in Elizabethan England," Ph.D. dissertation, University of Birmingham, 2008. See also Mallin, "Emulous Factions."

53. See Isaac Goldberg, *The Wonder of Words: An Introduction to Language for Everyman* (New York: D. Appleton-Century, 1938), chap. 12; and Joseph T. Shipley, *Playing with Words* (Englewood Cliffs, N.J.: Prentice-Hall, 1960), 77.

54. In the existentialist tradition of Kierkegaard, Heidegger, and Sartre, dread is analogously seen as a vindication of autonomy, despite its native associations with awe and reverence. In addition to Kierkegaard (see note 36 of this chapter), see Jean-Paul Sartre, *Being and Nothingness: An Essay in Phenomenological Ontology,* trans. Hazel E. Barnes (New York: Citadel, 2001); and Martin Heidegger, *Being and Time*, trans. John Macquarrie and Edward Robinson (New York: Harper Perennial, 2008). See also Paul Megna, "Better Living through Dread: Medieval Ascetics, Modern Philosophers, and the Long History of Existential Anxiety," *PMLA* 130, no. 5 (2015): 1285–1301.

55. Thomas Birch, ed., *Memoirs of the Reign of Queen Elizabeth*, 2 vols. (London, 1754), 1:134; see Partridge, "Images of the Courtier," 260–61.

56. TNA, SP 12/265, fol.16.

57. Folger MS, V.a.164, fol. 29^{v}.

58. CP 64/92; CP 68/4.

59. Quoted in Paul E. J. Hammer, "Shakespeare's *Richard II*, the Play of 7 February 1601, and the Essex Rising," *Shakespeare Quarterly* 59, no. 1 (2008): 10.

60. Folger MS, V.a.164, fol. 25.

61. CP 81/45.

62. CP 80/2; CP 79/74. When *An Apologie of the Earle of Essex*—a document, written two years earlier, vociferously advocating war with Spain—was published in May 1600, Essex blamed the corruption of his servants and the machination of conspirators working falsely in his name. See Hugh Gazzard, "'Idle Papers': *An Apology of the Earl of Essex,*" in Connolly and Hopkins, *Essex*, 179–200.

63. TNA, SP 12/265, fol.16^{v}.

64. BL, Cotton MS Galba D/I, fol. 136.

65. TNA, SP 12/239, fol. 93.

66. Henry Unton, *Correspondence of Sir Henry Unton*, ed. Rev. Joseph Stevenson (London, 1847), 264.

67. Quoted in Hammer, "Myth-Making," 627.

68. Birch, *Memoirs*, 2:101.

69. Hammer, *Polarisation of Elizabethan Politics*, 280.

70. Bacon, *Works*, 9:96.

71. See Paul E. J. Hammer, "The Earl of Essex, Fulke Greville, and the Employment of Scholars," *Studies in Philology* 91, no. 2 (1994): 167–80; and Paul E. J. Hammer, "The Use of Scholarship: The Secretariat of Robert Devereux, Second

Earl of Essex, c. 1585–1601," *The English Historical Review* 109, no. 430 (1994): 26–51.

72. See F. J. Levy, "Philip Sidney Reconsidered," *English Literary Renaissance* 2, no. 1 (1972): 6; James, *Society, Politics, and Culture,* 387ff.; J. H. M. Salmon, "Stoicism and Roman Example: Seneca and Tacitus in Jacobean England," *Journal of the History of Ideas* 50, no. 2 (1989): 205; and Joel Davis, "Multiple *Arcadias* and the Literary Quarrel between Fulke Greville and the Countess of Pembroke," *Studies in Philology* 101, no. 4 (2004): 407ff.

73. On Tacitus, see Edwin B. Benjamin, "Sir John Hayward and Tacitus," *The Review of English Studies* 8, no. 31 (1957): 275–76; Edwin B. Benjamin, "Bacon and Tacitus," *Classical Philology* 60, no. 2 (1965): 102–10; Kenneth C. Schellhase, *Tacitus in Renaissance Political Thought* (Chicago: University of Chicago Press, 1976); Alan T. Bradford, "Stuart Absolutism and the 'Utility' of Tacitus," *Huntington Library Quarterly* 46, no. 2 (1983): 127–55; Salmon, "Stoicism and Roman Example"; J. H. M. Salmon, "Seneca and Tacitus in Jacobean England," in *The Mental World of the Jacobean Court,* ed. Linda Levy Peck (Cambridge: Cambridge University Press, 1991), 169–88; Peter Burke, "Tacitism, Scepticism, and Reason of State," in *The Cambridge History of Political Thought, 1450–1700,* ed. J. H. Burns (Cambridge: Cambridge University Press, 1991), 479–98; David Womersley, "Sir Henry Savile's Translation of Tacitus and the Political Interpretation of Elizabethan Texts," *The Review of English Studies* 42, no. 167 (1991): 313–42; David Womersley, "Sir John Hayward's Tacitism," *Renaissance Studies* 6, no. 1 (1992): 46–59; T. J. Luce and A. J. Woodman, eds., *Tacitus and the Tacitean Tradition* (Princeton, N.J.: Princeton University Press, 1993); Malcolm Smuts, "Court-Centred Politics and the Uses of Roman Historians, c. 1590–1630," in *Culture and Politics in Early Stuart England,* ed. Kevin Sharpe and Peter Lake (Stanford, Calif.: Stanford University Press, 1993), 21–43; A. J. Woodman, ed., *The Cambridge Companion to Tacitus* (Cambridge: Cambridge University Press, 2009); Paulina Kewes, "Henry Savile's Tacitus and the Politics of Roman History in Late Elizabethan England," *Huntington Library Quarterly* 74, no. 4 (2011): 515–51; Alexandra Gajda, "The Earl of Essex and 'Politic History,'" in Connolly and Hopkins, *Essex*, 237–59; and Bradley J. Irish, "The Literary Afterlife of the Essex Circle: Fulke Greville, Tacitus, and BL Additional MS 18638," *Modern Philology* 112, no. 1 (2014): 271–85. On Essex and Roman history more generally, see Paulina Kewes, "Roman History, Essex, and Late Elizabethan Political Culture," in Smuts, *Oxford Handbook of the Age of Shakespeare,* 250–68.

74. See S. L. Goldberg, "Sir John Hayward, 'Politic' Historian," *The Review of English Studies* 6, no. 23 (1955): 233–44. For the changing curriculum at Cambridge, see ibid., 235; and more generally, Lisa Jardine, "The Place of Dialectic Teaching in Sixteenth-Century Cambridge," *Studies in the Renaissance* 21 (1974): 31–62. For Essex at Cambridge, see Hammer, *Polarisation of Elizabethan Politics*, 24ff.

75. Despite the innovations of politic history, recent scholarship has importantly cautioned us against the previous generation's teleological account of Renaissance historiographical development, which envisioned a secularization process by which early modern thinkers gradually came to acquire something like a modern historical sensibility. See David Womersley, "Against the Teleology

of Technique," in *The Uses of History in Early Modern England*, ed. Paulina Kewes (San Marino, Calif.: Huntington Library, 2006), 91–104; David Womersley, *Divinity and State* (Oxford: Oxford University Press, 2010), 8–10; and Alexandra Walsham, "Providentialism," in *The Oxford Handbook of Holinshed's Chronicles,* ed. Paulina Kewes, Ian W. Archer, and Felicity Heal (Oxford: Oxford University Press, 2013), 427–42.

76. F. J. Levy, "Hayward, Daniel, and the Beginnings of Politic History in England," *Huntington Library Quarterly* 50, no. 1 (1987): 4.

77. See Kewes, "Henry Savile's Tacitus," 525; and note 75.

78. Robert Johnson, *Essaies, or Rather Imperfect Offers* (London, 1601), D2–D3, for this and the next quote. For further discussion of Johnson, see Bradford, "Stuart Absolutism," 130–31.

79. Michel de Montaigne, *Essayes or Morall, Politike and Millitarie Discourses* (London, 1603), 554. See also Womersley, "Sir John Hayward's Tacitism," 49ff. For discussion of the relationship between rhetoric and effeminacy, see Jennifer Richards, "'A Wanton Trade of Living'? Rhetoric, Effeminacy, and the Early Modern Courtier," *Criticism* 42, no. 2 (2000): 185–206.

80. Goldberg, "Sir John Hayward," 243.

81. Benjamin, "Bacon and Tacitus," 107.

82. Johnson, *Essaies*, D4^{v}.

83. Bacon, *Works*, 9:25. Brian Vickers argues the letter was ghostwritten by Bacon; see his "The Authenticity of Bacon's Earliest Writings," *Studies in Philology* 94, no. 2 (1997): 248–96; and Hammer's refutation at *Polarisation of Elizabethan Politics*, 149 n. 200.

84. BL, Cotton MS Vespasian F/XIII, fol. 290.

85. Ben Jonson, "Conversations with William Drummond," in *Ben Jonson*, ed. C. H. Herford and Percy Simpson, 11 vols. (Oxford: Clarendon, 1925–52), 1:142.

86. Bradford, "Stuart Absolutism," 132; Henry Savile, *The Ende of Nero and Beginning of Galba: Fower Bookes of the Histories of Cornelius Tacitus* (Oxford, 1591), 3.

87. Savile, *Ende of Nero*, 3^{v}.

88. Jonson, "To Sir Henrie Savile," in *Ben Jonson* (vol. 8), lines 7–12. See also Womersley, "Sir Henry Savile," 314.

89. Savile, *Ende of Nero*, 6. See Bradford, "Stuart Absolutism," 146.

90. Womersley, "Sir Henry Savile," 342.

91. Kewes, "Henry Savile's Tacitus," 551. See also J. H. Waszink, "Henry Savile's Tacitus and the English Role on the Continent: Leicester, Hotman, Lipsius," *History of European Ideas* 42, no. 3 (2016): 303–19, which emphasizes a different context than Kewes but echoes her caution against anachronistic reading.

92. Kewes, "Henry Savile's Tacitus," 526. Malcolm Smuts similarly notes that "followers of the second Earl of Essex . . . read Tacitus as a guide to the many ways in which courtiers, spies and informers can manipulate a ruler's jealousies"; see Smuts, "The Politics of Royal Jealousy," unpublished talk, Renaissance Society of America Annual Meeting, Venice, 2010. I am grateful to Dr. Smuts for sharing his paper with me.

93. Savile, *Ende of Nero*, 3, 2^{v}.

94. Ibid., 3.

95. Alexandra Gajda, "*The State of Christendom*: History, Political Thought and the Essex Circle," *Historical Research* 81, no. 213 (2008): 426. Hammer observes that "if Essex and his inner circle could be said to have had any kind of guidebook for their actions," it was *The State of Christendom* ("Shakespeare's *Richard II*," 12).

96. Henry Wotton, *The State of Christendom, or, A Most Exact and Curious Discovery of Many Secret Passages, and Hidden Mysteries of the Times* (London, 1657), 5.

97. Ibid., 24; Gajda, "*State of Christendom*," 435.

98. Gajda, "*State of Christendom*," 439.

99. Hammer, *Polarisation of Elizabethan Politics*, 400.

100. *CSPS*, XVII, 423, for this and the next quotation. (Note that the State Papers Spanish restart their volume numbering with the reign of Elizabeth, so this volume is marked "Vol. IV, Elizabeth, 1587–1603.)

101. See Richard C. McCoy, "'A Dangerous Image': The Earl of Essex and Elizabethan Chivalry," *Journal of Medieval and Renaissance Studies* 13, no. 2 (1983): 313–29.

102. Hammer, *Polarisation of Elizabethan Politics,* 201.

103. Collins, *Letters and Memorials of State*, 1:362. See also Paul E. J. Hammer, "Upstaging the Queen: The Earl of Essex, Francis Bacon and the Accession Day Celebrations of 1595," in *The Politics of the Stuart Court Masque*, ed. David Bevington and Peter Holbrook (Cambridge: Cambridge University Press, 1998), 41–66; and Linda S. Shenk, "'To Love and Be Wise': The Earl of Essex, Humanist Court Culture, and England's Learned Queen," *Early Modern Literary Studies* Special Issue 16 (2007), http://purl.oclc.org/emls/si-16/shenwise.htm.

104. Hammer, "Myth-Making," 621.

105. BL, Egerton 2877, fol. 16–16^{v} ; "An Excellent Song on the Winning of Cales by the English," in *The Roxburghe Ballads*, ed. William Chappell and J. Woodfall Ebsworth, 9 vols. (Hertford, 1870–99), 6:402–3.

106. See Hammer, *Polarisation of Elizabethan Politics*, 211.

107. Edward Guilpin, *Skialetheia, or, A Shadowe of Truth, in Certain Epigrams and Satyres* (London, 1598), C8^{v}–D.

108. Ibid., C3^{v}.

109. On Essex and popularity, see Gajda, *Earl of Essex*, chap. 5.

110. Bacon, *Works*, 9:44.

111. Folger MS, V.b.142, fol. 47; Folger MS, V.a.164, fol. 38^{v}.

112. Robert Devereux, Earl of Essex, *An Apologie of the Earle of Essex* (London, 1600?), B2^{v}–B3. Hammer suspects that "a majority of his friends were men with whom he shared the special bond of going on campaign together"; see Hammer, *Polarisation of Elizabethan Politics*, 216ff., for further discussion.

113. TNA, SP 12/259, fol. 179^{v}; Folger MS. V.b.142, fol. 29.

114. Folger MS, V.b.41, p. 288, for this and the next quotation.

115. Collins, *Letters and Memorials of State*, 2:130–31.

116. CP 74/89.

117. Bacon, *Works*, 9:43.

118. Folger MS, V.a.164, fol. 37.

119. Essex, *Apologie*, B3.

120. CP 251/134.

121. CP 90/150.

122. TNA, 12/278, fol. 130.

123. Stephen Greenblatt, ed., *The Power of Forms in the English Renaissance* (Normal, Okla.: Pilgrim Books, 1982). On the topic more generally, see Leeds Barroll, "A New History for Shakespeare and His Time," *Shakespeare Quarterly* 39, no. 4 (1988): 441–64; Arthur F. Kinney, "Essex and Shakespeare versus Hayward," *Shakespeare Quarterly* 44, no. 4 (1993): 464–66; Jonathan Bate, "Was Shakespeare an Essex Man?" *Proceedings of the British Academy* 162 (2009): 1–28; Louis Adrian Montrose, *The Purpose of Playing: Shakespeare and the Cultural Politics of the Elizabethan Theatre* (Chicago: University of Chicago Press, 1996), chap. 5; Chris Fitter, "Historicising Shakespeare's *Richard II*: Current Events, Dating, and the Sabotage of Essex," *Early Modern Literary Studies* 11 (2005), http://purl.oclc.org/emls/11-2/fittric2.htm; and Hammer, "Shakespeare's *Richard II*."

124. TNA, SP 12/278, fol. 139.

125. Hammer, "Shakespeare's *Richard II*," 18.

126. Francis Bacon, *A Declaration of the Practices & Treasons Attempted and Committed by Robert Late Earle of Essex and His Complices* (London, 1601), K3.

127. For a concise account of Hayward's troubles, see the introduction to John Hayward, *The First and Second Parts of John Hayward's The Life and Raigne of King Henrie IIII*, ed. John J. Manning (London: Royal Historical Society, 1991), 17–34. See also Alzada J. Tipton, "'Lively Patterns . . . for Affayres of State': Sir John Hayward's *The Life and Reigne of King Henrie IIII* and the Earl of Essex," *Sixteenth Century Journal* 33, no. 3 (2002): 769–94; and Rebecca Lemon, *Treason by Words: Literature, Law, and Rebellion in Shakespeare's England* (Ithaca, N.Y.: Cornell University Press, 2006), chap. 2.

128. Bacon famously declared that Hayward "had committed very apparent theft, for he had taken most of the sentences of Cornelius Tacitus, and translated them into English, and put them into his text" (*Works*, 10:150).

129. TNA, SP 12/275, fol. 42[v]. Or, as Hammer puts it, Hayward treated a "childless sovereign troubled by rebellion in Ireland, facing widespread discontent over heavy taxation, and buffered by bitter factionalism at court and accusations that key royal councilors lacked sufficient respect for martial honour and the status of the peerage" (Hammer, "The Smiling Crocodile: The Earl of Essex and Late Elizabethan 'Popularity,'" in *The Politics of the Public Sphere in Early Modern England*, ed. Peter Lake and Steven Pincus [Manchester: Manchester University Press, 2007], 95–96).

130. Fynes Moryson, *The Itinerary of Fynes Moryson*, 4 vols. (Glasgow, 1907),

131. Bacon, *Works*, 10:150.

132. TNA, SP 12/278, fol. 80.

133. For the Cadiz affair (and what follows below), I follow Hammer, "Myth-Making." See also Wernham, *Return of the Armadas*, chaps. 7 and 8; and Tosh, *Male Friendship*, 144–47.

134. Lambeth Palace Library, MS 658, fol. 88 for what follows.

135. The document was to be titled "A true Relacion of the Action at Calez the 21 of June vnder the Earle of Essex, and the Lord Admirall sent to a gentleman in Court from one that serued there in good place" (ibid). "Calez" was the period's common designation for the modern "Cadiz."

136. See Hammer, "Use of Scholarship."

137. Lambeth Palace Library, MS 658, fol. 259v.

138. Hammer, "Myth-Making," 632.

139. Poem 1, lines 35–36 in Steven W. May, "The Poems of Edward DeVere, Seventeenth Earl of Oxford and of Robert Devereux, Second Earl of Essex," *Studies in Philology* 77, no. 5 (1980): 1–132; Alastair Bellany and Andrew McRae, eds., "Early Stuart Libels: An Edition of Poetry from Manuscript Sources." *Early Modern Literary Studies* Text Series I (2005), http://purl.oclc.org/emls/texts/libels /, A3, A4, A5. All citations of Essex's poems are from May's edition. On libels in the period, see May and Alan Bryson, eds., *Verse Libel in Renaissance England and Scotland* (Oxford: Oxford University Press, 2016).

140. Folger MS, V.b.142, fol. 50.

141. Bellany and McRae, "Early Stuart Libels," A7, lines 3, 11, 15, 14, 27.

142. Ibid., A8.

143. Ibid., A12, line 10.

144. Ibid., A9, lines 1–5.

145. Ibid., lines 7–8.

146. Ibid., A13, lines 12–14. According to Bellany and McRae, "Burghley Clowne" refers to "Thomas Cecil, 2nd Lord Burghley, Cecil's older brother."

147. Folger MS, V.b.142, fol. 49.

148. CP 83/67, for this and the following quotation. I discuss this document in Bradley J. Irish,"Libels and the Essex Rising," *Notes and Queries* 59, no. 1 (2012): 87–89. When I published this article announcing the document, I was unaware that it had been previously discussed in Andrew Gordon, "The Act of Libel: Conscripting Civic Space in Early Modern England," *Journal of Medieval and Early Modern Studies* 32, no. 2 (2002): 391. See also Joseph Mansky, "'Unlawfully Published': Libels and the Public Sphere in *Titus Andronicus*," *Shakespeare Quarterly* 67, no. 3 (2016): 293.

149. John Harington, *Nugae Antiquae*, 3 vols. (London, 1792), 2:225.

150. Folger MS, V.b. 41, p. 303.

151. Folger MS, V.a.164, fol. 47.

152. Ibid., fol. 25.

153. Ibid., fol. 29v, 27v, 29.

154. Ibid., fol. 80v.

155. Ibid., fol. 42v.

156. H. L. Stephen, ed., *State Trials, Political and Social*, 4 vols. (London, 1899–1902), 3:80.

157. Ibid., 3:78.

158. Hammer, "Shakespeare's *Richard II*," 14–15.

159. TNA, SP 12/278, fol. 207. The following quotations are from this account of Essex's prison confession. See Alan Stewart, "Instigating Treason: The Life and Death of Henry Cuffe, Secretary," in *Literature, Politics and Law in Renaissance England*, ed. Erica Sheen and Lorna Hutson (New York: Palgrave, 2005), 50–70.

160. Ibid., fol. 207v.

161. Essex, Poem 11, lines 265–70.

162. Ibid., lines 289–94.

163. TNA, SP 12/279, fol. 45, for this and what follows.

164. Essex, Poem 10, lines 1–5.

165. Essex, Poem 11. Subsequent citations parenthetical.

166. Howell and Howell, *Complete Collection of State Trials*, 1:1358–59. J. A. Sharpe has examined how "the civil and religious authorities designed the execution spectacle to articulate a particular set of values, inculcate a certain behavioural model and bolster a social order perceived as threatened"; see "'Last Dying Speeches': Religion, Ideology and Public Execution in Seventeenth-Century England," *Past & Present* 107 (1985): 148. See also Peter Lake and Michael Questier, "Agency, Appropriation and Rhetoric under the Gallows: Puritans, Romanists and the State in Early Modern England," *Past & Present* 153 (1996): 64–107. On the emotional scripts of the early modern execution, see Frederika Bain, "The Affective Scripts of Early Modern Execution and Murder," in Meek and Sullivan, *Renaissance of Emotion*, 221–40.

167. Howell and Howell, *Complete Collection of State Trials*, 1:1359.

168. Ibid., 1:1360.

169. Folger MS, V.b. 41, p. 315.

170. Ibid.; Stephen, *State Trials*, 3:86.

171. Stephen, *State Trials*, 3:87, for this and the next quotation.

172. Henry Wotton, *A Parallell Betweene Robert Late Earle of Essex, and George Late Duke of Buckingham* (London, 1641), 5.

173. See *OED*, "affection."

INDEX

Adams, Simon, 149
affect studies, 3, 5–6, 8, 181n10
Alba, Fernando Álvarez de Toledo, Duke of, 97–98
Alwes, Derek B., 132, 212n67
angry young man of privilege archetype, 62
Angyal, Andras, 26
Anjou and Alençon, Francis, Duke of, 134
Aristotle, 73
Arthur (king), 117, 122, 216n117

Bacon, Anthony, 150, 157–58
Bacon, Francis, 153, 157, 163, 166–67, 208n161, 228n128; on envy, 76, 91, 202n35; on factions, 148; on popularity, 161–62
Baker, Matthew, 138
Bakhtin, Mikhail, 31, 195n80
Barclay, Alexander, 66
Barlowe, Jerome, 20, 24–25, 34–35, 37, 41–43
Bates, Catherine, 110, 129, 131, 217n125, 219n150
Becker, Ernest, 141
Becket, Thomas, 24
Belsey, Catherine, 11
Berry, Edward, 130–31
Berry, Philippa, 213n75
Boleyn, Anne, 22, 45, 48, 59, 60
Bolingbroke. *See* Henry IV
Bridges, John, 81
Brigden, Susan, 77, 206n113
Brooke, William, 138
Buckingham, Edward, Duke of, 20, 43, 55–56
Burke, Kenneth, 74

Callard, Felicity, 8
Campana, Joseph, 3
Campeggio, Lorenzo, 23, 44
Camus, Albert, 106
Capitanio, John P., 13
Carleton, George, 174
Casimir, John, 99, 126, 134
Cassirer, Ernst, 113
Castelfranchi, Cristiano, 64
Catherine of Aragon, 22–23, 111
Cavendish, George, 21–22, 24, 32, 48–50, 52, 199n157
Cecil, Robert, 144–45, 153, 158, 162, 164, 167–69
Cefalu, Paul, 12
Chaloner, Thomas, 90–91
Chapuys, Eustace, 59, 60, 78, 79
Charles V, 22, 23
Childs, Jessie, 78, 90
Churchyard, Thomas, 33–34, 43, 160
Clarke, Simon, 13–14
Clement VII, 23, 44
Cobham, Henry Brooke, Baron, 146, 151, 168
Cockcroft, Robert, 3
Coke, Edward, 145, 168
Collinson, Patrick, 4, 146
Connolly, William E., 11
Cook, Amy, 12
Cooper, Robert, 110, 131
Copley, Anthony, 30
Cornish, William, 110–11
Cornwallis, William, 66, 148–49
Cotton, George and Richard, 61, 201n18
Crane, Mary Thomas, 12
Crewe, Jonathan V., 76, 204n74
Cromwell, Thomas, 52, 60
Cuffe, Henry, 151–52, 157, 167, 172–74
Cvetkovich, Ann, 5

Damasio, Antonio, 5, 8
Darwin, Charles, 25–26
Davison, William, 97, 100
Dawkins, Richard, 8
delinquency, 104
Devereux, Robert. *See* Essex, Robert Devereux, Earl of
Dickinson, Janet, 149
disgust, 5, 7, 16, 25–31, 56, 190nn36–39, 191n46, 192n51, 199n167; abjection and, 52–53; etymology of, 30–31, 195n74; Freud on, 191n45;

disgust, *continued*
Wolsey and, 14, 21, 25, 28, 32–53, 56, 199n160
Donne, John, 139
Doran, Susan, 96, 126, 134, 218n132
Douglas, Mary, 25, 28, 56
dread, 5, 15, 16, 140–43, 146–50, 172, 176–77, 224n54; etymology of, 147; Essex and, 15, 139, 146, 150, 153, 158, 164; Kierkegaard and, 222n36, 224n54; Surrey and, 90
du Bellay, Jean, 45
Dudley, John, 82, 89, 206n120
Dudley, Robert. *See* Leicester, Robert Dudley, Earl of
Duncan-Jones, Katherine, 107, 129, 130–31, 212n67
Dupré, John, 11–12
Dutch revolt, 97–99

Edward I, 83, 87–88
Edward VI, 17, 77, 82, 88; Surrey and, 58, 62, 84, 85–86
Ekman, Paul, 8
Elias, Norbert, 190n36
Elizabeth I, 15, 16, 98–101, 115–35; Essex and, 137, 140, 144–46, 153, 158, 159–60, 162–64, 172, 174; final years of, 137, 140, 146, 148, 166–67; Gloriana cult, 109, 123, 134–35; Leicester and, 95–96, 115–22, 126, 137; progresses of, 95, 106–7, 115, 134, 216n118; Sidney and, 128, 130, 132–33
Ellis, Hugh, 85
Elyot, Thomas, 67
emulation. *See* envy
emotion: politics and, 4–6; scholarship on, 3, 6, 8–10, 12–14; scientific models of, 8–11
Enterline, Lynn, 3
envy, 56–57, 63–67, 71–73, 76, 202n40; emulation and, 66–67, 73, 74, 91; etymology of, 65; in *The Faerie Queene*, 65, 93, 202n39; malicious vs. benign, 65–67, 69; Surrey and, 15, 58, 63, 69–71, 74–77, 90–91; vs. jealousy, 71–72
Erasmus, Desiderius, 22, 55, 90
Essex, Robert Devereux, Earl of, 15, 62, 105, 116, 137–30, 143–46, 148–77; ballads on, 160; Cadiz raid by, 144, 153, 160–61; Elizabeth and, 137, 140, 144–46, 153, 158, 159–60, 162–64, 172, 174; execution of, 140, 146, 172, 177, 230n166; poems by, 173–74, 175–76; poetic libels regarding, 167–69; on Tacitus, 156–57; uprising by, 5, 140, 145–46, 151, 159–60, 162, 165–67, 169–72. *See also* dread
Essex, Walter Devereux, Earl of, 143
Étampes, Anne de Pisseleu d'Heilly, Duchesse d', 86, 87
Etchegoyen, R. Horacio, 76

factionalism, 15, 140, 143, 148–51, 155, 157, 223n52
Fallon, April E., 26
Fitzroy, Henry. *See* Richmond, Henry Fitzroy, Duke of
forester figure, 107–8, 110–12, 128–31
Fox, Cora, 3
Fox, Richard, 21
Foxe, John, 51
Francis I, 22, 23, 78, 86–87
Frye, Susan, 120

Gajda, Alexandra, 143, 158
Gascoigne, George, 115–23, 217n119, 217n125
George (patron saint), 113
Gil, Daniel Juan, 3
Girard, René, 64
Giustinian, Sebastian, 32, 38, 40
Govan, Cassandra L., 105
Gowland, Angus, 180n5
Greenblatt, Stephen, 165
Guercis, Balthasar de, 35
Guicciardini, Francesco, 50
Guilpin, Everard, 161
Gwyn, Peter, 35, 48, 195n81

Habermas, Jürgen, 5
Haidt, Jonathan, 5, 27, 29
Hall, Edward, 44, 47, 51, 110
Hammer, Paul E. J., 153, 159, 165, 167, 227n95, 227n112, 228n129
Harington, John, 170
Hart, F. Elizabeth, 12, 185n46
Hayward, John, 166–67, 228nn128–29
Henry IV (of France), 144
Henry IV, 155, 161, 166–67, 173
Henry V, 78, 79
Henry VII, 21, 155
Henry VIII, 14–15, 55–56, 78, 89–90, 218n139; Arthur and, 117; Boleyn affair and, 22–23, 44, 48, 60; forester and wild man figures favored by, 110, 111, 113;

Metsys's engraving of, 19; physicality of, 19–20, 78; Richmond and, 59–61; Surrey and, 68–69, 78–82, 84, 88, 90; Wolsey and, 21–23, 38–41, 44–48, 53
Hertford, Edward Seymour, Earl of, 61, 62, 81–82, 86, 89
historical phenomenology, 7, 10. *See also* humoralism
Hogan, Lalita Pandit, 8
Hogan, Patrick Colm, 8, 9, 12
homoeroticism, 70, 73, 204n65
Howard, Henry. *See* Surrey, Henry Howard, Earl of
Howard, Jean E., 10
Howard, Katherine, 77
Howard, Thomas, 137
humoralism, 3, 6, 8, 10, 180n5

"Impeachment of Wolsey, An" (anon.), 24, 36, 39
Irby, Anthony, 39, 56

James VI (I), 151, 174
jealousy, 56, 58, 63, 64, 71–74
Johnson, Robert, 154–55, 158
Jonson, Ben, 156–57

Karant-Nunn, Susan C., 3
Kass, Leon, 194n71
Kenilworth entertainment (1575). *See* pageants
Kewes, Paulina, 157
King, John N., 217n124
Kinney, Arthur, 12
Kristeva, Julia, 52

Laneham, Robert, 115, 118–19
Leary, Mark R., 103
LeDoux, Joseph, 8
Lee, Henry, 123
Leicester, Robert Dudley, Earl of, 15, 94–106, 114–26, 130–36, 151, 152; Elizabeth and, 95–96, 115–22, 126, 137; Essex and, 143–44, 159, 162; Kenilworth pageant and, 115–23; Robin Hood and, 111–12, 131; Woodstock pageant and, 123–25, 218n132. *See also* rejection
Leicester's Commonwealth (anon.), 96
Leys, Ruth, 8
Lines, Candice, 68

Machiavelli, Niccolò, 50, 154, 161, 168
Mary I, 17
Maslen, R. W., 123
Mason, William A., 13
Massumi, Brian, 7
McCauley, Clark, 27, 29
Metsys, Cornelis, 19
Mattingly, Garrett, 20
Merrick, Gilly, 151–52, 165–66, 174
Meyers, Jonathan Rhys, 19
Miceli, Maria, 64
Montaigne, Michel de, 155
Montrose, Louis Adrian, 109, 130, 135
Moore, Peter R., 87
More, Thomas, 45–46
Morrison, Susan Signe, 195n80
Mouffe, Chantal, 5
Mucedorus (anon.), 112
Mullaney, Steven, 3

narcissism, 75, 95, 105, 204n72
nature/culture divide, 11–14
Naunton, Robert, 149
Nemas, Clara R., 76
New Historicism, 8, 9–11, 106, 165
Norfolk, Thomas Howard, Duke of, 43, 59, 60–61, 79–80, 82–83, 85, 87–90

"Of the Cardnall Wolse" (anon.), 24, 37, 39
Olatunji, Bunmi, at al., 27–28
Olmsted, Wendy, 3
Orgel, Stephen, 130
Ovid, 65, 137

pageants, 95, 106, 109, 112, 114; Kenilworth, 95, 115–23, 125, 135, 216–17nn118–19; *The Lady of May*, 95, 106–10, 126–34, 135; Norwich, 134; Woodstock, 95, 123–26, 217n126
Paget, William, 81–82, 205n99, 206n120
Palsgrave, John, 67
Papoulias, Constantina, 8
Parker, Geoffrey, 138
passions, 5, 6
Paster, Gail Kern, 3, 9, 10, 197n107
pastoralism, 108–9, 115, 128–30, 135, 213n70
Peele, George, 135
Percy, Charles, 165
Perez, Antonio, 157
Persius, 55–56
Petrarch, 6
Philip II, 97, 137, 138–39, 147–48, 158
Pilgrimage of Grace, 61

"political feelings" field, 5–6
Potter, David, 78
Protevi, John, 5, 13
Puttenham, George, 109, 201n21, 215n100

Raleigh, Walter, 137–39, 144–46, 151, 158, 164, 167–69
rejection, 15, 16, 94, 101–5, 114, 134; Leicester and, 94–97, 99, 101–2, 105, 123, 133; Sidney and, 94–95, 101–2, 105, 107, 132–32; wild man figure and, 112, 124
resentment, 52, 57, 63, 64
Reynolds, Bryan, 12
Richard II, 166–67, 173. *See also under* Shakespeare, William
Richmond, Henry Fitzroy, Duke of, 15, 57–63, 65, 83–84, 89–90. *See also* Surrey, Earl of: "So crewell prison"
Richmond, Mary Howard, Lady, 60, 86–87, 89
rivalry, 16, 56–57, 63, 71, 142. *See also* envy; jealousy
Robin Hood, 110, 111–12, 119, 131
Robsart, Amy, 96
Rosenwein, Barbara H. 181n9
Roy, William, 20, 24–25, 34–35, 37, 41–43
Royzman, Edward B., et al., 28–29
Rozin, Paul, 26–27, 29

Sacks, Peter, 76–77
Sackville, Thomas, 168
Salutati, Coluccio, 6
Sani, Fabio, 103
savage. *See* wild man figure
Savile, Henry, 156–58
Schaefer, Donovan, 6
schism, social psychology of, 103–4
Sedgwick, Eve Kosofsky, 204n65
self-esteem, 102–3, 105, 141–42
Seneca, Lucius Annaeus, 114
Sessions, William A., 79, 80, 81, 83–84
Seymour, Edward. *See* Hertford, Edward Seymour, Earl of
Seymour, Jane, 60, 61, 77
Seymour, Thomas, 83, 86
Shakespeare, William: *Henry VIII*, 20; *Love's Labour's Lost*, 128; *Othello*, 14, 72; *Richard II*, 161, 164–65
Sharpe, J. A., 230n166
Shenk, Linda, 126–27
Sherman, Gary D. at al., 28
Sidney, Philip, 15, 62, 94–96, 100–109, 115–16, 125–36, 144, 151; *Arcadia*, 133; Elizabeth and, 128, 130, 132–33; Essex and, 154, 159, 162; on hunting and hawking, 219n150; *The Lady of May*, 95, 106–10, 126–34, 212n67. *See also* rejection
Skelton, John, 31, 32–41, 168, 188n44, 189n28; *Collyn Clout*, 24, 38, 39; *Magnyfycence*, 23, 24, 44, 196n89; *Speke, Parott*, 23–24; *Why Come Ye Nat to Courte?*, 20, 24, 44
Smith, Richard H., et al., 69
Smuts, Malcolm, 226n92
sociality and political power, 4
Solomon, Sheldon, et al., 141
Southampton, Henry Wriothesley, Earl of, 146, 172
Southwell, Richard, 85
Spanish Armada, defeat of, 138, 147, 159
Spargo, R. Clifton, 204n72
Spenser, Edmund, 65, 73, 93–94, 112, 135–36, 148
Spolsky, Ellen, 12
Standen, Anthony, 150
Starkey, David, 4, 19
State of Christendom, The (author uncertain), 157–58, 227n95
status-seeking, 102
Stets, Jan E., 13
stigmatization, 210n36
Stow, John, 143
Strier, Richard, 6, 16
Stróbl, Erzsébet, 214n90
Suffolk, Charles Brandon, Duke of, 39, 55–56, 79
Surrey, Henry Howard, Earl of, 14–15, 57–63, 67–91, 101, 206n120; *Aeneid* translation by, 67, 68–69, 90; Arundel portrait of, 83–84, 86; elegies by, 57; emotional profile of, 61–63, 64, 105; later career and execution of, 62, 77–89; "So crewell prison," 57–58, 59, 61, 62–63, 65, 67–77, 84, 86, 87, 203n45. *See also* envy

Tacitus, Publius Cornelius, 154–58, 164, 166, 226n92
terror management theory (TMT), 141–43; religion and, 220n21
Thornton, Sarah, 114, 215n108
Tosh, Will, 143
Treaty of London, 22

Tribble, Evelyn, 12
Tudors, The (TV series), 19
Turner, Jonathan H., 13
Tyndale, William, 40
Tyrone, Hugh O'Neill, Earl of, 144–45

van der Delft, François, 81, 89
Vaught, Jennifer C., 3
Vergil, Polydore, 33, 78
Virgil. *See* Surrey, Earl of: *Aeneid* translation by

Walker Greg, 189n28
Walsingham, Frances, 144
Walsingham, Francis, 97, 98, 144
Whetstone, George, 113
Whigham, Frank, 37, 208n5
White, R. S., 3
Whitney, Geffery, 65
wild man figure, 112–14, 214n90; in *The Faerie Queene*, 136; Hercules and, 113–14, 117; in the Kenilworth pageant, 117–21; in *The Lady of May*, 127–28, 130–31; in the Woodstock pageant, 123–24
wildness discourse, 107–14, 118, 122, 130–33, 135, 214n96, 215n100
William of Orange, 97–98, 99–101
Williams, Kipling D., 105
Williams, Raymond, 16
Wilson, Thomas, 65, 72–73
Wintroub, Michael, 114
Withington, Robert, 110
Wolsey, Thomas, 5, 14, 20–25, 31–53, 55–57; *alter rex* designation, 14, 20, 48, 56, 187n9; background of, 21; Boleyn affair and, 22–23, 44–45, 48; downfall and death of, 44–53; physicality of, 20, 32, 35, 38, 195n81; poems against, 20, 23–25, 32–44, 195n80; Richmond and, 59; in Shakespeare's *Henry VIII*, 20; witchcraft accusations against, 39–40, 197n119. *See also* disgust
Womersley, David, 157
Woodstock entertainment (1575). *See* pageants
Wotton, Henry, 157, 177
Wriothesley, Charles, 50, 60, 85
Wyatt, Thomas, 57, 70, 197n111